PENGUIN BOOKS

I LIVED UNDER HITLER

Sybil Bannister was born in Uckfield in Sussex. After studying at Kensington College in London she went to Bonn for six months in 1933 to study German. While there she met a medical student whom she married in 1936 and they moved to Danzig (Gdańsk). On 1 September 1939, six days before their son was born, Hitler bombed the Polish garrison in the city and continued his advance into Poland. After the break-up of her marriage in 1942 and her survival of the first firestorm in Wuppertal-Barmen in 1943, Sybil Bannister's son was taken from her by the Gestapo in 1944, and only reunited with her in Hamburg in September 1945. Repatriated to England, just before Christmas of the same year, they returned to her father's house in Sussex, where she still lives. Her son has done very well in his career and is happily married. Since 1950 Sybil has often visited her trusted wartime friends in Germany.

SYBIL BANNISTER

I Lived Under Hitler

PENGUIN BOOKS

PENGUIN BOOKS

Published by the Penguin Group
Penguin Books Ltd, 27 Wrights Lane, London w8 5tz, England
Penguin Books USA Inc., 375 Hudson Street, New York, New York 10014, USA
Penguin Books Australia Ltd, Ringwood, Victoria, Australia
Penguin Books Canada Ltd, 10 Alcorn Avenue, Toronto, Ontario, Canada m4v 3b2
Penguin Books (NZ) Ltd, 182–190 Wairau Road, Auckland 10, New Zealand

Penguin Books Ltd, Registered Offices: Harmondsworth, Middlesex, England

First published by Rockcliff Publishing Corporation 1957
This revised edition published in Penguin Books 1995
1 3 5 7 9 10 8 6 4 2

Filmset by Datix International Limited, Bungay, Suffolk
Printed in England by Clays Ltd, St Ives plc
Set in 10.75/13pt Monophoto Baskerville

LIST OF ILLUSTRATIONS

All the photographs come from the author's collection with the exception of the following: 28 and 29 © Imperial War Museum, 22 © Stadtarchiv, Wuppertal, 23 is from W. Ispert, *Wuppertal, Aufsteig aus Trümmern und Ruinen*, Bonn, 1960.

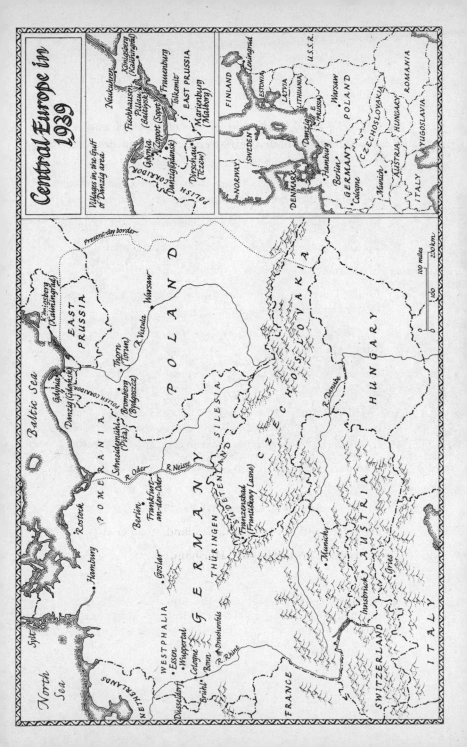

Central Europe in 1939

Villages in the Gulf of Danzig area

North Sea

Baltic Sea

Sylt

NETHERLANDS

Düsseldorf

Brühl

Bonn

Cologne

Wuppertal

Essen

WESTPHALIA

R. Rhine

R. Drachenfels

FRANCE

SWITZERLAND

Hamburg

Rostock

POMERANIA

Goslar

Berlin

Frankfurt-
an-der-Oder

R. Oder

THÜRINGEN

GERMANY

Franzensbad
(Františkovy Lázně)

SUDETENLAND

Munich

AUSTRIA

Innsbruck

Gries

ITALY

Gdynia

Danzig (Gdańsk)

POLISH CORRIDOR

Schneidemühl
(Piła)

R. Neisse

SILESIA

CZECHOSLOVAKIA

R. Danube

HUNGARY

EAST
PRUSSIA

Königsberg
(Kaliningrad)

Bromberg
(Bydgoszcz)

Thorn
(Toruń)

R. Vistula

Warsaw

POLAND

Present-day border

0   100   200 km
0   100   miles

Villages in the Gulf of Danzig area

Neukuhren

Fischhausen

Pillau
(Baltiysk)

Königsberg
(Kaliningrad)

Gdynia

Zoppot (Sopot)

Danzig (Gdańsk)

Dirschau
(Tczew)

POLISH
CORRIDOR

Frauenburg

Tolkemit

Marienburg
(Malbork)

EAST PRUSSIA

NORWAY

SWEDEN

FINLAND

Leningrad

DENMARK

Hamburg

Berlin

Cologne

Munich

GERMANY

U.S.S.R.

ESTONIA

LATVIA

LITHUANIA

Danzig

E. PRUSSIA

Warsaw

POLAND

CZECHOSLOVAKIA

AUSTRIA

HUNGARY

ITALY

YUGOSLAVIA

ROMANIA

This is a true story, but most of the characters and a few small places have been given fictitious names.

FOREWORD

Germany today presents the spectacle of a thriving and industrious country. Although it has many of the characteristics of the confident Germany of the Kaiser's day, there are certain very great changes in attitude of mind. My story begins when Germany was in the full tide of a rise in confidence of a very different kind – the exuberant emergence from depression between the wars under the leadership of Hitler – and it ends when that dream had been smashed and Germany lay hungry, divided and without hope, waiting upon the decision of the conquering armies she had brought upon her. In 1933, seven months after Hitler had become Chancellor, I first met my future husband, a German medical student. I left Germany in 1945, nine months after Hitler had died by his own hand.

This story is the account of my life as a civilian in Germany during the Second World War. I was the first of our family, as far as the records show, to marry a foreigner. At that time, if an Englishwoman married a German, she automatically took her husband's nationality; that is why I lived the life of a German subject when that country was at war with my own.

To a young woman marriage is a great adventure, an all-absorbing challenge to her resourcefulness to make it a success. When one has chosen to marry a foreigner and make him a home in his own country it is an even greater challenge. I was not exceptional among women of my age in having only a distant interest in politics. And I think my story shows that in busying myself in setting up home in a foreign land, and endeavouring to assimilate the way of life of my husband's people, I was in no position to assess their ways objectively.

The Nazi regime was not presented to England suddenly

as a complete scheme of life with all its worst features fully developed. We learnt bit by bit something of the form it was taking, and right up to the time of Munich there was no unanimity in England as to whether this was not just a German way of setting a demoralized country on its feet. By the time a clearer picture reached Britain, and the British view was more united, I was committed. I was married and a German subject.

These remarks may serve to explain how I was at first able to pursue wholeheartedly my self-appointed task of trying to make myself a good wife to my German husband.

But it was impossible to remain detached from the implications of the Nazi hold on Germany for long. Suddenly I was to find myself without the comradeship of my English friends in Danzig, then a marriage that failed and the desolation of life without my child. I was to find myself − an English-woman − alone in Germany.

ONE

It was the day of my wedding, 5 September 1936, and the weather was hot and sultry. As I dressed in my long organdie dress of pale apricot pink with darker spots, and put on my large picture hat, there were distant rumbles of thunder. The storm rolled nearer and nearer to the thirteenth-century church, St Margaret the Queen in Buxted Park and, as I walked up the aisle on my father's arm, there was a sudden violent clap of thunder directly overhead – an omen of things to come?

The two lanky young men standing before me were Germans, Kurt Falkenberg, my husband-to-be, and his elder brother Heinz. In the pew behind them their father, a doctor from Wuppertal, sat with his youngest son, Max. The family had been well established in Wuppertal for many generations. *Mutter*, the mainstay of the family, had died the Christmas before while I was on my first visit there, which had been a tragic blow for all of us. *Vater* had served on Germany's eastern front throughout the First World War, so *Mutter* had had the responsibility of bringing up the two elder boys alone and had suffered many hardships. These, however, were not as severe as during the disastrous inflation period which followed in 1923. *Vater* was of course home by then, but unemployment was rife throughout the country and in the cities food was so scarce that the population was at starvation level. *Mutter* had shown me a photograph of Kurt and Max then, and they were mere skeletons. Under a Government scheme they were sent to be fattened up on a Baltic baron's estate.

On the other side of the aisle my brother Reg and his wife Win were sitting with my sisters Muriel and Gwen. Reg's son Michael was my page boy. In 1914, Reg, aged sixteen and training as an electrical engineer, had posed as an eighteen-year-old and, like his faithful yeoman-farmer ancestors, joined the Army to defend his country. For most of the war he served in the front line in Flanders with the HAC. Except for the agony of knowing that he was in constant danger, we in the Sussex countryside lived peacefully, with no real hardships. We Bannisters can trace the family tree back as far as the seventeenth century, always in Sussex. The first of the de Banastres to set foot in England were followers of William the Conqueror, the last successful invader of these shores, who granted them pockets of land in various parts of the country. The younger sons had branched out into trade and the professions, and my father, the youngest son in a prosperous farming family, following the loss of both parents at an early age, was set up by his uncle and guardian, Tom Bannister, with a small property on the outskirts of Uckfield.

In spite of the extreme contrast between Kurt's and my family backgrounds, we were all immediately on good terms. We were both blessed with loving, broad-minded parents who wished only for us to be happy and who had much in common, both personally and culturally.

What had first attracted me to the German nation was their knowledge and appreciation of classical music at every level of society. From my earliest childhood singing had given me the greatest joy. On Sunday mornings we all went to church, and in the evenings I loved to sing hymns and songs with my mother at the piano. This yearning was nourished at my boarding school, the Welsh Girls' School (now St David's School) in Ashford, Middlesex. I knew, however, that I should not yet be able to earn a living as a singer, so I took an intensive year-and-a-half secretarial course at Kensington College and subsequently worked as secretary to one of the partners in a stockbroking firm in the City. In the meantime I started singing lessons in the evenings at Morley College, where I also joined a German class. When I started learning *Lieder* I found my knowledge of that language inadequate, so I decided to spend six months in

Germany. There I lived *en famille* with Herr and Frau Doktor Stockmann and their ten-year-old daughter in Brühl, between Cologne and Bonn. The Frau Doktor taught at the Lyceum (the girls' high school), and gave me daily lessons in grammar, literature and history. We never spoke a word of English.

In the late summer of that year, 1933, I met a tall, handsome medical student, Kurt Falkenberg. Our mutual attraction was immediate. I had never before met a young man who was both serious and lively, endowed with all the characteristics I admired. He was strong, clever, generous, sensitive, at home equally in the ballroom, the opera and the concert hall, in the consulting room or the operating theatre, skilled at swimming, canoeing, ski-ing, drawing, painting and sculpture. He seemed, with his tireless energy and keen perception, to be possessed by a restless demon. At that time he was at Bonn university, preparing for his final, fifth-year exams which he was to pass in spite of gadding about with me. We spent as much time together as we could, mostly in and around Bonn, walking along the Rhine or over the mountains and through the forests on either bank, swimming, visiting various museums and galleries, concerts and operas, dancing or sitting in the cafés frequented by students.

In September, not long after we had met, Kurt's parents and brothers drove over from Wuppertal for his twenty-fourth birthday (I was eight months younger). They picked me up from the Stockmanns to join them in a sumptuous picnic near the Drachenfels in the Siebengebirge. I was very shy in my youth and was now even more tongue-tied than usual, but *Mutter* was the life and soul of the party. She had a wonderful flow of language, inherited by Kurt, and soon put me at my ease. *Vater* was an easy-going man, intellectually extremely alert, fond of music and the arts, and a busy, first-rate family doctor, popular with his patients. The management of the household and its accounts, as well as assistance in the surgery, was taken on by his capable wife, who was greatly loved and respected by her sons.

As December drew near Kurt and I became more and more conscious that a parting would be unbearable without the prospect of a reunion, with the ultimate object of sharing our future. I would certainly have to adapt myself to living in Germany and renouncing my British nationality (compulsory at that time for British women who married foreigners). But a stroke of the pen could not alter my heredity. I was English-bred and nothing could alter that, nor did I dream that such an impossible transformation would be expected of me. I was young and confident, and may have overestimated my own capabilities, but the overwhelming odds against which I would have to struggle could not be foreseen. Brought up as I was, in a rural area and in a family who were not involved in international politics, I was ignorant of the ominous changes already starting to take place in Germany.

Following the completion of his studies in Bonn, Kurt now had to work for a year in a hospital before being presented with his medical degree. It was his ambition to specialize in gynaecology, which would mean another four years of study, working in a university hospital for women with – in those days – extremely small remuneration. Therefore, when we parted, it was for an indefinite period. I went back to my job in London and Kurt took a post as assistant in the Schneidemühl Hospital, some 150 miles east of Berlin. We corresponded fervently, but it was impossible to see each other before the summer holidays. We met in Hamburg, where Kurt took me to *Die Walküre* with Frieda Leider and Rudolf Bockelmann. The next day we travelled by steamer to the island of Sylt in the North Sea and stayed in a fisherman's hut in List, at what was then the wild northern tip of the island, surrounded by rare birds which were nesting in the sands.

Christmas 1934 gave Kurt only a few days at home, where

he was distressed to find his mother, usually the prop and mainstay of the family, very sick. By this time he had started his four-year training as an assistant in the Danzig State Hospital for women, under a well-known gynaecologist, Professor Dr Hans Fuchs. Danzig, now in Poland and known as Gdańsk, was a Free City on the north-eastern tip of the Polish Corridor. And it was an eighteen-hour train journey from Wuppertal.

The separation was proving a strain, and I grew anxious as Kurt's letters became less frequent and shorter. In the early spring of 1935 I wrote to ask him if he had changed his mind but before he could reply I was lying in hospital, dangerously ill with an acute infection of the antrum. Only skilled surgical intervention saved my life. A friend wrote to Kurt to tell him of this and, I learned later, he had gone to the coast and sat watching the waves for hours while he pondered on our situation. The thought of losing me made him desperate, and he decided that whatever obstacles there might be to our marriage they had to be overcome.

That summer I was still not strong enough to travel, so Kurt came to England to stay with us at home and meet my people. We went first of all to stay with Win's friends in Morecombe Lake, near Lyme Regis, and then on to Uckfield where Kurt was surprised to find that he felt completely at home from the moment he entered the house, as though he were my mother's own son. He was by now able to understand English fairly well but could speak very little. My relations could not speak a word of German, which led to many amusing misunderstandings.

The first thing that struck my mother was Kurt's fine, even rows of teeth. In those days, while many English people lost their teeth early in life, Germans had exceptionally healthy teeth. Impulsive and guileless as ever, she could not help exclaiming the moment after she had welcomed him, 'What beautiful teeth you have! Are they your own?'

Plans for our wedding in the following year were tentatively made, by which time Kurt reckoned he would be earning sufficient although he had not finished his training as a specialist.

He asked me to stay a few weeks with him in Danzig in December and proposed that following this we should both travel to Wuppertal-Barmen to spend Christmas at his home. His parents invited me to stop a day or two there on the way out to Danzig so that I could have a rest and avoid travelling by night.

I crossed via Dover, Ostend and Cologne, arriving late in the evening. It was of course a momentous journey. How would I like my 'in-laws'? Would they approve of an English wife for one of their sons? Certainly we had met once, but at that time there was no thought of a close relationship, and now we would judge each other from an entirely different aspect. I looked forward with interest to the climax of my holiday when I would be seeing the town where Kurt had grown up, and staying in the house where he had lived since he was just learning to walk.

The train journey through the breadth of Germany seemed never-ending, and it was particularly tedious having to cross and re-cross the Polish frontier, then at last the Danzig frontier. Before 1917 Danzig, together with East and West Prussia, had been part of Germany, but under the Treaty of Versailles Poland was granted the strip of land known as the Polish Corridor, which extended from Poland up to the Baltic Sea, thus cutting off East Prussia from West Prussia and creating two frontiers around Danzig (with Poland and East Prussia). Although Danzig was called a 'Free City', it was in fact a very small state measuring about 45 miles west to east and 25 miles north to south. To the south of the city and its suburbs there were beautiful lakes and forests and also arable land where peasants grew their products for the population in the city who were Germans. The Free City was under the supervision of a United Nations High Commissioner, but the Poles were given control of the Customs and the Post Office and were allowed to build a military garrison in a part of the harbour known as Die Westerplatte. The trains were, by international law, locked whilst going through the Polish Corridor via Dirschau (Tczew) to Marienburg (Malbork). Here passengers for Danzig had to change and proceed back again to Dirschau, then northwards to Danzig. The travel agency in London did not realize that a double journey between Dirschau and Marienburg had to be made each time and only issued a single ticket. The result was that the angry ticket collector delivered a lengthy tirade in Polish and, not understanding a word, I wondered what serious offence I had committed. After a while I guessed from his gestures that I was expected to pay for something, but he would not or could not accept German or English money, and finally gave up in despair. I was amazed that he did not speak German. This was the first instance I had come across the dogged determination of the Poles not to utter a word of a language so obnoxious to them.

I stayed in the Staatliche Frauenklinik in Danzig-Langfuhr, a suburb of Danzig, where Kurt worked, and was interested to watch the organization of a German university hospital from behind the scenes.

Although the hospital was administered by State officials, the chief surgeon, Professor Fuchs, enjoyed considerable powers within his own sphere. He lived in the hospital grounds, and had complete control over medical matters and staff.

For a time Kurt worked as his senior private assistant. In this capacity he assisted the Professor at his lectures and at all deliveries and operations on his private patients, accompanied him on his daily tour of the wards (followed by the usual cluster of underlings and nurses), and if necessary helped him in his consulting room.

While I was staying there Kurt was sole assistant in charge of the labour wards, where there was an average of one thousand births a year, and his working hours were even more erratic than usual. If a doctor was needed it was etiquette for the Sister first of all to call the assistant, who would then only summon the Chief if he could not cope with the trouble himself. This meant many disturbed nights, besides strenuous days. Kurt might have applied for another assistant to relieve the situation, but then he knew the interesting cases would be divided between the two, as well as the routine work. His fever to assimilate as much knowledge as possible in the shortest time drove him to persevere to the last. He soon operated skilfully, and his ability and keen interest were justly recognized by his Professor – so much so that his advancement was eyed with resentment and jealousy by some of the less energetic and less able assistants.

Professor Fuchs was an exceedingly kind, clever and chivalrous old gentleman. At a Christmas supper party I was placed next to him at the top of the table. On his other side was a lady assistant, who, for some reason unknown to me then, ignored me the whole evening, nor would she join in any conversation I had with the Professor. I thought she must be anti-British or anti-something or other. Perhaps the old Professor's all-seeing eyes perceived her secret passion for Kurt, which I discovered later was the reason for her peculiar behaviour. In any case, he handled the difficult situation with true diplomacy, now conversing with her about college or hospital, now bandying jokes with me in broken English, much to everyone's amusement. In the company of so many strangers, I was riddled with shyness, and but for Kurt on one side and the kindly Professor on the other, I would have felt more like bursting into tears than joining in a party.

On this first visit I did not meet any friends outside the hospital. While Kurt was working I spent many hours roaming about the city, which was the most beautiful I had ever seen, particularly because the old parts were preserved in almost perfect condition, unspoilt by many modern buildings. Although new shops had been built beneath the old houses in the main streets, they did not as a rule mar the façade.

The newer houses were outside the ancient walls and extended into more distant suburbs. The massive structure of the Cathedral, the St Marienkirche, rose strong and high above the gabled houses clustered round it, dominating the city. These houses, although now regarded as unhealthy and unhygienic, were once the homes of wealthy citizens, in the days when Danzig was the most important of the easterly Hanseatic harbours.

For Christmas Kurt bought me a very lovely water-colour landscape by a Danzig artist named Pasternack, a Customs official who spent all his spare time painting. The picture was of a small fishing boat on the edge of the water, with reeds and low dunes in the foreground. The scene on the remote, sparsely inhabited northern shore was captured with unfailing delicacy.

As we left for Barmen before Christmas I did not that year experience the severity of the winter in the east.

We arrived at Kurt's home on the day before Christmas Eve. During the last few weeks *Mutter*'s health had been steadily deteriorating and she had only with great determination managed to complete her preparations for Christmas.

In Germany festivities and the exchange of gifts take place on Christmas Eve. It was the custom in Kurt's home to start by having hot baths in the afternoon, one after the other, beginning with the youngest. After tea (or rather coffee) we waited in suspense for the sounding of the bell, supposed to be rung by the Christ Child, summoning us to the Christmas tree. I had hardly seen *Mutter* since we had arrived, and we wondered whether she would be able to face the ordeal of a full family gathering. To our joy and surprise, she was there in the festive room, dressed in her best black and white silk gown, standing under the Christmas tree, looking almost her normal self. This sacred moment had been celebrated in northern Europe thousands of years before the coming of Christianity to give thanks for the return of the longer days and sunshine after the winter darkness.

The long table in the 'official' dining-room was laden with presents, making a bright picture which gleamed in the soft candle-light. Nothing was packed in paper. There were no names showing for whom the presents were meant. But somehow everyone knew which was his or her particular pile of gifts, each grouped round a plate full of nuts, spiced biscuits, chocolates and sweets in many-coloured wrappings (*der bunte Teller*). After we had gloated over our own collection, a general tour of inspection followed. Each person's tastes and needs had been carefully considered, and as usual with all of *Mutter*'s purchases, the hall-mark was good quality. We then gathered round *Mutter* and gave her our presents one by one. Kurt had brought a shallow wooden bowl made by a woman in Danzig who specialized in that type of work, and I gave her a Liberty silk scarf. He handed her the bowl as she sat on the sofa and while she was contemplating it I laid the scarf on the bowl. This she quickly removed, however, until she had thoroughly examined the bowl, then she took up the scarf and in turn inspected it in detail. Although there were no signs of her normally gay, energetic spirit, it looked as though she were quietly enjoying the evening. Later we had the traditional supper of carp and went early to bed.

During the night *Mutter* suffered a serious relapse and our hopes for her recovery were dashed to the ground.

It had been planned for us all to motor to Langenfeld, on the Rhine, after lunch on Christmas Day, to see *Vater*'s mother, his sister and her two daughters. *Mutter* was too ill to come with us and we hated the thought of leaving her; but if we stayed, what could we do to help her? Also, Kurt's grandmother, who was over eighty, would be anxiously looking for us and would be bitterly disappointed if we did not turn up. In the end we decided to go, even if we only stayed there a little while. It was about an hour's drive in the car. There was always great competition as to which of the sons should drive, but at that time Heinz was undoubtedly the best driver. He was the eldest and had had longer practice. He drove swiftly and accurately, Kurt was inclined to be a trifle too rash and impatient, whilst Max was as yet a beginner. *Vater*, who was a shockingly bad driver, had long since ceased to lay himself open to his sons' indignant abuse, and handed the car over to them on every possible occasion. This time it was Kurt's turn.

Grossmutter was a bulky old lady, with typically Westphalian broad, strong features. She had a sweet, generous nature, but could be as stubborn as a mule. After her first husband (Kurt's grandfather) died, against the advice of the rest of the family, at the age of seventy-five, she married again. She once confided in me that she had never known what love was until she married the second time! However, her happiness was short-lived, for the old boy proved too restless and too much of a handful for her, and after a while they parted company, each returning to live with their own daughters. In the meantime *Grossmutter* had improvidently spent practically the whole of her first husband's money (most of it was given to her second husband) and now she was dependent on her children's charity. She was nearly blind, but managed to find her way from room to room, round the garden, or even went for a stroll down the country lanes. She knitted a good deal on enormous needles, and gave me some sturdy bedsocks, also a crocheted bath-mat and a bundle of kettle-holders. There was a bath-mat ready for each grandson when he married. Although she lived to hear of the birth of her first great-grandson (Manny), she died during the war before I was able to take him to see her. On that Christmas Day she sat holding my hand, peering at me with her dim, blue eyes, asking me about my home and England. The cousins said they had not understood why Kurt should want to marry a foreigner, but now, after seeing me, it was quite clear to them why he had made this choice. This was not empty flattery, but their genuine sentiment; I always found warm-hearted hospitality there and in the homes of all Kurt's relatives.

Although we were anxious to get back, in some ways we almost dreaded returning, because *Mutter* had been so ill. However, she was resting when we got home so we did not rouse her.

The next morning when *Vater* came to breakfast he said *Mutter* was sleeping. As time went on we thought it was strange that she did not come for her coffee, and Heinz went to see if she was awake. He soon reappeared, his face pale and distraught. When he opened his mouth to speak, no sound came. After a pause he whispered, '*Mutter ist tot*' (Mother is dead). *Vater* and Kurt hurried into the bedroom to see if they could save her, but the end had come.

The household had revolved round *Mutter*. Now the central figure had gone, and each one had to shift for himself as best he could.

I had intended returning to England soon after Christmas when Kurt went back to Danzig, but now the family asked me to stay on as long as possible to keep *Vater* company. Most mornings I spent in the kitchen watching Erna cook in the way *Mutter* had taught her, and writing down the special recipes. After surgery hours were over I went with *Vater* in the car on his visits, which were mostly in the town, and we had to twist and climb up the steep, narrow streets. *Vater* drove so recklessly that it seemed as though our lives were in jeopardy at every bend. The car screeched and groaned, but bore its batterings and scratches bravely. There had long been a debate in the family as to whether a new car was necessary or not. Now, without *Mutter*'s economical and procrastinating restraint, it was decided to embark on a Mercedes-Benz *Heckmotor*, a car with the engine at the back. No sooner was the decision made, than the shiny grey saloon stood at the door. This was of course like a new toy, which was fussed over by the boys even more than the old one had been.

On Wednesday and Sunday afternoons, when *Vater* had no surgery hours, we motored out into the country. This district is called '*das Bergische Land*', the hilly country, and is surprisingly beautiful and unspoilt considering it is only such a short distance from the largest industrial area in Germany.

About once a week we went to the theatre where *Vater* had season tickets, sometimes to a play, sometimes to an operetta or an opera. Whatever it was, I enjoyed these visits immensely. It was a fine theatre and the performances were excellent. In German theatres during the intervals most people promenade along the wide corridors at the back of the auditorium on each floor, where one also leaves hats, coats and overshoes with the attendants. Nobody sits inside the well-heated theatres in coats, and ladies like to show off their best party dresses. *Vater* was well known amongst the audience, who bowed sombrely to him when we passed by, as was befitting to a man so recently bereaved. They gave me a close inspection and obviously wondered who I was. After the performance we often called on the way home at a restaurant two doors away for a snack and a glass of lager, where the boys would join us. The owner's wife had known the family for many years. When I was introduced to her she said she was surprised to hear that I was not a relative – in fact she had thought I so closely resembled the Falkenbergs that I must be a daughter she had never seen before! At the time I found this rather consoling. Surely, I thought, it would be easier to live amongst people if I did not at every turn strike them as being a foreigner. However, I was sometimes told that I had only to walk into a room and it was obvious which country I came from. I remember much later, after I had lived in Germany for six years, a Viennese lady staying in the same hotel as I in Franzensbad (Františkovy Lasne) said she knew I was English immediately she saw me, although I was not even wearing English clothes then. Anyway, it was generally decided that our marriage would only involve a mixing of nationalities, not of races, as we were both north-European types . . .

TWO

For our honeymoon Kurt and I went first to the Lake District where I had booked rooms in a little white-washed cottage near Patterdale, at the foot of Helvellyn. Everything was spotlessly clean in this north-country home, and the food overwhelmingly good. We spent the lovely late-summer days walking near the lakes or climbing the mountains. Even on the lower, gentler slopes the scenery is awe-inspiring, and very beautiful in rather a dark, gloomy way, but I don't know anywhere more uncanny than high up amongst the lurking tarns and peaks. One day I had lingered a little behind Kurt and found myself surrounded by tall high rocks, silhouetted in a jagged outline against the sky. Suddenly a sharp wind sprang up. It howled and whistled through the crevices making a most mournful sound. Dark clouds swept across the sky. It was as though devils raced and danced around me, screeching into my ears. I tried to shout to Kurt but I could not hear my own voice. My cries were borne away, almost before they were uttered, by gusts of angry wind which lashed against me and stung like a whip. When I was able to recover my breath I tottered to the narrow gap through which Kurt had disappeared and fled down the mountainside. He was not far away, sitting in the grass waiting for me, sheltered from the wind. The clouds disappeared as fast as they had come. The sun shone serenely and we seemed infinitely removed from my nightmare.

After a week or two in the Lake District we moved on to Bearsden, near Glasgow, to stay with my brother and his wife, who took us for some wonderful drives through the mountains round Loch Lomond and the Trossachs. Kurt was again quite taken aback by the beauty of the countryside and was amazed that so little advertisement was made abroad. It was obvious to foreigners that a visit to London, the world's most important trading centre, was advantageous to businessmen, but it rarely occurred to them that the rest of the country might be worth seeing.

When we returned to Sussex the remaining few days were spent in packing and making arrangements for my goods to be sent direct to Danzig by ship. Kurt and I then travelled first of all to Wuppertal-Barmen. I had never left home for any considerable period without being desperately homesick, but this time to my surprise the pangs did not come. It was sad to say goodbye to my people, but I consoled myself with the thought that I would see them as often as if I had married and moved say to Scotland or the north of England, and still more often than if I had gone to Egypt or India, as one of my English suitors had wished me to.

We bought our furniture, carpets, china, glass, kitchen utensils and bedding in Barmen. Kurt gave me a pair of best quality skates and boots, and a pair of brown walking shoes edged with red, with red shoe-laces, with which I was highly delighted, because in those days the serviceable shoes obtainable in England were never pretty. We knew it would take several weeks for all our things to reach Danzig, so Kurt returned there alone when his holiday was over, and his father and I went to stay with a cousin, David, in Krawarn, near Ratibor in Silesia.

David took us for drives, sometimes in the wagonette through the country lanes, sometimes for longer rides in the car. It was a broad, sweeping land, softly undulating in wide slopes over a vast expanse of rich soil. The peasant population was a mixed bag of Poles, Russians, Czechs and Germans, but the people in the few towns dotted here and there were almost all Germans.

After we had stayed in Krawarn for about a fortnight, *Vater* travelled with me to Danzig where we arrived on 9 October 1936, and a few days later he returned to his home.

Kurt had found a suitable flat which was now vacant, but the furniture had not yet come, so he rented a room for me opposite the Klinik, in Posadowskyweg. The lady of the house, a widow called Frau Stein, was kindness itself and was to prove a good friend. She was a most efficient housewife and was always ready to give advice on the many problems which arose for me. Although she lived alone, she was for ever busy bottling, jam-making, baking, cooking, sewing and gardening, and was a fathomless source for good recipes. Sometimes she would buy a whole hare at the market, in its skin (this being the most economical way) and sell me half. She showed me how to roast it in the proper fashion, with strips of bacon fat threaded through the flesh, and basted with sour cream from which afterwards the sauce was made.

Our furniture and goods did not, of course, all arrive at the same time as they had been ordered from various firms in Germany, as well as one lot from England. This meant many visits to the Customs offices in Langfuhr and seemingly endless formalities.

In the meantime we had one divan made to our design at Sternfeld's in Danzig. When this was ready I moved into our flat to sleep, though I still had my meals in the Klinik because I had as yet no cooking utensils at home. Frau Stein lent me her sewing machine to make some of the curtains, but I could not get them all ready until the rest of the materials arrived from Germany. Curtains were the only household problem on which we found it difficult to make a decision. Both Kurt and I liked the English manner of having only non-transparent materials which could be drawn across when it was dark, with no net or lace curtains in the middle (as was the fashion in Germany). On the other hand we lived on the ground floor and found that passers-by could peer through the large windows in the daytime, which could be embarrassing, especially as the doctor's English wife seemed to be the centre of curiosity among the housewives in the neighbourhood. This therefore finally meant our having transparent curtains drawn, at any rate partly, across some of the windows.

We had three rooms, kitchen and bathroom, with our own central-heating stove in the kitchen. We disliked the idea of having the stereotyped double-bedroom, dining-room and *Herrenzimmer* suites, and decided to furnish the two rooms which were separated by sliding glass doors as sitting-rooms (with my divan and wardrobe in one of them) and the third room, which had a balcony, as a dining-room with Kurt's divan in the corner. Both divans were comfortable to sit on during the daytime, and another long sofa could be converted into a bed if necessary. By this means we had three living-rooms, and could easily accommodate one guest. When we had two visitors, Kurt would sleep in the Klinik, where he still had his bedroom and study.

By the time we were properly settled in our flat, the winter was upon us. Fortunately for my peace of mind, I did not realize that it was the worst possible time of the year to set up housekeeping in a climate where many food supplies were non-existent for several months during the cold spell. I had, of course, only been used to catering in our mild English climate where cucumbers, tomatoes, lettuce and many green vegetables can be bought nearly all the year round, also where imported apples, oranges, pears, bananas and other fresh fruits, as well as tinned vegetables and fruits, were available at reasonable prices, not to mention new potatoes early in the year.

In Danzig the frost was so prolonged and severe that between Christmas and May or June no vegetables came into the market excepting red or white cabbage, carrots, beetroot, onions, swedes or turnips. During periods of exceptionally cold weather, even these would not appear, as the ground was so hard that the peasants could not open their clamps. As soon as the home-grown apples had been consumed there was no fruit excepting a negligible amount of oranges and bananas, which were an exorbitant price owing to the heavy customs duties and the distance they had to be transported. Tinned vegetables and fruits were likewise so expensive that they could only be looked upon as a luxury. These circumstances explained the orgy of bottling and pickling in which efficient housewives indulged during the summer when there was a glut of cheap produce of every sort, including eggs. Every house or flat was equipped with a special cellar store-room in which there would be neat rows of bottled beans, tomatoes, carrots, peas, mushrooms, cherries, strawberries, gooseberries, red and black currants, plums, luscious fruit syrups, pickled gherkins, pickled cabbage, and so on, all of which could be drawn upon to concoct varied and sumptuous meals during the lean winter months. Meat was plentiful all the year round, although the beef and particularly the mutton was, to an English palate, rather tasteless. I soon discovered why pork was the most popular dish. It was by far the best quality for the money (veal being rather more expensive), and at the same time provided the necessary fats to protect one from the cold. All the same, it took several winters before I could get accustomed to eating the pure fat which was often served with roast pork instead of a gravy thickened with flour and made with stock. Duck and geese (the latter conveniently sold in portions if desired) were obtainable at reasonable prices in the market.

Butter, cheese and cream were quite cheap − in fact a good-sized bowl of whipped cream only cost about sixpence so that there was no difficulty in devising rich sauces or decorating fancy tarts and cakes. In the summer we were able to have strawberries or raspberries and cream nearly every day while they were in season. Kurt had often made my mouth water by telling me that barrow-loads of enormous juicy strawberries would be hawked round the streets every day at sixpence a pound during the season, and I would only need to walk outside the door to buy them. This was true except, as chance would have it, during my first summer, when even the medium quality did not sell under a shilling a pound at the market, and I waited in vain for their miraculous arrival before the house.

There were very few greengrocers' shops, and the freshest and finest produce was available at the market. In the centre of Danzig there was a market hall surrounded by a large market square, and a separate fish market down by the river. The Langfuhr Market had long since been transferred from the original Market Place in the main road (which was now a busy thoroughfare crossed by trams) to a side street, with the fish market at the bottom round the bend. This is where I did most of my shopping. On market days (twice a week) there was a seething hub of jostling shoppers crowding round the barrows which lined each side of the road, the robust peasant-owners (the women dressed in voluminous long skirts, aprons and shawls) standing behind them, touting their goods in loud voices. When I first went there I was quite amazed at the colourful display of flowers, fruit, vegetables, eggs, butter, cheese and meat. I took so long walking up and down, carried away by the absorbing spectacle, watching the experienced *Hausfrauen* picking their bargains, and trying to decide what to buy out of this abundance, that it was nearly lunch time before I realized that my string bag was still empty. (Shopping baskets were seldom used, except for small fruits or eggs.)

What intrigued me most at the market, however, was the variety of fish, many of them sold alive. At first I had no idea what they were called, so, not to be daunted, I just stood in front of my choice for the day and pointed out the ones I wanted, saying, 'These two please.' I would then identify them from the pictures in my *Davidis* cookery book (the German equivalent of Mrs Beeton's) and read how to cook them, or failing that seek advice from Frau Stein. At first I only tackled the dead fish, then one day, feeling more venturesome, I chose a live one, a fine, dark chap. I asked the woman to kill him, as I had seen others doing. She cut him through the back of his neck with a large, sharp knife, and popped him into my string bag. On the way home I felt him give a jerk every now and again and when I unpacked him, to my horror, he heaved and wriggled about in the bowl. To make matters worse, Kurt rang up to ask if he could have lunch early as he had to operate immediately after. I waited in vain for half an hour for the wretched creature to become inert, then in desperation I sharpened my carving knife and hacked off his head. Wriggling or no wriggling, I thought, he must be dead now. Needless to say I could not eat a mouthful, although Kurt said it was the best fish he had ever tasted. It took me some time to overcome these sensibilities, but later on I scorned dead fresh-water fish. However, I always remained squeamish about putting live crayfish into boiling water, and no matter how many I was cooking, I put them in one by one, waiting for the water to wallop each time to ensure instantaneous death. I could never bring myself to cook eels, although I enjoyed eating them, in dill sauce. An acquaintance told me that they wriggled for hours after they were dead. Once she left one in her sink, only to find it had vanished when she came back to the kitchen, and there followed a hectic search all over the ground floor before she finally tracked it down in some obscure corner. Another friend told me that she once bought a couple of eels at the coast, had them killed, and put them in a basket into the back of the car. When she arrived home, to her amazement, no eels were to be found. A week or so later she noticed a nauseating stench in the car which, in spite of cleaning and disinfecting, increased from day to day, until it became quite intolerable. She took the car to a garage for close inspection, whereupon the putrefied eels were discovered in the exhaust pipe! After hearing these stories, I only had the courage to buy smoked eels. I accumulated a considerable knowledge of fish and how to cook them by sampling different sorts each week, and before long I had outstripped the local housewives, most of whom were extraordinarily unenterprising in this respect, preferring the familiar *Pommuchel* (the name peculiar to Danzig for cod), which certainly were delicious, and far superior in flavour to the usual sort.

My first winter I tripped up badly over the potato question, because I did not realize in time that a good store had to be laid in. It never dawned on me that I would not be able to fetch them from the greengrocer down the road in small quantities as I needed them, until one day he suddenly had no more for sale. This was a rude awakening. After many enquiries I managed to get a sack or two delivered, but I had to pay a relatively high price for a poor quality. It was a worse tragedy of course when the fruit and vegetables also disappeared from the market, because, not having bottled any, I sometimes got no supplies at all, and was reduced to pickled cabbage, haricot beans or dried peas.

Another fiasco was my first big washing day. There were few laundries and it was the custom for everything to be washed at home. For this purpose every building had a cellar equipped with a tap, some sort of grate and a drain in the stone floor, also an attic in which to dry clothes in wet weather. In Kurt's home in Barmen there was a built-in copper, as well as large receptacles in which to soak and wash the clothes. His mother had an electric washing-machine and a centrifugal dryer installed. I knew I could not expect to find such expensive apparatus, but I was under the impression that all wash-cellars would have built-in coppers and wash tubs. Each flat in our block had use of the wash-cellar in turn once a month on certain fixed days, and the keys were passed round. I therefore had no opportunity of inspecting the cellar, nor did I think it was necessary, until it was my turn and the keys were handed to me. I had arranged for a washerwoman to come the next morning, so during the afternoon I took the washing down to put it in soak overnight. But alas! The cellar was empty. There were no tubs, no copper, nothing at all but a grate on which to heat a boiler. Now what should I do? It was too late to buy anything, on the other hand it was imperative that I should use the cellar the next day, as my woman would not be able to alter her plans at such short notice, and I would not have use of the cellar again for another month. I had no alternative but to face the derision of my neighbours and ask them to lend me the necessary equipment. This they did willingly, but it was obvious that they were aghast at what they thought was incredible stupidity on my part! From time to time various minor incidents of a similar nature occurred which made them think I was, to say the least of it, rather peculiar. These incidents, coupled with my English accent and my English hats, made them doubt my sanity. Their suspicions were confirmed one day when I rushed breathlessly up to the people overhead to warn them that the chimney was on fire. With scathing ridicule at my ignorance they pointed out that it was only being swept. I had returned from a shopping expedition to find my kitchen full of smoke and soot, which was belching from every crack in the stove, and from the ventilators above and below. Apparently the chimney-sweep would announce his visit on the previous day, from door to door, and when he came he would shout, 'Schornsteinfeger' through the building in a loud voice before starting. All ventilators would then be firmly shut, but those unfortunate people who happened to be out would find it necessary to springclean the kitchen on their return.

The stove was rather a worry to me at first. In a letter to my mother I wrote: 'Our stove which heats the central heating burns very well and economically. You just turn a tap on or off as the case may be when you want to heat the bath-water. The first time I turned it on, after about a quarter of an hour there was a *terrible* noise, clank, bonk, clank! I thought all the pipes were bursting and stood waiting for the flood. I am altogether in any case rather frightened of the whole process of central heating when I'm alone in the house. However, nothing further happened and my alarm was in vain. I'm terrified of pipes bursting! Someone told me I mustn't let the water boil. One day although the temperature on the stove was only 60 degrees (140 degrees Fahrenheit) it sounded to me as though it was boiling and I waited again for the flood, but nothing happened. I was told later that the noise had something to do with the circulation.'

I must say my neighbours were very good-natured and kind, but I felt a complete outsider. I knew I seemed odd to them, just as many of them, with their foreign ways, seemed odd to me, the difference being that I was the only one in my camp, whereas they all conformed to their pattern. They did not realize that among my own people I was no more of an oddity than they were among theirs. They struck me as being much more old-fashioned than we were in England. I discovered that if I bought a hat in London, it would be laughed to scorn in Danzig, but nevertheless would be the height of fashion there two or three years later.

The Danzigers were not only more old-fashioned in dress but also in their everyday habits, especially in the home. This was, however, largely due to climatic reasons and to the fact that Danzig was surrounded by hampering frontier restrictions.

The Poles, of course, had no harbour in their strip of land so, with the help of the French they set about building one, a masterpiece of engineering, at the little fishing village of Gdynia. Thus, although not robbed of their ancient harbour, the Danzigers found as time went on that their prosperity was threatened by Polish rivals a few miles away. Danzig, a natural harbour, with well-known and long-established trade routes, used to be the gateway to the east, but her connections with Soviet Russia had been severed since the war, customs barriers had been set up between Danzig and East and West Prussia, and now, to make matters worse, sources of trade with her only remaining neighbour gradually dried up, for as soon as the port of Gdynia was completed, the Poles naturally favoured the use of their own harbour for merchandise brought to and from Poland and the regions south of

Poland. Under these circumstances Danzig was denied the means of making an independent livelihood. The wharves and warehouses grew quieter and emptier. The mighty crane, called *der grosse Heinrich*, in the Schichau shipyards revolved less and less frequently with its heavy burdens. It became increasingly obvious that Danzig's only hope of survival was to turn to one of her big neighbours for help, and it was natural that she should turn to Germany. Not only was she linked to Germany through tradition, ties of blood and a common language, but her other two near neighbours, Poland and Russia, had decisively turned their backs on her. Hitler, notoriously overwilling to take advantage of any situation favourable to his purpose, eagerly stretched out his hands towards them.

So far as I could make out, the German minority in Poland was not badly treated (no worse than any minority is always treated), but although they naturally felt a strong affinity to Germany, they seemed to live in constant dread of being considered on too friendly terms with her, which would of course prejudice their standing with the Poles, indeed they might even be suspected of being secret agents. Few of them married Poles, and many were related to Germans in Germany. Their sons were sent to German universities (in fact so were those of most educated Poles). A number of the younger people, excepting the peasants and landowners, emigrated to Germany, where there was more scope for advancement.

My first contacts with these minority Germans from Poland (known as *Volksdeutsche*) gave me the impression that they were morose, suspicious and unreliable. It was not until I myself lived in the Polish Corridor in a world of fear and mistrust during the war, when every movement was watched, that I properly understood the position they had been placed in and their consequent reactions to people from the outside world. They appeared to be morose and suspicious because they were afraid of informers and of any new contacts which might heap further trouble on their heads, and they appeared to be unreliable because they lived from hand to mouth and could not vouch for the morrow. They resented their isolation and were envious of our freedom. Whilst they longed for friendship, they dared not become involved with foreigners for fear of being suspected of collaboration. They had little in common with the Poles, who in any case did not associate with them. There were German schools and they were allowed to speak German, but plays, opera, films and so on were naturally always in Polish. My singing teacher in Bromberg (Bydgoszcz), who had performed a good deal on the Polish Radio, told me she had been allowed to sing in any other language – English, French, Russian, Spanish, Italian or even Chinese if she wished – but never in German.

Class distinction was very marked. The rich Poles lived off the fat of the land, whilst the poor (who were in the majority) could not afford to buy butter. Even peasants who kept cows could rarely afford to eat the butter they made.

Through a laboratory assistant in the Frauenklinik, whose father was an architect in the Polish Corridor, we were introduced to some able *Volksdeutsche* craftsmen. They had great difficulty in keeping their heads above water and were only too pleased to be given orders for wrought-iron and wooden lampstands and candlesticks, copper ornaments, and hand-woven materials, carpets and rugs. We had to pay no customs duty on goods from Poland, so that the prices were extremely reasonable for the good quality materials and workmanship. What is more, we were able to make our own designs and order exactly what we wanted. When their representative first visited us, he showed us samples and photographs of their smaller pieces of work which were entirely to our taste. Although he said they were badly in need of customers, he seemed extraordinarily diffident and vague. After taking a note of the various things we needed he went off, leaving no address. However, a few weeks later he turned up again with everything we had asked for. In the course of conversation he happened to mention that he knew some men who made very fine furniture. When we questioned him he said, yes, there was ample timber available at reasonable prices, and yes, the men badly needed work, but again there was the same mysterious drawing back, so that we could not make out what he was really thinking. One moment he jumped at our suggestions, and the next he appeared completely uninterested. No doubt the reason for his peculiar vacillation was that he was torn between wanting to give the men work and the dread of becoming entangled in business and activities which might cause disapproval in Polish quarters. Eventually he warmed to our enthusiasm and designed some beautiful furniture for us from our sketches. Some of it was still undelivered when the German Army marched into Poland in September 1939, and he was amongst the thousand innocent *Volksdeutsche* who in Bromberg alone were massacred by the Poles before the town was taken. His transactions with us were not of course the cause of his murder. He just happened to be one of the unfortunate individuals of German blood who were on the spot to be sacrificed in the slaughter of revenge by a nation whose land was being invaded. Like many others, he was the victim of circumstances, and looking back, it seemed almost that he foresaw his fate.

In spite of the fact that Danzig was already more or less politically under the power of the Nazis when I first lived there, I was left free and unhampered in every respect until the war started. I naturally did not join any political movement or party – in fact I was never asked to. Although I still saw much good work being done by the Nazis for the poor, and their welfare workers were truly excellent, I did not wish to become involved in any politics. When the representative of the *Frauenschaft*, the Nazi Women's Group, called canvassing for members, she beat a hasty retreat when she heard I was English-born. There was one man, a cripple, living in a flat on the top floor of our block, who became most abusive because I would not hang out the Nazi flag on some festive occasion. This attitude was, however, only adopted by ignorant fanatics, and Kurt said such an incident would have never occurred in western Germany. In the outposts of eastern Germany those who were Nazis were much more narrow-minded than their western brothers. Their ardour was not tempered with the Rhinelander's *Gutmütigkeit*, nor with the Berliner's critical wit.

The standard of living was on the whole lower than in England, but a little money seemed to go a long way. Necessary foodstuffs, meals in restaurants, wine, beer, liqueurs, or seats in the cinema, theatre or concert-hall were not so expensive. There were outdoor cafés and restaurants in the woods or by the sea where a family could have a good meal and spend a pleasant day at a reasonable cost if they did not wish to take a picnic basket. The coast was studded with bathing resorts and fishing villages with wide stretches of sand in between, bordered by good paths running parallel to the sea for pedestrians and cyclists. Most roads had paths at the side for the exclusive use of cyclists, and as our flat was only ten minutes' ride from the sea, we could easily slip down for a bathe.

Small boats ran out to Brösen, Glettkau and Zoppot (Sopot) from the centre of Danzig, besides which there were buses and trams. Except at Zoppot, which was a fashionable seaside town with a casino and a Kurhaus frequented in the summer by throngs of international tourists, there were never any crowds. At the landing-stage in Zoppot German Seedienst steamers called for passengers to Stralsund to the west, and Pillau (Baltiysk) to the east, some of which went on up to Helsinki. The fares were fabulously cheap and, as the Baltic Sea is rarely choppy, these steamer trips were very popular. Some liners would come as far as Zoppot for summer cruises. Special dates for calling were arranged to coincide with the performances of the *Waldoper*, the world-famous Wagner Opera

Season which took place out of doors in the woods. There was a natural arena and stage, a clearance in a dip, surrounded by pine forests, which made a fitting background for the mythical scenes of the Nibelung Ring. The acoustics were excellent, but the voices were sometimes overwhelmed by the volume of sound from the orchestra, as the instruments were considerably nearer to the public. In spite of the fact that first-rate singers were engaged, the prices of seats were not exorbitant. I had a season ticket for the whole of the Ring, and went with an English friend, Miss Roberts, as Kurt was unable to get away for so many hours at a time each evening, and it was several miles out of Danzig.

It was easier for Kurt to go to the theatre in the town for which we rarely had to buy tickets as the authorities always liked to have a doctor in the theatre, and for each performance two seats were reserved for this purpose.

One of the star actors, Gustav Nord, was married to an Englishwoman whose mother, strangely enough, was a neighbour of my aunt in Rye. Herr Nord was a clever comedian, popular amongst the Danzig people because he played to perfection the rôles of the local humorist. He was a little man, with a large nose, a wide mouth, and an attractive voice, and although considerably older than his wife, he was very nimble on the stage.

Mrs Nord and I visited each other, but except for our English connections we did not have very much in common. After her mother died, Mrs Nord built a little house near the Städtisches Krankenhaus in Danzig with some money which had been left her. It had what Germans call a 'winter garden' (a little covered verandah with wide windowsills for plants), but was otherwise built in the English style, with an open fireplace in the drawing-room, which looked attractive but unfortunately could never be used as the German architects and builders had no experience in such matters and it smoked abominably. She had central heating as well, of course, as an open fire would have been inadequate. I was introduced to various people from the English colony at her house, and through the British Consulate I met Miss Roberts and Mrs Johnson, who became my best friends in Danzig.

Miss Roberts had worked in southern Germany for a considerable time and then in 1936 she got a job in the British Consulate in Danzig. She was a little older than I and had stood firmly on her own feet for so many years that she gave the impression of being very independent and somehow complete in character. In spite of having lived abroad for so long, she had remained fundamentally as English as anyone I have ever known. She rented a charming little top-storey flat in Zoppot with a wide sky-light in one room which had previously been used as an atelier. From the windows in her sitting-room there was a fine view, beyond the fir tops, across the roofs, to Danzig and the sea. The thought of her flat conjures up many happy memories. We returned there, or to my flat, for cosy teas or suppers after long walks in the woods and by the sea, and had lengthy discussions on all manner of subjects, heartily disagreeing on many of them. To be with her was like going home to England for an afternoon. We hooted with laughter over the foreign oddities, and compared notes in general over our impression of the Germans. It was interesting to find confirmation of my view that they were bad losers. She belonged to a fencing club and thoroughly enjoyed herself there, no matter whether she won or lost, but it was not long before she discovered how seriously the Germans took the sport, and that they were bent on winning at all costs. If there was any uncertainty, they would emphatically assert their claim to the point instead of insisting that their opponents should have the benefit of the doubt, as is usual in England.

Another adverse criticism we both had to make about the German character was the lack of any code of honour with regard to prying into other people's business. For instance, at home in England who would dream of reading other people's letters, wherever they may be left lying about? No doubt some English people would do so, but they would be considered intolerably inquisitive. Not so in Germany. There one must reckon that everything that is not under lock and key is liable to be pried into, especially if there is something which might be particularly interesting to the person concerned. In our flat I had an upright secretaire, which I kept shut, but naturally I never locked it. I had no secrets to hide, nor any private business, and I trusted everyone who came into our home. One day I was terribly shocked to find a relative of my husband, who was staying with us, quietly nosing through my letters and papers. When I remonstrated he was most surprised and not at all abashed. The desk was unlocked, and therefore according to his logic it was open to inspection.

However, such differences in upbringing and outlook can cause amusement when discussed with a friend who shares your point of view. No doubt we sometimes unknowingly trod on the Germans' toes just as much as they did on ours. It is only by living for many years among foreigners that the fine points of behaviour can be absorbed and their idiosyncrasies understood, which was probably one of the reasons why Miss Roberts remained entirely English, because she did not in fact either live or work with Germans, nor had she any wish to do so. Nevertheless she did adopt some German habits. Like most members of the middle classes she had a daily maid who did all the work except the cooking, and she would leave all the washing-up (even from the whole of Sunday's cooking) for the woman to do in the morning. We used to laugh when we thought how horrified maids in England would be if we served such a trick on them. This, however, was quite usual in Germany, where only one maid was kept, and even on her half day off as a matter of course all the dirty dishes from the afternoon and evening meals were left stacked up in the kitchen.

Mrs Johnson also lived in Zoppot, in a ground-floor flat. There was a lilac tree in the garden and she had a bed of mint which had grown from one little root someone had brought her from England, as there was none available locally. She gave me a root, which grew and spread like wild-fire, but unfortunately I could never get a really tasty piece of mutton to go with it! Mrs Johnson was half-English and half-Danish. She and her husband, who was in the shipping business, had previously lived in Riga and Petrograd (as it was then called).

It was from Mrs Johnson that I learned how to do the fine cross-stitch Russian embroidery and she lent me a lot of patterns. She stitched lovely borders on her linen face towels, and usually had a piece of work in hand. I had never seen this sort of embroidery before, although I was soon to become familiar with it at an exhibition of handicrafts by Ukrainians from south-east Poland which was held in Danzig. Here I was able to buy exquisite examples of brilliantly coloured embroidery, mostly on hand-woven linen — tablecloths, towels, mats, blouses and so on. There were also bowls, boxes and buckles of finely carved wood inlaid with mother-of-pearl. These things were made by the peasants during the long, severe winter when it was impossible to work out-of-doors. They were glad to raise money in this way, and being duty-free, the prices were very low compared with our standards; what is more, besides being so beautiful, the linen would wash and wear for a lifetime. The peasants, living hundreds of miles away from large towns and factories, were as yet unaffected by the industrial mass production of goods and their traditional handicrafts flourished. They would spin and weave linen and woollen materials, and make their own clothes. In the winter their coats would be lined with fur or sheep skins. They made the furniture necessary for their primitive existence. Very often the whole family was housed in a one-room hut into which the chickens would also be brought in the winter, and in some cases the only animals they could afford to feed. The rest of the cattle would be slaughtered in the autumn and the meat pickled or smoked.

In the corner of the room there would be a large square stove upon which the family slept when it was cold. They suffered great hardships after a bad harvest, and if they were unable to store sufficient food to last through the winter, they starved to death.

A daughter of the more well-to-do farmer would start spinning, weaving, crocheting, embroidering and lace-making for her bottom drawer as soon as she was old enough to practise these crafts, long before she thought of marrying. The more prosperous the family, the larger was her store of linen and other goods when she married. This was also the custom in Germany until comparatively recent times. I knew one very old farmer who still had rolls of hand-woven linen which his wife had brought into the marriage as part of her dowry. They had such vast stores of linen that they did not have any 'big washes' in the winter – in fact it was looked upon as rather degrading if this were necessary because it only showed there was not sufficient in the cupboards to last out until the spring! By this time, therefore, there would be an enormous collection of dirty linen, and several women would be busy washing for two or three weeks, the sheets being laid out on the grass to bleach in the sun.

The fine cross-stitch embroidery was popular in various places, each district having its own traditional patterns, some of which have been handed down from mother to daughter for hundreds of years. One of my favourites depicted a bold stag, with a little fir tree in one corner and an *Auerhahn*, a mountain cock, in the other, an ancient design (originating from Siebenbürgen, the 800-year-old German settlement in Romania) which was passed on to me by a friend of Kurt's some time after my eyes had been opened to the fascination of this work by Mrs Johnson.

In spite of the fact that she was only half-English, had lived abroad practically all her life, and even spoke English with a slight accent, there was nothing foreign about Mrs Johnson, or her home. Another English lady, Frau Beutter, who was married to a German and had lived in Danzig for twenty or thirty years, had become completely German in her habits and outlook, and yet the little German-born wife of the English parson in Danzig behaved like an English-woman and felt like one. These three were all happily married. Mrs Nord had remained more than partially English, and her marriage was not a happy one. I wondered if this was a coincidence, or was it essential for the wife to adapt herself entirely to her husband's nationality, in which case how would I end up?

Even though I no longer possessed a British passport, I was more or less accepted as a member of the British colony. Kurt and I were even invited to the official banquet given by the Consul-General, Mr Robinson, to celebrate the Coronation of King George VI on 12 May 1937. Kurt could not come to the dinner, so Miss Roberts called for me, and before leaving we listened in to the King's speech. Kurt found there was a good reception from some ultra-short-wave station and we were surprised to hear afterwards that it was 'Sydney calling', which seemed rather a roundabout way of hearing it!

THREE

I did not find it easy at this stage to make friends with German women, who probably in their turn thought I was as stiff as a poker. Except for Frau Stein, and later on, one or two doctors' wives, there was nobody I knew well enough or wished to call and see without a formal invitation. I was, however, very busy and taken up with my own domestic affairs and found the change in environment and style of living quite strenuous. On days when Kurt was operating or assisting Professor Fuchs he would usually have to be in the theatre by six o'clock at the latest. To avoid disturbing me he would creep out of the flat and have his breakfast in the Klinik. In the winter it was dark in the mornings until eight o'clock or more and I had the greatest difficulty in waking up at all. Sometimes it was well after nine before I roused. Then I would leap out of bed and hurry into my clothes, terrified that someone would ring the front door bell before I was dressed, and that I would be dubbed a lazy slut for evermore by the efficient housewives next door, who had probably been up and doing for hours. Fortunately we lived on the ground floor because there was one habit of the neighbours with which I would in any case have refused to conform and that was to wear bedroom slippers indoors nearly all day long, ostensibly because the sound of shoes reverberated into the flat below.

Though time never lagged as there was always so much to do, the first winter still seemed never-ending. It was not the intense cold that I minded so much as the *length* of the winter. Indeed, in spite of the prolonged low temperatures outdoors, I felt warmer indoors than I had ever been during the mildest of winters in draughty, badly heated English houses. In every building, house or flat there were double windows and snug central heating or decorative tiled stoves standing about six or seven feet high. The water and drainage systems were so constructed that frozen or burst pipes were unheard of. Our central heating stove maintained a steady, comfortable temperature throughout the flat, supplied us with hot water, and could be used for cooking or for keeping pots or dishes warm, all at no more expense than one open coal fire. In midwinter it was impossible to leave the windows open for long, otherwise everything in the room, plants and so on, especially those near the window, would become frozen. We found that the best way to keep the place fresh was to open all the windows and doors wide for a short period, to give a good draught through, every now and then, especially after meals. While this 'airing' was in progress the temperature of the water in the central heating boiler shown on a thermometer would visibly sink very fast as the cold blast chilled the pipes.

The secret of keeping warm outdoors is to start off warm, wrap up in a fur coat, overboots, mitts (*not* gloves), a cap or scarf over the head and ears, and then keep moving. Knowing that I was going to live in a cold climate, my parents had wisely given me a thick fur coat. When out of doors for any length of time it was necessary to give one's nose and chin a good rub now and again to prevent frost-bite. The only part of me which I could not keep warm when carrying heavy loads while shopping was my fingers. They would ache and sting then in an unbearable manner. The biting wind swept down the narrow market street, and everything I bought or touched, including fish, would be frozen hard. The fat, red-faced market women (looking fatter than ever in their innumerable layers of skirts, scarves and shawls) beat their hands across their chests and stamped their feet on the ground in an effort to keep warm while waiting for customers.

We started off usually in November with fairly heavy falls of snow. Sometimes it got a little warmer again, but most years the November snow stayed on the ground until March, April or even May, as the temperature did not rise much above freezing point until then. It was swept off the roads, but the little clumps did not melt away, and the countryside remained white all the winter. I have some letters written home which my mother kept. On 20 December 1937, I wrote: 'Ever since I came back from Neukuhren (10 November) we have had snow on the ground.' Exactly a year later, on 20 December 1938, I wrote: 'Hilde and I went shopping and to the market this morning and bought my Christmas tree . . . My word, we simply *froze* up at the market. A snow storm came up with an *icy wind*. The temperature in the day time is 17 degrees Centigrade below freezing point (just above zero Fahrenheit) as I have just se·n in the paper, and that's what it felt like too. People are going about looking like a lot of mummies wrapped up from head to foot. Even your chin and ears freeze . . . The rivers are frozen thick enough to bear horses and sleighs.' In places where ferries were normally used, cars and other traffic would drive across the frozen rivers. In January and February it was still colder. Even the sea would freeze then, and you could walk on the ice as far as the end of the pier and further. Miss Roberts told me the first winter she was in Danzig the sea froze out as far as the Hela peninsula which is twenty miles away.

It was interesting to compare the climates, and notice how much later flowers blossomed in Danzig than in England. On 3 February 1938, I wrote: 'Fancy snowdrops out already! They won't be out here for *weeks* yet.' In March, while in England there was a profusion of primroses in the woods and gardens were full of daffodils, we were still 'in the depths of winter with snow lying very deep on the ground'. 'There is of course no sign of a bulb shoot coming up in anybody's garden and I do envy you folks being able to pick a bunch of daffodils' (26 March 1939). It was not until 15 April 1939 that I wrote: 'The snowdrops and crocuses are in bloom out here now,' and on 3 May 1939: 'It is still cold and the trees are only just beginning to sprout.' But then, once the spring started, things moved quickly. On 15 May 1939, 'Our fruit trees are beginning to blossom now and from every window we look out on to green lilac trees and green trees and bushes and fruit trees. It really is beautiful now the spring has at last wended its way up to Danzig town.'

Accustomed to the short English winters, when frost only appears in spasms, as the weeks and months of icy weather dragged on and on through November, December, January, February and March, and still there were no signs of a real thaw, I began to wonder that first winter whether the spring would ever come again. Indeed it did not come in the form that we know it – at first a gentle, almost imperceptible stirring of nature, followed by a gradual unfolding of leaf and flower. At the beginning of May the trees would be bare, but within a fortnight everything would be green and the fruit trees in blossom. By the end of May we would be thrust into the hot, dry continental summer almost before we had had time to unravel our winter mufflers. On 25 May 1937, I wrote: 'We have already had some *scorching* days – hotter than I've ever had in England, but now it is just perfect – sunshine all day long, but a cool breeze. We are so looking forward to our sea trip.'

We had a number of people coming to stay with us during our first summer, so we planned an early holiday, travelling by Seedienst Ostpreussen steamer from Zoppot to Helsinki, and on up through Finland, by train, lake-steamer and coach, as far as the Arctic Sea in time to spend the longest day of the year in the land of the midnight sun. The Finns struck us as being sturdy, industrious and straightforward, with a keen sense of beauty, and they were always helpful and friendly towards tourists. The pale northern landscape, with the enormous forests, the thousands of lakes, studded with little islands, and the myriad changing lights reflected in the water, held us spellbound. We were sad when our holiday came to an end.

Before leaving for Finland we had one visitor; Kurt's elder brother Heinz had motored up to Danzig with some friends and had stopped a night or two with us. That was the first time we had had anyone to stay because nobody had felt attracted towards our savage winter. As Heinz was the first member of Kurt's family to see our home, I was anxious to make a good impression, and was much relieved when at every meal he complimented me on my cooking. Heinz, like every German visitor we ever had, was most surprised that I could cook, but I could never get a satisfactory explanation of why they were surprised. I asked them if I looked too stupid, but no, that was not it; I just didn't look as if I could cook! A former friend of Kurt's, Lotte Niemann, and her husband, an officer in the Army, came to stay with us early in the summer and passed the same verdict on my cooking and household management, so that I felt I had passed my first tests satisfactorily.

Our next visitor was my brother's wife from Glasgow, who enjoyed prowling round the old town, sunning herself by the sea and generally finding out people's views concerning every subject which interested her. It was good to have this first link with home since I had left England.

Kurt's younger brother Max also stayed with us and was there when my sister Mu arrived from England in August. She stayed until mid-September, thus giving us plenty of time to show her round, as she was of course interested in our everyday routine, shopping, cooking and washing, besides the usual holiday activities, and Mama and Father were most anxious to have a first-hand description of every detail.

It was the first time that Mu had been to a German-speaking country and she did not understand a word of the language. When Kurt had a long or complicated story to tell, he sometimes could not speak quickly enough in English and reverted to German. In this way I had practice in interpreting and was highly praised by Kurt for the progress I had made.

Mu helped me with my work to give us more free time,

and liked to come with me to the market, which for her was an interesting novelty. On our way to Langfuhr Market we would call in at the Café Blum for coffee and cakes, which were an added attraction. They had luscious nut, chocolate and mocca gâteaux with oodles of whipped cream, also many sorts of pastries and cakes, but although I always intended to sample the latter, I never could, because it was impossible to eat any more after succumbing to one piece of the irresistible gâteau.

There was also a Café Blum in Danzig, run by the same people, which was a popular meeting place in the afternoons. Here too there were rows and rows of delicious cakes on counters where, as is the custom in Germany, you made your choice and were given a chit which you passed on to the waiter at your table, who brought the cakes with the coffee. Practically nobody drank tea, but the coffee was excellent.

Nearly every day we went out somewhere. We often cycled to different places along the coast. I used Kurt's bicycle which, once on the saddle, was easy enough to ride, but getting on and off was tricky. One day, when riding up the narrow street from the ferry on the other side of the Vistula towards Heubude, I nearly knocked down a little boy who suddenly decided to cross the road in front of me and I was unable to dismount quickly enough. The disadvantage of Heubude was the plague of mosquitoes which swarmed out in the evenings if there was not much wind. On the sands they were bad enough, but on the path which ran along the edge of the woods parallel to the sea, it was quite impossible to stand still for one second without being severely stung. Even while cycling the beasts attacked our legs if we went too slowly or free-wheeled, so that our homeward journeys were invariably at top speed. The coast on our side of the river was not infested as the woods did not come down so near to the shore.

On 5 September, the first anniversary of our wedding day, Kurt, Mu and I had a celebration lunch in Danzig and then went on a small boat from Danzig harbour to Zoppot. It was a gloriously sunny day, and we finished up by having coffee in the open-air Café Lucas on top of the cliffs near the Polish frontier. We wrote a postcard home while we were sitting there, which showed the café, with the tables and large mushroom sunshades in the foreground, and the sea beyond. The especially harmonious and happy day was unfortunately marred by a misunderstanding about the jokes that Mu and I made about Mama while writing this card; Kurt was bitterly offended because he was very fond of her and thought we were unkind. He did not understand that had Mama been there she would have enjoyed the jokes as much as any of us, if not more. We were trying to describe the events of the day in a nutshell, and were laughing because Mama would be sure to want to know, amongst other things, exactly what we were wearing. This was a standing joke in the family in which she heartily joined.

One day, my sister and I went to Marienburg. We spent most of the time looking over the castle and had lunch in a restaurant in the *Rathauskeller* (the old Town Hall cellar) where we chose fried fillet of pork, served in the east German fashion with fat instead of thickened gravy, and *Pfifferlinge* (a small edible toadstool) which Mu had never eaten before.

I was only beginning to learn about edible toadstools. Kurt's family had become experts during the First World War and in the period of inflation afterwards when food was so scarce. They made expeditions to the surrounding woods in the autumn to gather a store of nourishing fungus which could also be bottled for use in the winter. In eastern Germany, where the food shortage had not been so great, many people, excepting the poor peasants, were almost as ignorant as I was about the various sorts which can be eaten and enjoyed, but the *Pfifferlinge* and *Steinpilze* were universal favourites. At first I swore to Kurt that there were no edible toadstools in England; however, on one of the first walks we took when he came to stay with us before we were married, we found hosts of *Pfifferlinge*!

Soon after Mu left us Kurt went to Neukuhren, a small fishing village, in East Prussia, on the Samland coast, where he had to do two months' military training on the medical staff at an Air Force camp. He left Danzig on 30 September, and after he had found somewhere for me to stay and I had cleared up the flat, I followed him.

During the daytime, while Kurt was on duty, I made the best of the sunny autumn weather. It is a lovely coastline, with a long stretch of yellow sand by the sea, above which are high sandy, earthy cliffs, mostly covered with trees and bushes. On the eastern side of Neukuhren the cliffs slope down lower and lower until they become mere sand dunes, which are skirted by pine woods.

Most men who had to do a term of military service complained about the hard work, but Kurt looked upon it as a holiday. He certainly had to be on duty early in the morning, but he was free at one o'clock on Wednesdays and Saturdays, at four on other weekdays and had every Sunday off. It was a treat for him to be able to sleep all night long without being wakened by the wretched telephone and to know when he went to bed that he could stay there until the next morning. It seemed quite strange to us both to be able to make plans ahead and say tomorrow at half past four we would do this or that and the next day we would go here or there. It made us realize what an easy life most people have in comparison with a doctor's. When their hours of work are over, no matter how short or long, men in other professions are free. Not so a doctor, still less a gynaecologist working in a hospital where the most difficult and urgent cases are brought for treatment, operative or otherwise. It is not only the irregular hours and emergency calls which are a strain, but also the weight of responsibility for human lives. Delay may be fatal. One slip and the patient may never recover. Every day there are literally *vital* decisions to be made.

After I had been in Neukuhren for about a fortnight I went up to Tilsit, near the border of Memel, to stay with Hauptmann and Frau Niemann, and then returned to Neukuhren for a few days before going back to Danzig on 11 November 1937. Kurt did not finish his military service until 26 November, but now that I had some friends I did not mind being alone for a time.

After Kurt married it became quite the fashion for the young doctors in Danzig hospitals to do likewise. At that time it was still difficult for married doctors to find hospitals in Germany where they were allowed to train as specialists.

A young doctor in the Klinik, Dr Schneider, with whom Kurt was friendly, had married and lived further down our street. Not long afterwards another assistant married, but we had no contact with them, I think mainly because there was some curious rivalry between him and Kurt. A Dr Maisel, who was already married, came to live in the next block of flats. He had not been working very long in the Klinik when he was taken ill with a tumour on the brain just when his wife was expecting her first baby. We did not have the usual Christmas festivities amongst the medical staff in the Klinik that year as Dr Maisel was just having his operation in Berlin and nobody expected him to survive. When Frau Maisel had to give up her flat owing to her husband's prolonged illness, from which there were faint hopes of recovery, she stored her furniture, and asked me if I would like to borrow her piano, an offer which I gladly accepted as it gave me the opportunity to practise singing again.

It was during this winter that I started skating in earnest. I made my début in the open-air rink near the Sporthalle in Langfuhr, about ten minutes' walk from our flat. On my first attempts I tried to go in the mornings when the children were at school, as I felt such a fool slithering about and falling down every other minute, whilst the smallest nippers were cutting miraculous figures as if they had been born on skates. Naturally they could not conceive the possibility of an adult being a beginner and thought it very comic to see a grown woman floundering on the ice like a clown. One of the most difficult manoeuvres was to negotiate the route from the changing hut to the rink, between a narrow opening in the fence and down a slope. I usually crashed into the wire-netting and then slid down the slope, landing with a bump at the bottom.

As soon as I could steer my way moderately well without falling down too often, I preferred to go in the afternoons or evenings, in spite of the increased numbers on the rink, because there would then be music blaring out of loudspeakers and it was much easier to swing along to the rhythm. A girl who worked in the laboratory at the Klinik, came to my rescue sometimes and, holding hands, we would float round together. There was no pleasure in taking a rest, unless the sun was shining, as it was too cold, but it was a most invigorating sport. By the end of the evening the surface of the ice would become very rough. It would then be covered with water from hosepipes, and by the morning it was as smooth as glass again.

I soon decided that I had started learning much too late ever to become proficient in figure-skating. What I loved best, when I was more experienced, was to skate up the River Mottlau, which was swept free of snow for this purpose for several miles as far as a little guest house. Two of the nurses took me with them whenever they made this expedition. We rarely met or passed anyone else as we swung along the winding river between snow-clad fields, the silence only broken by the swish of our skates skimming over the ice. With no tiresome experts cutting figures across our path, we covered the ground rapidly, then after a short thaw round the stove at the restaurant and a steaming hot cup of coffee, we sped homewards through the pale winter twilight. To me this was much more fascinating than going round in a circle for hours on end. On the whole, however, the rinks in Danzig were much more popular than the river, no doubt because the surface of the river was not smooth enough and the passage swept free of snow not wide enough for elaborate figure-skating.

It must have been during my first winter in Danzig that I attended lectures given by Professor Le Baume on the Early History of Man, at the Technical High School, one of the courses taken by full-time students, which anybody was allowed to join in as a 'visitor' at a reasonable cost. In January 1938 I joined Professor Haferkorn's Interpreters' Course in English which was held twice weekly. On Tuesdays about twenty came, mostly professional men who needed the language for their jobs, but on Fridays there were only about five of us, which gave us greater scope for individual practice. Professor Haferkorn spoke perfect English with perfect diction, in fact so much so, that he could only be recognized as a foreigner through this very perfection. The native never bothers to speak with such accuracy! By far the most difficult task in this course was to remember the exact wording of long passages which Professor Haferkorn read from articles out of German newspapers and *The Times*. We were supposed to interpret these in a flash, as though we had recording instruments in our minds and needed only to press a button in order to produce an accurate translation.

Learning that I was English-born, the Professor asked me to become his assistant, and at the end of the term he paid me the portly sum of 80 Gulden, which I did not feel I had deserved because I picked his brain much more than he did mine. But of course the mere fact of being English was sufficient, as it stimulated interest amongst the students, and it was good for them to hear an English voice. I went to Professor Haferkorn's study about an hour before each lesson to correct papers and to help prepare the work. During the lesson I read out the English passages to be interpreted. Sometimes I would give short lectures, and discussions would follow. I also helped him in the examinations. He sat at one end of the table pretending he could understand no English, and I sat at the other end pretending I could understand no German. The victim sat between us and had to interpret the conversation we carried on through him. I enjoyed every minute of the work and was sorry I could not continue the next winter owing to a period of uncertainty with regard to Kurt's new job, and to my preoccupation with the expected arrival of our baby in the following summer.

FOUR

Kurt managed to get the Whitsun weekend of 1938 free and we went for a little cycling tour. We set off on the Saturday by bus for Königsberg (Kaliningrad). Once we were out of the busy town, we hardly saw any traffic, and cycled between thick pine woods, every now and then catching a glimpse of the water through the trees. It was ideal weather for cycling – sunny but cool. We stopped on the way for rests in the shade of the trees, sometimes calling at restaurants for a glass of milk and covered about thirty miles that afternoon. When we arrived in Fischhausen, a small fishing town, I went into a grocer's shop to buy a few things and to ask where we could find a night's lodging, only to be told that there was not much chance in the town, and the nearest guest house was seven miles away. We were not satisfied with this reply, and while we consumed ice-creams in a dairy, we made further enquiries, with better results. Yes, there was a guest house down the road on the right-hand side. Here Kurt received a frigid welcome by the barmaid who apparently thought we were not married (a mistake which a lot of people used to make). When the buxom landlady arrived, 'all was in best butter' (as they say in German), and we were taken to a clean, but sparsely furnished room. After a good night's rest we started off again at dawn when the countryside was at its best and before it got too hot. By midday we were near Pillau (Baltiysk) and rested on the sand by the sea, where Kurt had a bathe. The water was too cold for my liking, but I could not resist the opportunity of swanking in my new two-piece swimming costume (a bright blue, with white dots all over it). After lunch in an open-air restaurant on the seafront, we crossed over on a ferry to the narrow strip of land between Pillau and Bohnsack called the Frische Nehrung, which was thickly wooded, with a sandy shore on either side. There were only one or two fishing villages and one holiday resort, as no motor traffic was allowed. On the path between Neutief and Narmeln (about seventeen miles) the only people we met were two or three cyclists. One man, who was cycling alone, had apparently had a dip and had not bothered to dress. As soon as he saw us, he beat a hasty retreat behind some bushes, not before we had caught a glimpse of the peculiar spectacle. He could not have felt any cooler cycling in the nude, because the sun must have been beating down on his bare flesh. On this day we cycled on during the early afternoon, as we were not sure whether we would find lodgings in Narmeln, which would mean pushing on a good deal further before dark. As a matter of fact our misgivings were not without foundation, but fortunately we discovered there was a steamer leaving shortly for a town called Braunsberg on the other side of the Haff, where we could be sure of finding accommodation.

The next morning we set off for Frauenburg where there was a beautiful cathedral, dating back to the thirteenth century, built on a hill overlooking the Haff. We had looked up the road on a map in our hotel and found one marked 'side road' from Frauenburg to Tolkemit, which skirted the edge of the water. Unfortunately it deteriorated into a mere sandy track full of cart ruts. It took us up hill and down dale through woods near the coast for about ten miles. Half the time I had to push my bicycle, as I kept being shaken off, but it was impossible to pause for one moment without getting bitten all over with mosquitoes.

We had only just arrived at an hotel in Tolkemit when a terrific thunderstorm burst overhead. The rain poured down in torrents, and within a few minutes the street in front of our restaurant became swamped with several inches of water, much to the amusement of the village children, who paddled up and down in great glee after the storm had abated as though they had never had a chance to paddle before. Later in the afternoon we boarded a steamer for Kahlberg. The next day was our last and we had a lovely run home in perfect weather. Altogether in three and a half days we cycled about a hundred and forty miles, and thoroughly enjoyed ourselves, although I must say I would advise anybody who is not well upholstered to avoid carrying a rucksack on a cycling tour, and to equip themselves with proper saddlebags for the purpose.

At this period I spent much time and thought in studying the language, and a vast field of exploration in the realm of German literature was thus laid open to me. I had slogged at French for years at school and had never experienced the thrill of the sudden raising of a curtain upon undiscovered riches, in the way that German literature was revealed to me by learning the language quickly with adult perception. Long before I could understand all the words, I enjoyed reading poetry and prose, with my ear only attuned to the rhythm and sound. I thus unwittingly stumbled on the surest test of style. If the style was bad (for which Germans use the very expressive word *Kitsch*) there was no music. If the style was good, even without understanding many words, their significance would be conveyed through the atmosphere they created, through the tune and rhythm, and through the rate of motion. I was almost sorry when I learned to understand the exact meaning, because as soon as the text conveyed definite ideas, it was impossible to concentrate solely on listening to the music of the language.

For some time after I married considerable concentration was necessary to carry on any complicated lengthy conversation in German, although I thought in German almost from the beginning. It was easier to understand when directly spoken to by one person only, but it was much more difficult to pick up the gist of discussions taking place in a room between various groups at the same time, as one can automatically when one's brain is properly 'tuned in' to a language. There was one thing I never learnt and never shall, and that is to do sums in German. I had always been top in arithmetic and mathematics at school, but Kurt is to this day firmly convinced that they are my weak subjects because I was so slow when trying to reckon in German.

Understanding jokes was another problem which often led to embarrassing situations, because people become highly offended if you do not find them amusing, and a joke explained loses its point completely. I developed a technique of going into fits of laughter when everybody else did. This did not work, of course, if I was the sole audience, when I had to be very careful not to burst out laughing in the wrong place.

German newspapers were mostly written in such poor style that they were scarcely readable. The droning voice of the radio announcer, in spite of his clear diction, was particularly remote, the more so because he rattled off dull or startling news alike, in the same monotonous tone.

Goebbels' speeches were easy to follow, but very uninteresting. As I listened I could always visualize the gaping movements of his enormous mouth, which we saw often enough in close-ups on the news-reels.

I liked Hitler's voice, with his rolling Austrian accent, until the point in his speeches when he would become so overwrought that he screamed. This ruined the effect of his arguments because the noise vibrated so painfully on the eardrums that they failed to drive home.

FIVE

Kurt finished his four years' training as a gynaecologist under Professor Fuchs at the Staatliche Frauenklinik in the summer of 1938, and decided he should study general surgery for a year. He was offered a post as assistant to Professor Klose, the chief surgeon in the Danzig Städtisches Kranken-haus, to start at the end of September 1938. That is why I did not travel to England in the spring, as originally in-tended, but waited until September, when Kurt could join me and take a holiday in between his change of jobs. We gave up our flat in Posadowskyweg, as Kurt had to live in the immediate vicinity of the hospital.

The hospital had recently requisitioned the corner house opposite their main entrance. On the ground floor of this house there were five good-sized rooms and a kitchen. Two of these rooms had been allotted to an unmarried doctor and the rest were in the process of being converted into a self-contained flat with a separate entrance and hall, and a new bathroom. We were promised this flat when it was ready and decided it was worth waiting for. It was a well-built house with two or three large windows in each room. We were given the three rooms on the sunny sides of the house, overlooking the garden, two of them leading on to a nice balcony. We were allowed to use the garden, which was tended by the caretaker who lived in the semi-basement, a carpenter employed by the hospital. We also had a share in the fruit harvest (chiefly cherries) and I was given a piece of ground to do just what I liked with. The flat was above ground level, so that when the trees were in blossom they were a wonderful picture outside our dining-room window. The architect who designed the alterations was very co-operative and adopted several suggestions which we put forward, such as making a hatchway between the kitchen and dining-room, fitting a cupboard in the hall, building a rounded archway in the passage instead of a square-shaped one. He also ordered a sensible sink and draining-board, and a large gas stove – modern fittings which at that time were not to be found as a matter of course in every German flat. The whole house was centrally heated from a large stove in the cellar, and there was of course a big wash-cellar and an attic for drying clothes in bad weather.

Until our flat was ready, we were allowed to rent two furnished rooms in the main building of the hospital, where there was, however, no kitchen, so we had our meals brought along the corridor from the resident doctors' dining-room (the so-called 'Casino'). We waited, impatiently, for the work to be finished. At first we were told it would only be a few weeks, then they said, 'You will be in by Christmas.' When Christmas came the necessary alterations to the central heating system were still not done and the painters had not started work, but 'It will certainly be ready by January.' The weeks dragged on into months, and it was the middle of February 1939 before we finally moved in.

In the meantime something of great personal importance was taking place. Kurt and I had long since hoped to see the arrival of a newcomer to the family. After we had been married for over two years he sent me to Professor Fuchs for treatment on 13 December 1938, which had immediate effect, and I was listed in his records as yet another success. For this reason, and because Kurt had been a favourite pupil, the dear old man took a particular interest in the case, and kept me under his special supervision.

Whilst we lived in the furnished rooms I suffered from the usual nausea and had ridiculous fads about food, a condition which was aggravated by the fact that I had no cooking facilities, and could never choose what I fancied. The hospital smells of sickness, disinfectants and anaesthetics made me feel quite ill. Worst of all, we had to pass through a little passage where our neighbours washed their babies' clothes. After coming through the hospital corridors, this was always the last straw, and I literally had to hold my nose as I dashed through, until I could fling our windows wide open to gulp in the fresh air. From the moment that we moved into our flat I was cured of my nausea. We wondered whether it was just coincidence, or the psychological effect, or the lack of smells and the freedom to choose my menu.

We had a busy time getting everything clean after the workmen had left, but we were delighted with our new home. Our furniture showed up well against the pale cream-coloured walls and the polished parquet flooring which was in every room. We had chosen the plain sunshine wallpapers which were not usual in Germany, but which were much admired by everyone who saw them. The dining-room was particularly attractive. Our new suite was ready before we moved in, and the light-coloured wood shone clean and warm. Over the sideboard we hung our latest acquisition, a very beautiful still-life oil painting by the Danzig painter Paetsch, showing a phyllocactus with its puce blossoms hanging on drooping stems, a bulbous wine flask and some rosy apples, on a table draped with a pale grey glossy cloth. Another Danzig artist, Zeuner, had painted my portrait for Kurt and this we hung on the opposite wall, over the couch. At the top end of the couch, furthest from the window there was an unusual little alcove with a rounded arch overhead.

We hung my Pasternack water-colour on the only large wall-space in the drawing-room, two of the walls having windows and the third a french window, also a door leading into my bedroom. Although there was a large window as well as a french window along the length of one side of my bedroom, it was nevertheless rather dark because the roof of the balcony was outside. I made the flimsiest cream-coloured net curtains with pale green dots, and we bought a fine hand-made carpet of sheep's wool in a natural shade with a dark brown border and a few brown flecks on it, with a pile about one inch thick, which it was fascinating to walk on with bare feet. Near the window I had my sewing table and armchair made in the old-fashioned style with a high back and projecting head rests on each side.

I was much occupied in preparing my baby's clothes and reading numerous books on the subject of baby welfare. I had never handled a baby, and was very grateful to the kind Sister in the babies' ward at the Frauenklinik for some much-needed practical instruction. Kurt also gave me many useful hints and I felt quite safe with a specialist in the house. He had always wanted me to have our children at home and to treat it as a family event (as his mother had done). Our little maid Hilde only wanted to work in the mornings, so I had to ask her to find another job, because we decided to look for a daily help who would be capable of running the household whilst I was laid up, a girl who could be left to mind the baby for short periods when necessary. For the arrival of the baby and for a few weeks afterwards, we planned to engage a nurse to live in.

On 15 January 1939 I wrote home, to Kurt's father and to his grandmother, telling them our news. I did not mind whether the baby turned out to be a boy or a girl, although much later, when I knew this would be my only child, I was glad he was a boy. The Falkenbergs naturally wanted a boy, as it was the first-born of the new generation.

The coming event caused lively interest in my family. We asked Mu if she would care to come over for a holiday in September. It was Kurt's suggestion in the first place and he said he would do his best to make the holiday interesting by taking her about, as there was still quite a lot of Danzig which she had not seen. The theatre would probably also be open for the Winter Season by then. I wrote: 'It would be wonderful to have someone here who belonged to me and to feel I was not so far from you all.'

I was thrilled when she replied that she could come. There followed much correspondence about the layette and my dear ones made beautiful garments most of which Mu was going to bring with her, but which lay unused in England whilst I listened to the thunder of the fighting on the Polish frontier a few miles away, wondering whether I would be alive to give birth to the child whose tumultuous presence within me was all too manifest.

Whilst Kurt was working as assistant to Professor Klose in his private wards, the President of the Senate, Herr Greiser, was one of the patients.

The President was so grateful to the hospital staff that he gave a large dinner party about the middle of February 1939 when he had recovered from his illness. He invited Professor Klose and his son, Kurt and me, two other doctors and about ten nurses, all of whom were fetched and taken home in large limousines. We started the evening with an hour of music. Frau Greiser (his second wife, a petite blonde) was a professional pianist and played very well. Professor Klose played the violin and viola, and his son the violin. After this enjoyable little concert we were given a fabulous dinner, with wines and champagne, served by numerous lackeys in livery. Herr Greiser was a typical example of the German dual character of those times – in private life kind-hearted and considerate, in public life cold and calculating – although by what I later heard when he was made Gauleiter of Posen, he was not nearly so ruthless as some Nazis in high positions. He must have known I was English, as everyone else did, but he made no reference to this fact. Little did he or I guess that eight months later we would be at war with one another.

SIX

During the summer of 1939 I went for long walks every day to keep fit and was always glad to find somebody who would go with me. I now lived further away from Frau Stein and Frau Schneider, who were not great walkers anyway, and the only other German friends I had were Herr and Frau Dr Basler, who both worked as doctors in the hospital. At the weekends, if Kurt was on duty, Miss Roberts and I would spend hours walking through the woods, usually followed by a cosy meal at her flat or mine. She had been rubbing up her French by talking to a Dutch friend, Dr Oosterhof, in return for conversation in English, which he was anxious to learn. As she was now so busy at the Consulate she asked me if I would care to give him English lessons. He came twice a week and I enjoyed the lessons as much as he did. He introduced me to Frau van der Maesen de Sombreff, the wife of the Dutch Consul-General in Danzig, who also wanted me to give her English lessons, and in March 1939 she started coming twice a week, so that I had a pleasant diversion from the usual household duties.

I wanted to have a new maid well trained in good time before my confinement so we started making enquiries in March. There was a law in Germany and Danzig whereby girls of all classes, whatever profession they intended to take up, or even if they wanted to stay at home, had to work one year on leaving school either on the land or in an approved household. They had to be prepared to be maids of all work and were supposed to learn cooking, washing, ironing, baby welfare, etc. There was a set wage of about one pound a month (and food of course), which was five shillings less than I paid Hilde, who only worked in the mornings. There were plenty of these girls looking for decent jobs, as the school year had just ended, and we had over a dozen applicants in answer to our advertisement. I chose a girl of sixteen from the secondary school. She looked good-tempered and reliable, of sturdy build and with no nonsense about her. She was the only daughter and had helped in the house at home. It was her ambition to train as a children's nurse when she was old enough, so she looked forward to the arrival of my baby. Her name was Alice and she started to work with me on 1 April. It did not take long for her to pick up the daily routine and she soon learned to cook simple dishes. I was therefore confident that by early September she would be capable enough to carry on alone under the supervision of a nurse.

At the end of April Kurt went to Stuttgart as accompanying doctor to a team of thirty-six men from Danzig competing in the finals of a 25-kilometre march and other sports contests. He was only away four days, nearly half of which was spent in travelling. He arrived back tired out and filthy dirty. Nevertheless he had enjoyed himself. In Danzig it was still cold and the trees were only just beginning to sprout; but he said it seemed like walking into paradise down there in south-west Germany, where the fruit trees, chestnut and magnolia trees were in full blossom. The gardens were full of flowers and everything had looked fresh and green.

On 3 May I had a letter from Mu saying she had definitely booked her passage on the United Baltic Lines steamer sailing from London on 24 August and that she hoped to be able to stay until the middle of October. This news caused great excitement.

Kurt was offered a job as locum for two and a half weeks in June to take over the practice and private nursing home of a gynaecologist in Goslar. As I was not able to take part in any strenuous tour that summer, such as mountain-climbing or cycling, he decided to accept this job as part of his holiday. Dr Schuster was the only gynaecologist in that district and had his own operating theatre, so that it would be good experience and something Kurt had always wanted to try out, added to which he thought the change of air would do me good. The prospect of walking in the Harz Mountains and inhaling the bracing air of the pine forests was certainly very appealing. For the first and last time in my life I was more sensitive to heat than to cold. I could not bear a stuffy atmosphere and the least suspicion of a thunderstorm upset me.

Following our visit to Goslar, Kurt had to do four weeks' military service in East Prussia. We travelled back to Berlin together, then he flew to Königsberg and I to Danzig. My garden had made rapid strides during my absence and I was able to cut some lettuce each day. Alice and I had plenty to do. We went shopping together, and I taught her to cook and bake. I was busy with my knitting and sewing, and went for long walks every day. I spent two weekends with Kurt. The first time I went on the Seedienst steamer from Zoppot (Sopot) to Elbing (Elbag) and from there by train to Königsberg. It was unbearably hot on land, so that the three-hour sea trip was doubly enjoyable. My husband met me at Königsberg and we spent the afternoon and evening in the country about fifteen minutes' train journey out of the town. Even though we kept in the shade, it was so hot that we had to sit and rest until the sun went down, but we were pestered by mosquitoes all the time. The next day it was cooler, and we wandered through the countryside to a restaurant on the edge of a lake. We were so near Königsberg and yet in the heart of the country, amid rolling cornfields, woods and lakes. There is nothing spectacular about East Prussia to attract many visitors from afar, and it is difficult to describe its beauty. The appeal lay partly in the very fact that tourists were not catered for on a large scale except on the coast. There were pleasant hotels and restaurants, with a certain number of holiday-makers, but the main work of the inhabitants was agricultural. Visitors were very much a side-line, and quickly became absorbed in the local life. Most of them in any case came from East Prussian towns (all very small in comparison with the western industrial cities). The hardworking peasants and farmers produced the chief corn supplies for western Germany from their rich, fertile soil. There was no opulence, only a moderate prosperity, the slow reward of patience and diligence. The land emanated an atmosphere of quiet austerity, as though the people were perpetually hardened to meet the adversities of nature and the challenge of the nearby frontiers.

The next weekend I went on an old bus over very bad roads to Elbing where Kurt met me. We found lodgings for the night in Tolkemit on the south side of the Haff. As we sat on the terrace of an open-air café overlooking the water we spoke of the subject which had been uppermost in my mind for some time, and Kurt's attitude towards it influenced my decision, which, as things turned out, was to determine the course of my life, and that of my son for a number of years to come.

Our baby was due to be born in two months' time, and it was no longer possible to shut our eyes to the fact that political developments in Danzig were working up to a climax. The ever-increasing pressure of Germany upon her Polish neighbour seemed to signify that Hitler meant to force a decision over the return of Danzig to the Reich in the near future. For fear that Poland would not cede to his demands he would probably wait until the Prussian corn had been harvested, but he would no doubt act before the winter set in.

During the early part of June there were some fifty cases of Danzig officials refusing to carry out the instructions of the Polish Customs. By the end of June a *Freikorps* of 4,000 was reported to have been formed. SA men were nightly preparing defences around the Free City. Approaches for pontoon bridges were in construction on both sides of the Vistula. All Danzig owners of lorries and trucks were ordered to leave them overnight at military police barracks for inspection, after which each vehicle was numbered and returned to its owner. Hundreds of horses were assembled. On 25 June 1,000 SS men from East Prussia and a number of high SS officers from Germany arrived ostensibly for sporting contests with the local SS. A considerable number of these visiting SS men remained. More and more young men appeared in uniforms similar to Danzig SS but with the death's-head emblem on the right collar and 'Heimwehr Danzig'· on their sleeves. Former barracks were occupied. Houses were requisitioned for the storage of ammunition. Two thousand men were working twenty-four hours a day in shifts on construction of barracks to accommodate 10,000 men. All approaches to some hills and a dismantled fort near the hospital (where I frequently went for my daily walk) were closed with barbed wire and marked '*Verboten*'. The walls surrounding the shipyards bore placards: 'Comrades, keep your mouths shut lest you regret the consequences.' At the end of June the German Government notified the Polish Government that the warship *Königsberg* would visit Danzig for three days on 25 August. (Actually it was the *Schleswig-Holstein* which came on the appointed day.)

The pressure of events was bearing down upon us with increasing intensity. But still we hoped that a peaceful solution would be found. Even the Poles did not think that Germany would go to the length of risking a general war in connection with Danzig, but felt rather that she would gradually strengthen her position there and try to weaken Poland's authority in the hope that Poland would finally be reduced to accepting some solution which would be favourable to Germany. Further, Germany would in the meantime no doubt assiduously propagate the idea that Great Britain and France would not implement their guarantee as regards Danzig, and thereby endeavour still further to undermine Polish morale. The Polish Government was of course aware that the gradual remilitarization of the Free City of Danzig could prove dangerous to them, but they did not seem seriously alarmed. Even if they were, there was not a great deal they could do to meet this danger.

We were walking on a volcano. The question was, would the volcano erupt, and if so, when? My personal problem, so closely knit with political events, was whether to stay in Danzig to have our baby, or to go home to England. My people strongly advised me to go home, where I would be out of the danger zone. From the beginning there had always been this pull of divided loyalties between my home and my husband, my motherland and my adopted fatherland. Now compromise was no longer possible and the breach we had always dreaded seemed almost inevitable. Standing at the fork in the road, whichever turning I chose would lead me away from loved ones. The suggestion to return to the lap of my family, to be enveloped in their all-embracing mantle of security, was infinitely appealing to the primitive instincts of motherhood. This, at first sight, appeared to be the obvious course to ensure the immediate safety of our offspring – but other instincts made me aware that the future of my marriage was at stake. Quite apart from the fact that I could not bear the thought of being separated from Kurt, was it right to risk breaking up our newly founded family for my own comfort and the evasion of *probable* trouble? Would I thus be depriving the child of the possibility of growing up with his father, and with brothers and sisters? After taking the risk of marrying a foreigner, was it fair to snatch the child away from him before it was born? If I went to England and subsequently war broke out, I would be cut off from my husband for an unpredictable number of years, after which time, having fought in opposite camps, it might prove impossible to find a path of mutual understanding. If I went to England and there was no war, then no advantage would have been gained; on the contrary, such a step might cause a rift in our marriage which could never be healed.

When we spoke about it as we sat on the café terrace in

Tolkemit, without any hesitation Kurt said I should do exactly as I wished. All the same I could see I had thrust an arrow into his heart and that it would be a bitter disappointment to him if I went. The idea of trying to persuade me to stay would never enter his mind, nor would he try to alter my decision by intentionally showing any resentment or disappointment if I decided to go. But he did not want me to *want* to go. My actual departure would not be so poignant a blow as the fact that I wanted to go.

We had many difficulties to face in our marriage, both from within ourselves as well as from without. I had made many blunders. I think I was subconsciously aware that the lack of some intangible quality in my character withheld us from the complete fulfilment of our hopes of a free and happy relationship. Years later Kurt told me he thought it was because I was English and he was German. Whatever the reason, we seemed powerless to effect this delicate adjustment. I was not wise enough to withdraw within the stronghold of my own individuality and to wait for time and goodwill to bring us nearer. Instead, I pressed too closely upon Kurt's personality, without sufficient regard for the inner preserves of his identity. I had left my home and country, but was not yet capable of standing on my own feet. This immaturity caused me to lean too heavily upon him and prevented me from exercising any patience. During the many hours I spent alone each day I worried over trivial matters, instead of brushing them aside with a sweeping gesture. The knowledge that I was not altogether contented did not ease Kurt's mind and he slipped ever further from my grasp.

The expectation of parenthood brought about many changes and as the months went by we seemed at last to be treading a path together. I had a mission and a task other than that of being Kurt's wife. I was proud to bear a child, and the new responsibilities helped to give me self-confidence and a stronger foothold. We both looked upon it as an event of the greatest importance and Kurt was happier because I was beginning to be more independent.

Now it was impossible to risk shattering this new hope of a firm foundation to matrimony by walking out at the climax. On the contrary, the tender plant must be nurtured to prevent it withering before it had spread out strong enough roots to survive.

I wrote home:

I have thought it out very thoroughly and have come to the conclusion that the right course is for me to stay here. It would be much easier and pleasanter for me to come home where I am certain of the love and care which only a mother, father, sisters and a brother can give but I feel if I left now I should funking something at the last minute and backing out of my responsibilities. I feel I must see things through if you can understand what I mean. After all, everybody hopes for a peaceful settlement and in any case the present condition of affairs may continue for months by which time Baby would be well on the way in the world. And *if* I came home and then nothing happened after all, I should have run away for no cause and Kurt would have been robbed of one of the most important events of his life . . . I feel if I left now I should only be doing so because it would be so much easier for me and because I feel too weak to face things through and follow my goal to the end.

SEVEN

Kurt came back from his military service in the middle of July and had one day, a Sunday, free, before starting work again at the hospital. We made the best of this opportunity and took the eight o'clock bus to Meisterswalde, and then walked from there to the Mariensee, a very beautiful lake surrounded by woods. We walked about fifteen miles in all, which was not a bad effort for me at that stage.

I had kept very fit on the whole, but a week after our outing to Mariensee I was not at all well. On the Saturday afternoon Kurt was free for a few hours and we went for a walk along the sea-coast between Brösen and Gletkau, thinking the sea breeze would revive me. Coming home in the crowded tram I felt very ill indeed, so Kurt suggested we should get out into the fresh air. As I stood up I dropped in a dead faint. The tram with the people in it seemed to turn a complete somersault, and the next thing I remember was lying on a bench on the footpath under the trees along the side of the Hindenburgallee, with Kurt anxiously standing by me feeling my pulse. After I had recovered a little he went off to telephone for a taxi. He was no doubt only gone a minute or two, but to me it seemed an eternity. The ground and the bench I was lying on were rocking in such a terrifying manner that I clung tightly to the sides for fear of rolling off. Kurt put me to bed as soon as we got home and kept me there for several days. After violent attacks of vomiting I felt much better and fortunately suffered no worse effects. Kurt assured me that the baby's heartbeats were as strong as ever, which I needed no telling, as the internal boxing match continued with relentless vigour.

No doubt the incessant worry about the international situation, with its repercussions in Danzig, contributed towards my feeling so unwell.

I had a letter from Mu saying that she had been advised not to come over in September. Soon after this there was a slight easing in the situation as we heard rumours that the Gauleiter Herr Forster (one of Hitler's mouthpieces) had said the Danzig question could wait until the next year or even longer. This rumour (which was later substantiated by official documents issued by the British Government) spread like wild-fire. It gave us renewed hope that a peaceful solution by means of negotiation might be found if Hitler did not intend to bring matters to a head peremptorily. This subtle change was soon reflected throughout Europe. The next time I heard from Mu she wrote that she might after all be able to come over. Our frame of mind vacillated from day to day according to the latest news.

In August our nerves were shattered by reports of further trouble between Polish and Danzig Customs officials. These squabbles had flared up before, but now the affair was particularly ominous, because, for the first time, the German Government openly intervened in the dispute between the Polish Government and the Danzig Senate, stating that if the Poles continued to cause economic losses to Danzig, the Free City would have no choice but to seek other opportunities of exporting and importing goods. In plain language: Germany would open the Danzig–East Prussian frontier. The Poles retorted that they would look upon this as a *casus belli*.

Still more ominous was the fact that the German press now began a heated campaign against the alleged persecution of the German minority in Poland. This seemed to point to a widening of the area of dispute and looked as if Hitler did not intend localizing his claims to Danzig and the Polish Corridor. These complaints about the persecution of minorities rang a familiar note in our ears. Similar stories had been put in circulation before the German Army marched into Czechoslovakia.

Official Polish circles adopted a restrained attitude but

nothing could curb the hostility of the population, their fanatical patriotism whipped into a frenzy by fear and hatred. My friend, Mrs Johnson, had moved from Zoppot to Gdynia, and she advised me not to visit her there because she did not consider it safe for me to cross the Polish frontier on my German passport. Not long afterwards she came to say goodbye as she was leaving for England. One by one all the English left, excepting the consular staff. Some of them moved off early and took their furniture with them. Others only took clothes and valuables.

During August military preparations were speeded up in Germany, but in spite of all the measures which had been taken in Danzig we were not in any position to defend the city. The whole of our Polish frontier lay open for the Poles to march straight in should there be an outbreak of hostilities. In the daytime I was haunted by fears that in the event of Germany attacking their country the Poles would seize Danzig, the only vulnerable spot, and seek vengeance on us. Or I imagined myself as a refugee, being trundled off in a cart, having to beg for bread and shelter, or having my baby by the wayside with no proper attention. At night I would have the most terrible nightmares and wake up in a bath of perspiration. I dreamed that my baby would be taken from me and left to starve, or that ruffians would mutilate his little body, scorch out his eyes with red-hot pokers, and cut off his tongue in my presence, while I was powerless to stop them. In broad daylight I would tell myself that these were the aberrations of an overwrought mind and that such brutalities could never be inflicted in our civilized age. A few weeks later I was told by eye-witnesses that thousands had actually been tortured to death in this way . . .

The Danzig people did not show undue alarm at the trend of events. They all went about their business in the usual way and it was generally considered unlikely that Hitler would risk a war. We did not know that he and Stalin were already dividing the spoils of a conquered Poland. The announcement of the Non-aggression pact between Germany and Russia on 23 August came as a complete surprise to us as to everyone else.

Hitler pressed still more urgently with his demands upon Poland, and all attempts at mediation failed. The Polish and German Armies were now fully mobilized and were standing face to face. As we waited, in agonies of suspense, it seemed that nothing short of a miracle could prevent an open clash.

Kurt was called up into the Air Force and sent to a field hospital directly behind the frontier. On 28 August I wrote home:

Well, I am of course still alone at home but Kurt was able to come home to tea yesterday which was very cheering. He is confident that everything will turn out all right and let's hope he's right and what's more that everything will be peacefully settled *soon*. This suspense is enough to get on anyone's nerves. Kurt rang me up this afternoon and said he hopes to get home tomorrow for a short time, too. When he comes everything is quite different. All alone here one is inclined to get blue. I feel like smashing the radio to pieces, it so gets on my nerves, but in spite of that I feel I must listen to all the news and keep myself well informed ... Well, well, folks, it's just a case of keeping your pecker up.

That was the last letter I was able to write direct to my home for six years.

EIGHT

About five o'clock in the morning on 1 September 1939 I was suddenly awakened by the roaring of guns which seemed to be firing almost on top of us. 'This is the end,' I thought. I leapt out of bed and dressed as quickly as I could, trembling so violently from head to foot that I could scarcely grasp my clothes or stand on my shaking legs. I seized my keys and handbag, and rushed out. I did not know where I was going except for a vague idea of trying to hide in a cellar in the hospital. I ran into the caretaker on the main staircase of our house. He told me that Forster had broadcast a Proclamation at 5 a.m. declaring that Danzig had returned to 'the great German Reich'. The shooting and explosions were in the town, where the Poles were defending their Post Office, and in the harbour where the Westerplatte (the fortress occupied by the Poles) was being bombarded by the German warship *Schleswig-Holstein*, which had duly arrived (instead of the *Königsberg*) according to the notification by the German Government of as long ago as 30 June. The caretaker said there had been no warning of air-raids and I would do best to make some hot coffee before any further developments occurred. I took his advice and felt a little better for it; then I switched on the wireless to hear reports from England and from Germany. Hitler had issued a proclamation to the German Army. German troops had crossed the Polish frontier. I wondered whether Kurt was in the midst of the fighting and whether I would ever see him again. Where had the Germans started advancing? Would the Poles retaliate by attacking Danzig? How long would it be before England declared war?

Alice, my daily help, did not turn up at her usual time. An hour or so later she telephoned to say that she had been unable to get through the town as the streets were blocked owing to the fighting. My sole companion that day was darling little Pinkie, our Siamese cat. She sensed I was in trouble and never left my side. If she could not sit on my lap she continuously rubbed her soft head against my legs, or jumped on to my shoulder to lie like a little fur cape round my neck as I paced up and down my rooms. I could not trust myself to talk to anybody, because I could not control my tears. In any case all the people I knew in the neighbourhood were on the hospital staff and were frantically busy. Patients were being transferred from some parts of the Städtisches Krankenhaus to make room for the wounded. Most of the young doctors had been called up and the Professors had to make do with a skeleton staff and the help of any females available. Professor Klose, Kurt's chief, was to be responsible for all the most serious surgical cases which could be brought out of the firing lines. During the morning ambulances started to roll past my windows bearing the first victims.

Miss Roberts rang me up to tell me that she was sorry she had no time to call and say goodbye. They had of course been working day and night in the Consulate and she had a rush to finish packing the little baggage she would be able to take with her. The acting Consul-General had been given permission to leave by car with his staff, and they were escorted by SS men to Königsberg. After staying the night there, they continued their journey to the German–Lithuanian frontier, from whence they proceeded northwards and crossed over to Finland, eventually sailing to England from Bergen in Norway.

With Miss Roberts' departure my last link with England was severed. Now I had to face the music alone.

The next day I was surprised to wake up and find myself still alive. I was a little calmer now. The guns were still firing in the harbour and at the frontier, but the Poles in the Post Office had been routed and all was quiet there now. They had fought on, men and women, shooting down from the windows, until finally they had been smoked out, like vermin.

I had not much food in the larder so I ventured out to the little shop on the corner of the next street, and down the road to a kind nurseryman who sold me lovely fresh tomatoes. If he only had a few he always kept them specially for me. Butter had been rationed in Germany for some time and we heard that other commodities were also to be rationed now. People were buying stores of butter, fats and coffee, so I did likewise. Remembering the boxes full of 'Palmin' (a vegetable fat) which Kurt's mother had always kept in her store cupboard I bought as much as I could get hold of as I knew it would keep indefinitely. I listened to what people were saying. As with me, the first frenzy of alarm had passed. Everybody reckoned the Poles would fight to the last man, but that the German Army would make short work of them. The war would soon be over. *Nobody* believed that the English would move a finger, and they all laughed me to scorn when I said we were in for long and bitter warfare. I never heard anything mentioned anywhere about the French attitude. It was always 'the English'.

This was the second day and still there was no declaration of war from England. Reports of the Prime Minister's speech in the House of Commons on 1 September, saying that the British Government would fulfil their obligations to Poland if the German Government did not immediately withdraw their forces from Polish territory, had not reached the man in the street in Danzig, nor had he heard news of the complete mobilization of all the English Forces. I knew England would stand by her word. I knew the English were tough and determined, but I also knew that their Army was not nearly as strong as the German Army. My heart bled for the Poles even more when I thought that my own country might suffer the same fate. Even the Germans marvelled at the bravery of the Poles, who stuck to their guns although they knew they did not stand a chance against the overwhelming odds.

Kurt turned up unexpectedly for an hour or two on the afternoon of 2 September. In spite of the critical situation he had been granted short compassionate leave to see how I was standing up to the shock. It was a great relief to see him and he was very kind. He was able to arrange for the nurse to come on 4 September instead of on the 11th, as had been originally planned, so that I should not be alone at night. He told me that he did not think England would declare war and that he understood agreement would soon be reached. I did not want England to leave Poland in the lurch, but I so earnestly longed for a last-minute miracle to stop this awful war and to prevent the outbreak of hostilities between our two countries that Kurt's steady confidence once again quieted my fears for a time. I do not know whether he really believed what he said, or whether he was only trying to calm my nerves. As soon as he had gone, tormenting doubts returned. How *could* an understanding be reached? The Germans would never withdraw their troops from Poland now the advance was in full swing. If they did not, England would certainly implement her promises. There seemed no way out of the dilemma.

The news that England had declared war on 3 September came like a bombshell to most people in Germany and Danzig. Everywhere there were bleak faces and a hushed atmosphere, as in the presence of death. The realization came to them suddenly that neither the form that it would take, nor the end of the war, could be foreseen. Immediate relief to Poland by means of large-scale attacks by air on Germany's western frontier and industrial centres was anticipated. The dreaded plight for the Germans of having to defend western and eastern frontiers simultaneously now appeared to be unavoidable. Would the French and English forces advance before the German Army had finished off Poland? Would Danzig be cut off from Germany and left to starve, or would the Poles seize the town before German troops could cross the Corridor? I listened day and night to the gunfire on the frontier only a few miles away, every minute imagining it was drawing nearer.

It must have been either on 3 or 4 September that I ventured into the town, because I know my nurse had not yet arrived. Besides buying fats and coffee beans, people were trying to lay in stores of soap and washing powder – contrary to orders we had received not to start hoarding. Knowing that I would shortly need a good supply of these things, I decided to go on a shop-to-shop search to see what was available, as my local grocer had sold out. I had quite a satisfactory expedition and was on my way home in the tram when we heard the drone of aeroplanes overhead. Nobody knew whether they were German or Polish. I sat tight and prayed I might get home safely. As I alighted the noise of the planes came nearer and nearer. It was a few minutes' walk to our house and there was nowhere to shelter, so I made a dash for home. I sped up the hill as fast as my shaking legs would carry their heavy burden, my heart thumping as though it would burst. Then there was a deafening roar of planes making a headlong dive, followed by repeated loud explosions. I ducked and cringed along by the garden fences, feeling as though I had been hit every time. The roaring and detonations continued, seeming louder and louder. I thought I would never get home. At last I reached the steps of our house.

As I looked back down the hill, in spite of being on the verge of collapse, I could not help being horribly fascinated by the spectacle below. The sun was shining brightly. Large planes were diving, like monstrous silver-gleaming birds, one after the other at a tremendous speed. It looked as though they could not fail to crash, but, with finest precision, they rose again just before they touched the ground. At the spot at which the nose of each plane had been pointed there followed a terrific explosion. They were creating an inferno.

I still did not know whether they were German or Polish planes, nor what their target was. Later we were told that they were German Stukas bombing the Westerplatte; but still the Poles did not surrender. Everyone was amazed at their pluck and determination.

The nurse, as it happened, came only just in time. On 5 September we thought it advisable to ring up Kurt, who was allowed to come home for one night, and it looked as though the baby would be a present for our third wedding anniversary. It was one of my husband's theories, based on his experience, that women always show their fundamental temperament at childbirth. For instance a woman with a phlegmatic character would usually be exceedingly slow in giving birth to a child, whereas an energetic woman would be very quick. If this be true, I should by nature be abounding in energy! Kurt and the nurse turned in for the night thinking there was no urgency or necessity to wait up. I did not want to disturb them prematurely, and, being a novice, I did not recognize the alarm signals, with the result that when I did call them, after sticking it for an hour or two, they had a hectic rush to get everything ready in time. It was necessary to delay the birth and Manny was therefore not born after all until 3 a.m. on 6 September. Kurt was back at the field hospital on duty at 8 o'clock. After I heard the baby cry and Kurt told me it was a boy I slept contentedly for twelve hours, little dreaming of the struggle they were having for the baby's life! When the nurse picked him up to wash him she found he had stopped breathing. His heart was still beating, and Kurt massaged him, poured hot and cold water over him alternately, then massaged him again, for nearly an hour, when at last he began to breathe again. As a consequence of this necessarily rough treatment the poor mite had a streaming cold and an infection of the eyelids.

When I woke up it was like emerging from another world and I could not think what the snivelling, snorting little object was, lying in the cradle beside me.

The nurse and Alice got on well together, no doubt bound by a common interest in the stirring incidents of the war seething around us. I did not want the radio in my bedroom so they were able to listen in as much as they liked. At two o'clock, however, when the report of the German High Command was given out, nurse would leave my door open into the drawing-room while I was feeding Manny as she could not bear to miss the news. Although I felt I simply must hear this too, it upset me every time. The voice of the announcer blared forth the reports of German triumphs. I shuddered to think of the fate of the Poles. At the same time the selfish urge for self-preservation made it impossible to curb exultant relief when Danzig was out of danger. We were told afterwards that during the first days of the war the Poles could easily have encircled Danzig and besieged the city, where there were insufficient defences. Although Poland had received repeated warnings, they had in the last instance been caught unawares, and in any case they were on the defensive, not on the offensive.

As soon as I got up I switched the wireless on to English stations, and was rather shocked to hear that their reports were always out of date. I knew this to be so, because we were kept well informed of the position on the front lines through the wounded, who were sent in constant streams to the already overcrowded hospital.

Towards the end of August 1939, fearing the worst, I had written to a friend of mine in Sweden, Baron von Langen, asking him if it would be possible, in the event of war, to pass on news of a personal nature to my parents. As soon as I was sufficiently awake after Manny was born I wrote to tell him that we had a son, and he was good enough to send on my letter, which finally arrived in England on 28 September. Up to April 1940 I was able to correspond indirectly with my people in this way. On 5 November 1939 I wrote to Baron von Langen: 'There are only two sorts of letters which really interest me now – one is from my husband and the other "aus Schweden". Whenever my maid sees the Swedish stamps she rushes with great glee to me with your letters!' The post was very irregular. From Christmas until March I heard nothing from home at all, then I had four letters in one week.

Miss Roberts moved to Rotterdam in the middle of November 1939 and immediately started another route for our letters, until April 1940, when it was accidentally discovered that some other member of the Consular staff there was doing likewise; whereupon they were all questioned; and to everybody's amusement it transpired that quite half of them had been forwarding letters to foreign countries, keeping it dark from each other in the belief that they were the only offenders. They were then asked to promise not to continue this practice, but were still allowed to write themselves. At about the same time Baron von Langen received an official warning from the Censors and was not allowed to forward any more letters. After this, except for messages sent through the Red Cross and occasional notes forwarded by one or two friends who seized any opportunity that occurred, I had no more direct communications from home. Baron von Langen was most kind in writing letters himself to my parents when he heard from me, and vice versa, and in sending photographs of Manny which I am sure were more eloquent than any written descriptions.

NINE

Before the news of the birth of a grandson had reached my parents, Poland had been completely overrun and inexorably crushed, and the spoils divided between Russia and Germany in accordance with their previous agreement. As new territory came under German occupation, so the task of administration of the hospitals and other public works fell into their hands. It soon became obvious that the Germans intended to reinstate themselves as firmly as possible in the Polish Corridor, which was now called West Prussia. Since this land had been taken away from Germany after the First World War, it had been intensively colonized by Poles from the south, who had been allotted the key positions. These so-called 'Congress Poles'* were now evacuated into southern Poland. Those who were taken as prisoners of war were not allowed to return to the Corridor, even if their families lived there. In any case most of their wives and children had fled to the south before the German attack. Most of the Poles who had lived in the Corridor before 1914 were allowed to remain, but they were the minority and nearly all of them poor working-class people. There was therefore a number of important posts to be filled without delay by Germans. While Kurt was still in the field hospital two of his colleagues, who had also trained under Professor Fuchs, had been sent to take over the women's hospitals in Graudenz and Schwetz. Herr and Frau Professor Fuchs were among the first visitors to congratulate me on the birth of our son, which I found most touching as I knew how overworked the Professor was. He told me there remained the biggest women's hospital in the Corridor (Bromberg) which could not yet be re-opened as it

* The term originally applied to the inhabitants of those parts of Poland not absorbed into Prussia after the Congress of Vienna in 1814.

was still being used for the wounded. The civilian population of the Bromberg district was without a gynaecologist of any sort and the need for maternity beds in particular was most urgent. Not long after Professor Fuchs called, Kurt was ordered to Bromberg, still in the capacity of an Air Force officer, to take charge of the gynaecological and maternity section for civilians in that district (Poles and Germans). This was no easy task because firstly the Army would not give up the wards and operating theatres in the hospital, and secondly he had no assistants and no nursing staff. It was therefore a veritable pioneer work. By working night and day he could for the time being manage without an assistant, but nurses and beds were essential. From experience in hospitals staffed by various types of nurses he had long since formed the opinion that the Diakonissen nurses were the most efficient; belonging to a Protestant Order, most of them were well-educated girls from good homes, who looked upon their work more as a calling than the means of earning a living. The Danzig Städtisches Krankenhaus, where Kurt had last been working, was staffed by Diakonissen nurses, and the matron, at his request, immediately telephoned her headquarters in Berlin, who promptly responded to her SOS by sending a midwife, a theatre sister and a sister to take charge of the newly-born babies' ward, with a promise of more help as soon as the initial arrangements had been made. The first two, Schwester Martha and Schwester Helene, had returned from Alexandria at the outbreak of the war where (on King Farouk's instructions) the Diakonissen-schwester had managed the staff and training school for nurses in the women's hospital. They were therefore accustomed to teaching foreign nurses and to organizing the work under mixed nationalities. The third nurse was a younger girl from Berlin. With this skeleton staff and as much equipment as he could muster at short notice, Kurt set off at dawn one morning in a lorry plastered with red crosses. It was in more ways than one a journey into the unknown. Although he and the driver were armed, they would not stand much chance against a hold-up by groups of Poles who were roaming the sparsely populated countryside. If they successfully completed the 150-mile drive, they were not sure of a good reception by the military authorities who were in charge of the hospital, still less by the Poles in the town. At the beginning of the war Bromberg had been the scene of one of the worst massacres on record when about one thousand German civilians had been slaughtered by the enraged Poles before the German Army took the town. On Sunday 3 September, the wave of hatred and crime reached its zenith. This day was afterwards always referred to as 'Blutsonntag' (Blood Sunday). Many of the Germans living in Poland had fled into the Reich before the war started. Those who had stayed and could not find safe hiding places were the victims of most terrible brutality, although they themselves had no connection with the Nazis as their families had lived in the Corridor for many generations and had been severed from Germany since 1918. Men, women and children, even babies, were slowly tortured to death in an indescribable manner under the eyes of their relatives. Women and girls were raped. Their homes were ransacked. Their barns were set on fire. Their cattle, horses and poultry were let loose. Stray cows were not milked and were left to suffer the most agonizing death.

When the German Army advanced they took reprisals. Members of the German minority who had escaped death crept out of their murky concealment – half demented, hungry creatures, their hearts in turn now burning with hatred and revenge. Every Pole who was reported to have taken part in the massacre of the Germans was peremptorily shot dead without any trial. The German civilians, who begged, borrowed or stole firearms, personally set about retribution. After a few weeks the town was quiet by day, but every night murder was rife. In spite of house-to-house searches the Poles managed to conceal their pistols, and for months it was not safe to go out after dark unarmed.

The evil spirit aroused by these hideous deeds pervaded the town and left its mark on every living soul. Even the bricks and mortar seemed infested. And here it was that Kurt arrived, after an unexpectedly peaceful journey.

He decided it was no good waiting for the Army to relinquish his wards in the large new hospital on the outskirts of the town, and obtained permission to take over a private nursing-home in the Weltzienplatz which had been confiscated from a Polish gynaecologist. There were only about ten beds and the place was filthy from top to bottom. Before he could take in any patients every corner had to be scrubbed and disinfected. No matter how many extensions he annexed in the neighbourhood as time went on, the Clinic was always overcrowded, with long waiting lists. (He finished up with over eighty beds for women and forty for babies). To add to his difficulties he had an accident on his bicycle early in October and broke his left collar-bone. He was sent home to rest, but returned on 17 October, although he was still in considerable pain. By 1 November he was operating again.

For obvious reasons the Polish and German patients had to be put into separate wards. Most of the fathers of children born there had been killed in the war or in civilian riots and the women of both nationalities poured out their tragic stories. Kurt still employed some Polish nurses but they could only be put on duty in the Polish wards because the *Volksdeutsche* (the former German minority) would not be attended by them.

There was great eagerness amongst these Germans to prove that they were *Volksdeutsche* as they had the whiphand and enjoyed advantages over the Poles. Some semi-*Volksdeutsche* and some Poles swung over to the Germans, and were then allowed *Volksdeutsche* identity cards, with consequent privileges, if they swore to conversion to the German cause. At first this question was not so pressing. It was not until food became scarce and strictly rationed, when the Poles received much less than the Germans, that they were hard pushed to a decision. As time went on it also became increasingly difficult for Poles to earn their living. Some doggedly testified their nationality to the end, which proved admirable courage and patriotism. Nevertheless it could easily be understood why, for instance, out-of-work parents of half-starving children succumbed to the temptation of professing adherence to the Germans whilst in their hearts they were deeply antagonistic.

Everything was done to stamp out the Poles in the Corridor. The Congress Poles were expelled immediately. By night the Gestapo would swoop down upon them in their homes and turn them out into the street, without giving them a chance to take their belongings. Those Poles who were allowed to remain were spurned and oppressed unless they became *Volksdeutsche*, and were made to move out of the best houses and flats into dismal quarters – again always by night. Carts trundled through the dark streets loaded with women and children huddled on top of their hastily packed goods. They were forbidden to speak Polish. They obviously continued to speak their own language at home, but if they were overheard in the street they were punished. Germans and Poles were segregated on every occasion, the Poles being given the remains after the Germans had taken their pickings. They could only work as labourers because no German would shop in a Polish store, nor go to a Polish doctor or dentist, and as the Germans were the only people with money it very soon meant bankruptcy for any Pole trying to set up independently even if he did get permission to do so – which was unlikely. All official positions were of course given to Germans – mostly to *Reichsdeutsche*, much to the annoyance of the *Volksdeutsche*.

The estates previously owned by Poles were allotted later on to Baltic German estate-owners who, under the Russo–German Agreement, were given the option to be evacuated from Lithuania, Latvia and Estonia where most of them had been domiciled for many generations. Hitler had handed over those states (which were not his to dispose of!) to Stalin as part of his reward for not interfering when Poland was attacked. Nearly all the Baltic Germans chose to leave the land of their forefathers rather than remain under Communist rule. Those who remained lived to regret it. Rejected by the native population, robbed of their property by the Communists, they were outcasts in a land where they had for centuries been the aristocracy. Some of these poor wretches managed to escape afterwards into Prussia, but unless they had come under the official evacuation scheme at the appointed time, they received no compensation from the German Government for their losses and remained penniless refugees, dependent on the help given to them by their Baltic friends. Compensation for the officially evacuated was liberal, as far as we could make out, but these Baltic Germans were never satisfied.

They were sick with longing for their old way of life, undisturbed by Nazis, Communists, wars and all the other distressing turmoils into which they had been thrust. None of them felt at home in West Prussia and vaguely hoped one day to return to the Baltic States. They had been uprooted, but represented a society too conservative to be capable of survival on new soil. For this reason they clung desperately together, in an endeavour to preserve their own traditions, resenting contact and interference from outside. In the Russian manner, they had been accustomed to wide family circles. Two or three generations lived under one roof perfectly happily – grandparents, great-aunts and uncles, sons, daughters, wives, husbands, cousins, grandchildren and great-grandchildren – no relative would be turned away. Riding, shooting, picnics and sledge parties were favourite pastimes. Visitors were entertained on a lavish scale and always stayed for at least a few days at a time owing to the great distances they lived apart. The native population of Lithuanians, Estonians and Latvians had worked for them as servants and labourers. Having been a ruling class since the twelfth or thirteenth century they still looked upon it as their right to be supplied with menials. More than anything they now longed for their own beautiful countryside. Perhaps I enjoyed their confidence because I too was in exile, and they had a deep admiration for English literature and music. One of my Baltic friends was a musician, and he composed songs especially for my voice, setting to music the poems of his compatriots. Every now and again he would ask me to sing these at his home before a gathering of friends and relatives. On one occasion I sang a song cycle which started off in a light-hearted vein, becoming sadder and finishing with a song called '*Am Grabe*' ('At the grave'). His mother lay very ill in the bedroom nearby and died a day or two later. By the time our recital was finished the whole company was in tears.

It was little wonder, with so many clashing personalities and interests, that Bromberg was a centre of intrigues and contention.

TEN

I first went down to Bromberg in November 1939 and stayed about two weeks. I did not enjoy the four-hour journey in a crowded train with Manny and all his trappings, but there was no alternative because Kurt wanted me to look over some houses. It now seemed certain that he would remain there and that I would have to move as soon as arrangements could be made. It was a bleak day when I travelled and soon afterwards we had our first fall of snow. Coming from my beautiful Danzig, Bromberg struck me as exceedingly dull, with no shape or style of its own – a mere jumble of buildings. The only pretty part was down by the River Brahe, where old granaries still stood as a reminder of the early use of these waterways, long before the sprawling town had arisen round about them. On the Schwedenhöhe there were huts and hovels, with no made-up roads. In another part there were ultra-modern villas scattered between pre-1914 houses. There was quite a nice theatre near the river, but it was not yet functioning. The new hospital on the outskirts of the town was lavishly designed for a population where domestic labour was cheap and plentiful, with corridors so wide and so long that the area to be cleaned and heated was for wartime standards extremely uneconomic. One of the most attractive buildings was the Dürerschule, built in between the wars and designed by a German architect, the father of the girl who used to skate with me in Danzig. Here local German craftsmen had been employed to carry out fine wrought-iron work, woodwork, carving and painting. It was a strong point in favour of the Poles that they had allowed the erection of this school for the German minority.

There was little life in the town, except for informal gatherings of a few *Volksdeutsche* and imported Germans (known as *Reichsdeutsche*), who spent long hours in the evenings eating, drinking and talking together, as the latter had not yet been joined by their wives and lived mostly in furnished rooms confiscated from Congress Poles. A few of them would still be seen defiantly flaunting their furs, jewellery and perfumes, but they were fast disappearing as their property was taken from them and they were forced to leave the district.

The houses which we had permission to view had all belonged to Congress Poles. The better ones were quickly being snapped up, which was the reason why Kurt wanted to earmark one as soon as possible. We looked over all sorts and sizes. Most of them were either empty or occupied by German grass-widowers, but one very large house was still inhabited by the owner's wife, who had not yet been turned out because she was German-born. The poor woman was quite distraught. She had not fled from Bromberg because she expected to be left undisturbed when her countrymen occupied the town. A few weeks prior to our visit her husband, a Congress Pole, had been marched off by the Gestapo without any warning and she had neither seen nor heard of him since. He had never been involved in any political activities and, owing to some illness, had not been fit for Army service. She had made frantic appeals to her relatives who had come from Germany to help her, but all in vain. It was impossible to obtain any information about her husband. Now that we had been sent to look over her house she realized that she was also to be deprived of her home. She implored us to find out what had happened to her husband and what accusations were being made against him. We tried to comfort her and needless to say we did not ask her to show us round. I could never have lived there, however much I had liked the house. When Kurt complained to the authorities that we had been sent to a house still occupied by the owner's wife, he was told that the man had been shot that morning, and she would have to quit immediately. No one Kurt spoke to knew why he had been shot. When he asked why the wife had not been informed he was told, in no uncertain terms, to mind his own business. This was only one instance of the tragedies which were an everyday occurrence. Even the empty houses we inspected were impregnated with memories of bitter experiences. I kept asking myself – how could this be right? How could we ever live happily in one of these homes haunted by the misery of our predecessors? But what alternative had we? Kurt had to carry on with his work and we had to live somewhere near.

We finally decided on a modern house five minutes' walk from the Clinic which had been designed and inhabited by the architect who had planned the new main town hospital, a Congress Pole whose entire family had fled before the Germans entered Bromberg, none of whom had been heard of since. The outside was ugly – a grey box with a flat roof – but inside it was compact and conveniently appointed, and suited our requirements. What appealed to me most were the large windows in every room, letting in every inch of sunshine, the pleasant drawing-room with a rounded alcove and windows on three sides, including a french window leading on to the terrace, and the pretty little walled-in garden with a small swimming pool in the centre. The dining-room had windows extending nearly the whole length and breadth of two walls. Upstairs there were three good-sized bedrooms and the maid's room was on the ground floor next to the kitchen. Both the kitchen and the maid's room were very small by our standards, but quite attractive in comparison with the dreary, poky little places in other houses.

The Sisters in the Clinic had fitted out a large room for me and baby, and I had my meals with them, presided over by the genial midwife, Schwester Martha, who was acting as Matron. The cook and general factotum for the medical and nursing staff was a Polish woman who turned out the most delectable dishes.

In Germany and Danzig no foodstuffs whatsoever could now be bought off ration, also no soap, soapflakes, synthetic coffee, cocoa or tea. The latter all through the war was only available in minute quantities from the chemist on a doctor's prescription and coffee was non-existent in the shops. I managed very well in Danzig, because, although Manny ate nothing, I received a ration card for him just the same; as a nursing mother I also had extra milk rations. The system of rationing had been prepared before the war so that it could be put into operation at short notice. It was, however, not easy to organize the distribution of goods in the newly acquired foreign territory until sources of supply had been rounded up and the farmers compelled to hand over their produce to State-controlled centres. Therefore, for a considerable time everything was unrationed in the Corridor and they were unhampered by any shortages.

Similarly, the process of establishing every other State department was necessarily slow – even though Germans are notoriously efficient at organizing government machinery. The greatest suffering was caused by the temporary lack of jurisdiction. Hitler had indeed tampered with German Statutes in the Reich; nevertheless a man would be given a fair trial according to the existing laws. In Bromberg up till about January 1940 the Army, Gestapo and the Party took control. There were no trials and no appeals could be made. What law and order prevailed was achieved by the crudest methods of suppression and harsh punishment. Even after German civilian law had been established, the Gestapo overruled any court if they wished, as in all other parts of the Reich.

Kurt's Clinic, where everyone was engrossed in good work, was a haven amid the abounding strife and terror. It was interesting to see Kurt's new sphere of activity, but how glad I was afterwards to be back in Danzig, a town unbesmirched by countless misdeeds.

Kurt had hoped that the house we had chosen would be

ready for us early in 1940, but after the grass-widowers moved out and before we could get final permission to take possession the house was neglected, and the heating pipes burst as they had not been properly drained off. Work on repairs and renovations could not be started until the thaw set in, which meant waiting until the spring. In the meantime everything that was removable was stolen from the house, even some mirrors which had been fixed to the walls, and all the metal handles on the radiators. It was a particularly severe winter that year. The sea was frozen hard right out as far as one could see.

Snug as we were in Danzig, Manny and I could not stay on there indefinitely, as it would be needed by the hospital for another doctor's family now that Kurt was no longer employed there. However, as he was not yet officially demobilized, no pressure could be put upon us. In any case the hospital authorities were very kind to me; also the doctors and nurses were always ready to help and give advice.

Manny had a little red birthmark on his instep which Professor Nast, the skin specialist, removed with an electric needle. Professor Klose, the chief surgeon, gave me treatment for a septic thumb which he thought he would have to cut open (in those pre-penicillin days) when fortunately an improvement set in which made it unnecessary. The children's specialist and the nurses gave me many hints on baby welfare and feeding. In spite of the fact that it soon became too cold to wheel such a tiny mite outdoors, Manny grew and thrived after his unpropitious start in this world.

Kurt managed to come to Danzig for a short holiday at Christmas, and after that we did not see him again until early March, when Manny and I again spent a few days in Bromberg. Work had not begun on our house (snow was still one and a half feet deep) and as Kurt had heard of another larger one which he thought might be more suitable, he wanted to have my opinion. We nearly decided on the bigger one but in the end reverted to our original choice.

1. My father's family from Uckfield, Sussex, c. 1899. Thomas Bannister, the bearded gentleman sitting in the front, was my father's uncle and his guardian.

2. My mother's family from Tonbridge, Kent, c. 1888. My mother, Louisa King, is second from the right.

Above 3. My elder sister
Muriel (Mu), brother Reg
and sister Gwen, Uckfield,
1907. I was born three years
later.

Left 4. Myself in 1917.

5. In the summer of 1934, Kurt and I spent a holiday in List on the Island of Sylt in the North Sea.

6. Kurt came to England in 1935 and together we stayed at Morecombe Lake, near Lyme Regis, Dorset.

7. Kurt and I were married on 5 September 1936.

8. *Left to right:* Gwen, father, mother, Reg, Kurt, myself, Reg's son
Michael standing in front of Vater, Kurt's elder brother Heinz, Mu,
Reg's wife Win and Kurt's younger brother Max.

9. Our first Christmas in Danzig, 1936.

10. Kurt and myself on the first anniversary of our
wedding, 5 September 1937.

11. Mu and myself on a pleasure boat, Danzig, 5 September 1937.

12. Pre-war Danzig showing the medieval crane gate on the far right.

13. We frequently went bicycling, especially to Brösen on the Baltic coast which was only a few minutes away from Danzig-Langfuhr where we lived.

14. Fishing nets drying at Brösen.

15. The coast at Neukuhren on the Samland coast where Kurt had to do two months' military training at an Air Force camp, 1937.

16. Kurt sitting under a portrait of myself, August 1939.

17. Sewing in my bedroom just before Manny was born, August 1939.

On this visit Manny and I stayed in the house in a parallel road to the Clinic which had been converted into a Nurses' Home and made easily accessible by knocking a hole in the wall between the two gardens. By this means Kurt had made room for twenty women's beds in the Clinic, and also had thirty in the hospital, which had at last been handed over by the Army. This, however, entailed his having constantly to rush from one hospital to the other, and he was looking forward to the time when alterations to the house adjoining the Clinic had been completed so that he could have all his patients under one roof.

After overcoming the women's initial mistrust of a specialist still so young (he was only thirty) his private practice grew steadily. Some of the patients coming to see him for the first time were shocked by his youthful appearance and would probably have preferred to turn tail had they not been reassured by his competent manner. Even greater was the confusion of one patient who had no possibility of retracing her steps because she had come across the Vistula in a small rowing boat (with her own Polish nurse and much paraphernalia) just before the river froze. As the bridges had been sprung during the fighting there were no means of returning until the ice was thick enough to bear vehicles. Judging by the sound of Kurt's voice over the telephone she had pictured him to be rather elderly, with a long beard. Imagine, therefore, her astonishment when, lying in bed, the door opened and a young man entered, who could be none other than the Chief, followed as he was by the usual retinue of nurses and others. Her misgivings, however, were soon dispelled. In fact, she won such faith in Kurt that she asked him, Manny and me to stay for a holiday in her castle for as long as we liked when her second baby was due.

In spite of the uphill work, I think the nurses enjoyed those pioneer days as much as Kurt did. The strict formality of a large hospital, where doctors only appeared as white-coated superiors, was, under the circumstances, quite out of place. Beds and the concentration on his patients of any help available were more important to Kurt than private apartments for himself, so that all visitors were entertained in one large dining-sitting-room, whether they were nurses, State or medical officials, or the Chief's wife and baby. This part of Poland, although fast being absorbed into the Reich, was still a foreign country to the Germans, and Bromberg was a refuge for travellers passing between the north and south. There was always a sense of living at an outpost or in a colony, much more so than in Danzig, where we were only cut off by distance, not by internal dissensions between mixed nationalities. When we visited Germany, it was like travelling into a different country.

I dreaded moving to Bromberg more and more as the time drew nearer. I hated the thought of living in that dull, miserable town, and of leaving my beloved Danzig, and my cosy little flat. This was the happiest home I ever had abroad, no doubt because it was here that Manny was born and because the months before Kurt was called up were the most harmonious we ever spent together, bringing hopes of a more propitious future.

These hopes had in the meantime borne no fruit. Since the day when England and Germany were at war an impenetrable wall had sprung up between us, not so much a barrier of enmity as of reticence. Kurt's withdrawal was such that from that day onwards I no longer knew what his personal thoughts and feelings were. He was not unkind. On the contrary he was sympathetic to my difficult position. The clash between our two countries was a crushing blow to both of us and we were no doubt over-sensitive to each other's reactions. Outwardly there was no noticeable change. We did not squabble, and discussed amicably all matters of a practical or impersonal nature. But for me at any rate there was an inexplicable void. Kurt may have been so taken up with working out his inner problems that he was not aware of any sudden difference in our relationship. The balance of his temperament was so easily affected that whenever anything moved him deeply, either in a pleasant or unpleasant way, he needed considerable time and opportunity for reflection before he could adjust himself to the new situation.

It was not surprising that the war should have a profoundly disturbing influence upon us and that it was impossible for us to see eye to eye on many issues. Also I knew Kurt's mind was much taken up by his work. He seemed more and more to be leading a life of his own from which I was excluded, so much so that while I was on the short visit to Bromberg in March, he actually accepted an invitation from the owners of the Hotel Gelhorn and went to the party alone without telling them I was there, from which I could only conclude that my presence would in some way have been an embarrassment to him.

I hoped that when we were once more living together, with the common interest of our baby and of establishing a new home, the ever-widening gulf could be bridged. This was my only consolation for moving to Bromberg.

Kurt came to Danzig in his car to fetch us, for which I was very thankful, particularly as Alice, my maid, had been offered a good job in the Post Office to start work on 15 April, the day the furniture van was coming. Through Gustav Nord I had been able to buy two tickets for the front row of the Dress Circle for a gala performance of *Tristan and Isolde* which happened to be taking place just on the Saturday evening previous to our move, with famous guest artistes, as though it had been especially planned to be our grand farewell to Danzig. I looked forward with great eagerness to the prospect of seeing this first-rate performance in Kurt's company. Surely here was a sphere of mutual enjoyment which transcended the horrors surrounding us? But he arrived, tired out, with a streaming cold, and although he enjoyed music as much as I did, he could hardly keep his eyes open during the performance.

ELEVEN

The work on our house took longer than had been antici- pated so that Manny and I had to be lodged temporarily in the Nurses' Home.

In the meantime I spent much time working in the garden. It had not been touched since the end of August of the previous year when the owners had fled, with the result that there were many gaps to be filled where those roots or tubers which do not stand the frost had perished. We had no idea what the surviving plants would turn out to be and after the thaw anxiously watched them peeping out of the ground. There was a vacant strip of land next to our house which had been used as a vegetable garden and which we were allowed to rent. This was empty except for some pumpkin plants and a bed of strawberries both of which bore prolific fruit. I had the rest of it dug and as soon as possible set about sowing early vegetables of every description. I also bought a lot of young plants from a helpful nurseryman who gave me a number of hints, as this was my first attempt at growing vegetables. I do not know whether it was skill or beginner's luck, but we had the most amazing crops. Kurt, a town- dweller, had never had vegetables fresh from the garden and I felt most gratified when he said they were the best he had ever tasted. Apart from the pleasure of achieving satisfactory results, the outdoor work, with Manny cooing in his pram beside me, was soothing to my nerves, shaken as they were by reports of the new offensive. As I tilled the soil, the west European states fell like ninepins before the advancing German Army. With a rapidity which even astounded the Führer they marched towards the Channel. Now only that narrow strip of sea lay between them and England, and soon the Blitz began. Although everyone was not a little proud of the military achievement there was no rejoicing.

Even to Hitler and the Nazi leaders the conquests in western Europe were only expedient in so far as they hoped thereby to avoid war on two fronts simultaneously. With the West laid low, they could then proceed eastwards, which was their ultimate aim. Hitler did not want to fight the West, but when his efforts to persuade the English to allow him a free hand in eastern Europe proved in vain, he impatiently decided to crush their opposition by force. Goering boasted that he would soon establish air supremacy, which was essential before a landing in England could be attempted. When this plan was thwarted through the heroic Battle of Britain, Hitler was foolish and cocksure enough to imagine that England's resistance had nevertheless been sufficiently lamed to be of no further danger. He underestimated the determination and recuperative powers of the English, which he considered to be no stronger than those of the French. But there could be no comparison between the two countries. In France there was no real unity of purpose and they did not possess the natural defence barrier of the English Channel. Nevertheless the outlook was indeed black during the summer of 1940 as wild rumours spread about plans to land on the south coast. It was almost as though everybody in Germany was spellbound by the magician Hitler. The Army so far owed their success to his initiative, to his intuition in spotting any weakness in his opponents and to his courage in grasping each opportunity that occurred, even though it might involve some risk. The impression was of a mastermind at work which could not fail in its purpose. The Germans did not doubt that if Hitler decided to land in England he would devise some successful means of doing so. It was said that he would leave most of the population to starve to death as it would be difficult enough to ship food to his own soldiers.

During my enforced wait until we finally moved into the house on 1 June, I was busy making what preparations I could in advance. I was able to have curtains made from a bale of hand-woven linen Kurt had bought from the widow of the man through whom he ordered our furniture while living in Danzig before the war. There were countless odds and ends necessary besides larger items such as another pair of armchairs and a chesterfield. The latter we had made by an old-established *Volksdeutsche* firm called Pfefferkorn. Amongst other things we bought a grand piano. The old cooking stove (which had also heated the bath water) was removed and replaced by a large gas oven and a geyser. The larder was not very spacious, so Kurt bought a refrigerator which just fitted in a cupboard under the stairs. We had all the walls inside the house distempered in pastel shades which were the best background for our pictures. Manny's room was equipped with a large cot with white metal bars top and bottom and webbing stretched along the sides. I bought a deep, white chest of drawers with a raised ledge along the back and two sides to keep a mattress in place so that it was comfortable to dress baby on it. He had his own small bath on a stand and of course a play-pen. This was the only room for which we had no carpet and I managed to find a Polish one, hand-woven in bright colours. To tone with this I sewed coloured borders on the natural linen curtains and hung gay wooden plaques of fairy-story figures on the walls. I had an electric ironer installed in Manny's room so that we could keep each other company while I was busy with the laundry. This proved to be the most useful gadget I ever possessed. After a little practice I became so proficient that the only articles which had to be ironed by hand were blouses, dresses and shirts. I left my maid to use it once, but never again, as she promptly ruined the heating clamp by leaving it on too long, and I had to wait months for a replacement. She was a Polish woman of about forty-five called Valentina, hard-working, efficient and an excellent cook. She loved Manny, who called her Tina, and was good-natured; only her heart was smouldering with hate for all Germans. She had broad Slavonic features and dark eyes which flashed with pleasure or anger according to her mood. When she had her afternoon off she would doll herself up to the nines so that she was hardly recognizable as the same person. She spoke German fluently but with a strong Polish accent. When Stefaniac (a man who worked at the Clinic) came once a day to rake out our central heating stove in the cellar, he and Valentina would have long, excited, whispered conversations together in their own language, which is so full of strings of consonants that it is like a perpetual tongue-twister. Valentina and I got on together well enough, except when she pinched things and then showed great indignation that I suspected her because she was the only possible culprit. To avoid this unpleasantness I locked up everything, including the food store cupboard in the cellar.

Dishonesty was rampant throughout the town, partly because the spirit of looting was still prevalent as a form of revenge, and partly because there was dire need among the Poles. All the same, even before the war I gathered it had been impossible to leave the milk on the doorstep or to hang a linen-bag on the door-knob for the baker to fill with hot rolls early in the morning (as was the custom in Germany) for fear of their being stolen. The milkman always had to ring the bell and wait for a jug to be brought. It was not safe to leave a bicycle for one moment unguarded or without a chain and padlock.

The German police who were by now installed in Bromberg were even more pompous and bombastic than in the Reich, and bursting with self-righteousness among these thieving underdogs. The sight of a German policeman never induces that feeling of friendly protection which one invariably experiences in the presence of an English policeman. The German police always look suspicious of everyone. Whenever I had to go to a Police Office to register a new address I felt I must watch my step or I might land in gaol. There was never a joke, never a bandying of words. They were much too important for that. One day I was sauntering diagonally across a quiet road, not knowing that this is strictly *verboten*, when I suddenly heard a stentorian voice behind me booming, '*Geradeaus gehen!*' (Walk straight across!) Startled, I took to my heels. Glancing over my shoulder I caught sight of an indignant policeman, purple in the face with anger. This aroused my contrariness to such an extent that thereafter it gave me great pleasure to walk diagonally across every road I could. If these police aggravated me, it can be understood to what a pitch of fury they stung the Poles – not merely because they represented the nation who had invaded their country and caused such hardships, but also for the very reason that they were efficient and insisted on law and order. The Poles so much preferred a free and easy *dis*order. What we might consider the most admirable or lovable qualities in both, acted as red rags to each other. The hard-working thoroughness and perseverance of the German was misconstrued as calculating ambition and avarice, his exacting cleanliness and tidiness as small-minded fussing over trivialities. On the other hand the Germans looked upon the unmethodical individualism and tolerance of the Poles as laziness, their haphazard habits as undisciplined and uncivilized. Whatever they thought of each other, I was an outsider either way.

When the German civilians followed up the military conquest of Poland they naturally came upon far worse havoc and disorder than would be likely to prevail in times of peace. To appease their conscience they pronounced the Poles as incapable of establishing a well-organized, independent State. The sharp contrast between the standard of living of the rich and the poor in Poland struck them as unfair and barbarous. Valentina and other Poles told me that before the war the poor people could never afford to eat anything but the cheapest foods. They were no better off now because their rations were so small. Germans employing resident Polish staff were given German ration cards for them which allowed much more than on Polish cards. The farmers were the best off since, no matter how strict the regulations were, there always remained a good margin for their own consumption and for purposes of barter. Right up to the time that the Russians advanced, the farmers lived as well as they had ever done in peacetime. Then they lost more than anyone else. For the time being, however, they prospered and obtained goods which no money could buy. For a piece of fat bacon they could get leather. For butter the cobbler would make a pair of shoes. They would line their coats with their own sheepskins, make soap from bones of cattle, bake their own bread. When petrol was short they would drive traps or sleighs. Their horses were well fed, their larders well stocked. To encourage maximum output they were paid well for their goods.

Sometimes, especially at Christmas time, Kurt would be given presents of food from his country patients. For anyone adept in the art of persuasive negotiations (which he and I were not) it was possible to obtain various extras off ration in exchange for other goods or services rendered. When I first set up house in Bromberg, in June 1940, theoretically meat, butter and sugar were rationed, but in practice I could buy what I wanted within reason, as control of food supplies had still not been strictly imposed. I dealt with the same tradesmen as the Clinic who never needed their full share as there were always so many newly-born babies entitled (on paper) to rations. Gradually restrictions became increasingly severe, but in comparison with densely populated industrial areas we remained well fed until we fled from the advancing Russians at the final breakdown in January 1945.

After meat, butter and sugar rationing had been organized in Bromberg, came flour, bread and milk, and then all other foodstuffs, as had been the case in the Reich since the beginning of the war. We did not have ration books but were issued once in four weeks with one coloured sheet of paper per person, printed with various squares marked off for meat, butter, margarine, cheese, etc. (Meat included sausages and offal.) A certain number of squares would be for white wheat-bread, cakes or flour, so that if you ate too much of the former you could buy no flour for cooking. Most of the bread squares were for rye-bread and could be spent on pumpernickel, wholemeal rye-bread, or what they called grey bread (a more refined and consequently more tasteless and less nourishing rye-bread). One slice of wholemeal rye-bread is as nourishing and filling as about four to six slices of white wheat-bread of the same size, besides which it keeps fresh for several weeks if stored in a cool place. Very early on, cornflour was only issued to young children. Soon milk was only allowed to be sold for children; the younger the child, the more he got. Milk powder was not available but skimmed milk was sold on ration for adults. We had to register at a fish-shop where we were given a number on a card. When there was a supply of fish the numbers (say 500–600) which were due to have their rations were written on a blackboard in the shop-window. On the day that your number was posted up (about once in four to six weeks) you had to queue up for your allocation per head, as the best fish was always sold out quickly. There were no spreads such as cheese, potted meat, fish paste, or peanut butter, not even mayonnaise or sauces. Even the unholy concoction called synthetic coffee was rationed. Having meals in a restaurant was no help because you had to give up meat, fat and cheese coupons, also white bread coupons for rolls, cakes or pastries, and then came away feeling you could have made much better use of them by cooking something at home. The choice of desserts in restaurants, even in peacetime, was always meagre; now at best you would only be offered a small portion of stewed fruit (if you were lucky). Saccharine was very difficult to come by. I never had a sweet or a chocolate all through the war.

Nevertheless in Bromberg we could not grumble. We were always able to buy a winter store of potatoes which were very scarce in some parts of Germany. In the summer we had ample fruit and vegetables to bottle for the winter months. All down one garden wall we had morello cherry trees which bore luscious fruit, ideal for cooking.

In one sheltered corner of the garden there was a summer-house where Manny would have his afternoon snooze when it rained. In the fine weather he was out of doors all day long and was as brown as a berry, with hair bleached like a platinum blonde! He loved his new home and garden, but objected to being taken into strange houses unless I carried him. When we went to stay in a country castle at Lukowo in August at the invitation of Frau von Oldenheim, it took him several days to settle down.

This had once been an attractive estate, indeed still was, except that it was badly neglected. The ownership of the property was in debate – in fact the legal proceedings never were concluded. Alex von Oldenheim was the younger of two sons. His father was a German with Polish sympathies and married to a Polish princess to whom the elder son remained loyal. Alex, who had always felt himself a German, joined the German Waffen SS and consequently had bitter feuds with his relatives. When Poland was taken the father was imprisoned, his property confiscated, and Alex nominated as trustee to the estate. As he was on active service, however, his wife had to manage the best she could. She put her furniture in about nine large rooms on the first floor of the castle (which was in better repair than the ground floor) and in some of the guests' rooms in the annexe. The kitchens were in the basement, so that it was not exactly a convenient *ménage*. The main part of the castle, built on a hill, had been designed by the famous Berlin architect Schinkel. It was beautifully proportioned, with the windows of all the main rooms facing south, overlooking what had been well-planned terraces, lawns and flower-beds, with green pastures and wooded parkland in the background. A gap had been hewn through the trees opposite the castle about half a mile away to reveal a distant landscape where the River Vistula swept through the broad valley. The symmetry of the building had been marred by the addition of an annexe on the east side. A few minutes' walk away down a fine avenue of trees there was another small castle, a little baroque gem, which, although now derelict, retained its charm. Beyond this there was an avenue of smaller trees (down a very steep hill), pollarded to avoid obstructing the view from the little *Schloss* across the wide stretch of country below. The branches of these trees formed a shady tunnel over the paths leading down to a lake, which was in reality a dead arm of the Vistula. There was a diving board reaching out beyond the muddy bank into the clear deep water, and nearby a rowing boat in the boat-house. Kurt went into Bromberg (about ten to fifteen miles away) most days and had to be available on the telephone day and night. All the same it was a pleasant change for him, as well as for Manny and me, and he often had time to go for walks in the evenings.

It was here that West Prussia began to cast its spell upon me. Up till then I had had little opportunity of seeing the surrounding country, except for my journeys between Danzig and Bromberg, when at a transitory glimpse it appeared to my disgruntled eye as dull as the town itself. There was at first sight nothing to attract attention – even less than in East Prussia. Its beauty lay in the peace of undisturbed solitude, in the vast expanse of land where only the keen observer could probe the hidden treasures. The sea was hundreds of miles away so that, although we were further south than Danzig and East Prussia, it was much colder in the winter as we were more open to the icy Siberian winds, and in the summer the earth became parched in the hot, dry air. East Prussia is softer and richer. We had no coastline and no famous beauty spots; indeed one had the impression that nobody ever spent holidays in the country. People either lived there on their estates and travelled abroad and to the mountains in the south, or they were too poor to have any holidays at all. There were very few wayside guest houses or cafés, for the population was too scattered to warrant their existence. The difference between the town-dweller and the country-dweller was much more pronounced. Nobody, for instance, would dream of living in the country for pleasure only, driving to and fro to the nearest town every day to work, as is done so often in England. If your job was in the country you lived in the country, if it was in the town you lived in the town. Even the wealthiest estate owners in West Prussia would rarely own a town establishment as well, and if they did it would usually be as far away as Berlin and would be used more as a *pied-à-terre* on their travels than as a town residence in our sense of the word. The class of business or professional man who retires to live in the country had been non-existent throughout Germany since the inflation period of 1923, when all investments became worthless.

Only the main roads leading directly from one town to another were made up, otherwise there were cart tracks which, in the Bromberg district, were often sandy. There was one lane at Lukowo, which Kurt and I explored, leading through thin fir woods sprinkled with juniper bushes to a beech wood on a hillside. Beyond this the path broke out into open wasteland with hidden ponds encircled by silver birches, high above the valley of the Vistula. We could see for miles into the haze of a distant horizon. Turning to each other, the same thought sprung to our minds simultaneously – what a lovely place to build a house! Although Kurt had not been brought up in the English tradition the idea of having a country house had always appealed to him. He was fond of the unusual and it would give him the greatest pleasure to live in a house made to our own design (our taste in these matters invariably coincided). Also it would partly fulfil the aspirations lying behind his original choice of profession – to be a forester.

But one of the main reasons why a country house attracted him was that it would not only provide him with a retreat from the worries of his work, but also, conversely, his work could be an excuse to retreat from his wife and family. Before we were married I was sometimes disturbed by this tendency of his to withdrawal, of not wishing to share everything with me as I would have wished to share it with him, but I dispelled such misgivings with the thought that our rare meetings and the distance of one or two thousand miles between us were not conducive to the exchange of confidences. Soon after we were married, however, it was obvious that he could not reconcile himself to the renunciation of the advantages of bachelorhood. Not that he begrudged having to keep a wife from the financial point of view – on the contrary, like his mother, he was economical, but at the same time extremely generous. Every penny he earned, all his worldly possessions, were there to be shared with me without a quibble. No, it was his personal freedom of thought and action that he wished to retain. My personality did not inspire him with the desire to give all and receive all in a fusion of mutual interests. Neither our love for Manny nor the common interest in our new home in Bromberg proved to be a bond strong enough to bridge the gap existing between us which was now widened by the fundamental difference in approach to world affairs, so closely affecting our daily lives. Perhaps if there had been no war, if we had had a large family and a country house, we might have found a basis of lasting understanding. Who knows?

I noticed that Alex von Oldenheim practised similar tactics of withdrawal. In fact in a number of ways he was not unlike Kurt in character. He too was over-sensitive. Beneath a cloak of quiet, almost sinister self-possession, he had a turmoil of conflicting elements and a wild, restless temperament which threatened to break out of control at the least provocation. He had the same sort of mind as Kurt which reacted instantly, enabling him to make lightning decisions. Before the war he had been a racing motorcyclist, representing Poland at international contests and bringing home many trophies, which were displayed in a cabinet in the salon. When he married he promised never to race again.

Nina, his wife, was the elder daughter of a *Volksdeutsche* family which had for generations owned an estate about thirty miles away. Although her father had the *von* title of nobility, he gave the impression of coming from farmer stock. Her mother, an energetic, handsome, nervy woman, was obsessed with hatred of the Nazis, and expounded her views to me at length, knowing that I would not inform on her. She was, however, not always discreet in choosing her audience and was subsequently imprisoned for eight or nine months. These misfortunes, coupled with the hatred and fury burning in her heart, brought on a nervous breakdown. After her release she was more embittered and incautious than ever and would have been put into gaol again had it not been for the advance of the Russians, after which she no doubt suffered an even worse fate than under the Nazis, unless she escaped to the West.

Nina had her mother's fine figure, also her nervous energy, and had a constant flow of humorous conversation. As soon as she came into a room, the company (including her husband) would be dominated by her presence. She watched him like a lynx – and no wonder, for he was the most handsome man for miles around.

I cannot remember whether Alex was at home on our first visit there, but we saw him frequently later on when he was wounded in the knee and sent back from the front for a lengthy convalescence. Both Alex and Nina were keen horsemen. Sometimes we would go for drives in the trap, taking the children with us. Even before petrol shortages, this had been the favourite method of transport except for long journeys, and of course in the winter the horse-drawn sleigh was much safer than the car, besides being infinitely more pleasant. As the children grew older these joy-rides became more and more popular. Alex adored his baby daughter, Gisela, who at a very early age learned to twist him round her little finger. Manny sometimes went into her nursery to play and I bathed him there, but they were too young as yet to appreciate each other's company. Manny, as usual, spent most of the day outdoors – in an arbour when it rained. Valentina, sociable as she was, enjoyed herself at Lukowo as much as anybody, helping in the kitchen, chatting to the Polish staff and farm labourers. She cooked Manny's meals, did his washing, kept our rooms clean, and otherwise lent a hand wherever she could. All the same she was essentially a town bird, and when the time came, was probably glad to get back to her own cronies.

TWELVE

After our return to Bromberg I continued to play tennis at the club I had joined earlier in the summer. Kurt had given me a beautiful new racquet for my birthday. The games I enjoyed most were with a young girl called Helga von P., daughter of the Chief of Police. Her mother used to invite me to their house where I always felt very much at home. They had lived in Berlin for many years, associating with cosmopolitan society, and had none of the narrow-mindedness of many of the people of Bromberg. Her father was one of the old school, a kindly gentleman, with pro-British tendencies, who refused to allow his police to knuckle under the local Gestapo, with the result that after a losing battle with the Chief of the Gestapo in Bromberg he was removed from his office and imprisoned. From that time on his health failed. One lung was removed and he was then set free, a broken man. The ironical tragedy was that after the collapse of Germany, when he fled to the West like all the rest of us, he was delivered over to the Poles by the British authorities because he had been Chief of Police in Bromberg, and he subsequently suffered a miserable death in prison. Thus, like many others, he was first of all punished by the Germans for being an anti-Nazi, then by their enemies for being a Nazi.

Apart from Helga, I made no friends at the tennis club. They divided themselves into two cliques – one made up of *Volksdeutsche* and the other of *Reichsdeutsche*. As I fitted into neither of these categories, there was no place for me. Kurt was very well known by then, being somewhat of an enigma on account of his early professional success coupled with his personal reserve, and everybody was curious to see his wife, '*die Engländerin*', as I was always called; when I appeared the hum of conversation lulled, while they eyed me as though I were a rare museum piece. I went there because I loved tennis, not because I enjoyed their company, which was no doubt a further reason why their circles were not opened to me.

Frieda, the wife of Kurt's younger brother, Max, had her first baby, Volker, in October 1939, and was living with my father-in-law at Barmen while Max continued his medical training, at the same time serving in the Navy. He was stationed at Königsberg, where he was studying at the university, and there was a possibility of his being able to come to us for Christmas. We were comparatively near, and the journey to Barmen would have taken too long. We therefore decided to invite Frieda, her baby and *Vater*, who had not yet seen Manny, to join us. The family party was thus complete excepting for Kurt's elder brother Heinz, a lawyer, who had been called up and was training in the north of Germany. The children got on very well together and it was interesting to observe the differences in character even at such an early age. Manny was persevering, independent and self-willed; he was extremely interested in technical matters, fuddling with his hands or building with his bricks, and he would busy himself quietly for hours if he found an intriguing object, trying to see how it worked. Volker on the other hand was quick and impatient, wanting to be here, there and everywhere, never stopping long over anything. He was as sharp as a needle, a jolly, affectionate little chap, and easily managed. He much preferred to potter about wherever there was company, and was not at all interested in playing by himself.

Vater had to return to Barmen after Christmas, but Frieda stayed on to take care of Manny while Kurt and I went away for three weeks. Had Kurt known that this was to be his last holiday until after the war, he might not have threatened to turn back from Berlin, where we were held up on account of heavy snowstorms. Excited at the prospect of my first winter visit to the mountains, I tried to prevail on him to wait until the journey south was possible. He was like a cat on hot bricks. 'What a waste of time it is with so much work to be done in Bromberg!' he complained. 'Tomorrow we will definitely take the train home if we cannot travel to Munich.'

When we finally arrived in Innsbruck even Kurt's spirits began to soar and I was at once captivated by the picturesque old town. It was a centre for students and sportsmen, who all seemed gay and carefree. I could understand the Austrians when they spoke to me personally, but when they talked among themselves their accent made it impossible to pick up a word, least of all a joke. We stayed a day or two in Innsbruck to give us time to buy our skis and other necessary equipment, then very early in the morning we set off by bus to Gries.

At Gries we left our luggage to be carried up on a donkey-sleigh and started on a four-mile climb up the mountain to our hotel at Kühtai. There was no road and we had to keep to the well-trodden footpath or we might have sunk in deep snow. The sun was shining brilliantly, glistening on the icicles and on the shimmering mountains, which were studded on the lower slopes with dark fir-trees laden with thick snow. I have never seen anything so beautiful in my life. It was lovelier than any fairyland that could ever be imagined. It surpassed all my dreams. Throughout our stay there I remained so enraptured that not even the worries of the war, Kurt's complete absorption in his private thoughts, nor embarrassment at my gauche attempts to conquer the art of skiing penetrated beyond the surface to disturb my peace of mind.

The hotel was 6,000 feet above sea level, near the top of a mountain, and the only other sign of habitation was a Youth Hostel about 200 yards away. It was essentially a centre for serious skiers, because, except for the pathway down to Gries, you could not set foot outside without skis. There were no shops, no cinemas, and nowhere to parade chic outfits. Kurt retained the student's disdain for the mondaine type of woman who stayed in popular winter resorts not to enjoy the sports but to display her wardrobe and attain the tan necessary to advertise her superiority on returning to town. For this reason he did not even want me to wear my fur coat. The first person we saw in the receptionist's office on arrival was a sophisticated, made-up dame in a ravishing ski costume and a fur coat! Kurt and I exchanged amused glances. Every guest was suitably dressed, some of them very smartly, and there was not one who could not ski well, in fact they were nearly all experts. I had no idea how to begin, but Kurt optimistically said I would soon find out. The first morning I crept slantways up a hill with him, and there he left me, continuing his way on a long morning's tour. I did not even know how to turn round. In the end I lay down on the slope, stretched my legs in the air and rolled over until my skis were facing in the direction of the hotel. If anyone was watching from below, it must have been a funny sight. My difficulties were by no means at an end. If I fell over once, I fell over a hundred times. I thought I would never get back alive. After this we decided I had better take lessons, which of course was the only sensible thing to do. I knew I was starting (as with skating) too late in life ever to become a champion, but I soon learned enough for what might be termed utilitarian purposes; that is to say I was able to get up or down any slope that was not very steep – not perhaps as fast as some, but I got there – and I could join in the simpler tours organized by the ski instructor. One of the favourite runs was to a little guest house two or three miles down the other side of the mountain. Oh, the exhilaration of those downward runs! Before the climb back we were able to fortify ourselves with *Glühwein* (hot spiced wine) – the most popular drink in that district – or real coffee, an unheard-of luxury. The landlord was one of those German inhabitants of the South Tyrol who had been forced by Hitler to abandon their homes, as a sop to Mussolini. When he moved from there he brought a supply of coffee with him which had still not been exhausted.

Once on our way back from a run we were caught in a snowstorm. We had to keep in a close crocodile or we would have lost sight of each other, and we were thankful to have a guide to lead the way. Sometimes it was warm enough to sit in the sunshine wrapped in rugs. Kurt was not interested in talking to any of the other guests and we usually went to bed early after dinner, tired from the day's exertions. I was always awake at dawn because from my bed I could see the mountain tops and I loved to watch the colours change as the sun rose – from deep blue, to pale blue, then finally to a delicate pink, while far below there were still dark shadows.

THIRTEEN

The return from our mountain eyrie to the hub of civilization was quite painful, like jumping off the moon. We had neither read any newspapers nor listened to the radio, and it was difficult to pick up the threads again as we were plunged into the nightmare of reality.

Our great joy was to see darling Manny, as bonny and cheerful as ever. Frieda had of course managed the household very well, and her only trial had been the bitterly cold weather. Neither she nor Volker had put their noses outside the door since we left them! She planned to travel to Barmen soon after our return. Before she left I was unfortunately taken ill. Kurt had given me some treatment which had exactly the opposite effect to that intended. I was seized with violent pains and a few days later was running a high temperature.

I asked Kurt to have me moved to the Clinic, because I thought with proper nursing I might recover more quickly. Valentina had been a brick and done everything she could without one complaint about the extra work and I hated having to let her wait on me. Kurt had been kind, though distant as usual. For some unknown reason he did not want me to go to the Clinic, but I finally persuaded him to change his mind. This, however, was a mistake on my part, for as a result the gulf between us grew even wider. He visited me every day in the same way as he visited all his private patients, accompanied by the Sister, but rarely stopped to talk. I was lonely and miserable, and I missed Manny, none of which helped towards a rapid recovery. When the summer came the heat was insufferable in bed. The door and french windows were flung wide open day and night and I lay there listening to the never-ending rumble of army lorries and gun-carriages moving along the main road up to the Russian frontier. The sultry air and the advancing troops were ominous signs of coming storms.

Although preparations for the large-scale attack on Russia could not be hidden from us in Bromberg, when it was finally launched we were stunned by the news. What would be the outcome of this hazardous venture? I do not think there were many who in their hearts did not at that moment fear it must be the beginning of the end. At any rate all hope of a speedy conclusion of the war was now out of the question. This time I was not alone in forecasting years of battle ahead. The Russians were looked upon as formidable enemies, and yet before long reports of the German Army's rapid advance belied logical prediction. Once more the magician had waved his wand.

Sorry as I was for the Russians, I could not keep being profoundly relieved that Hitler had shifted his target. So long as he was busy in the East there was at least no danger of a landing in England.

We heard from *Vater* that Heinz (Kurt's elder brother), who had married early in the year, had been sent to the front in northern Finland.

When I was at last on my feet again Kurt decided to send me to Franzensbad in Sudetenland for a moor-bath cure. Manny travelled with me to Berlin where Grete (Heinz's wife) met us and took Manny back to Barmen with her. *Vater* came to Franzensbad (Františkovy Lasne) with me and we stayed in the Hotel Imperial, where the rooms were comfortable enough and the service good, but the food hardly sufficient to keep body and soul together. Kurt had given me an introduction to Dr Holzer, a dear old chap who reminded me of a bumble bee. He, and his father before him, had been *Kurärzte* in Franzensbad for years. After an examination, he prescribed the number and temperature of my baths, which then had to be booked at the Bath House. Besides this I had to drink the waters regularly. I looked upon the whole thing as rather a joke, but carried out all the doctor's instructions because I knew it was costing Kurt a lot of money. I started off by having baths three or four times a week and finished by having them every day. You got undressed in a cubicle, then when your bathroom was free and cleaned the woman would have the hot muddy sort of peat wheeled in through a low door opening on to the yard. When the temperature had been checked according to your prescription, you had to climb into the tub and immerse yourself in the mud, all but head and hands, which was rather revolting until you were used to it. To the touch it was only warm, but after you had been lying in it for a few minutes, you could feel the heat radiating and penetrating into every muscle, into all your organs and into the very marrow of your bones, until by the time you had finished (after about twenty minutes) every ache and pain would be soothed and you would be sweating like a pig. When you rang the bell the woman would come to spray off the mud with a hose and you were not supposed to wash yourself too much with soap and water as the minerals which soaked into the pores continued to have a beneficial effect. One of the strictest rules was that you must wrap up warm and go straight to bed for two hours. If this overlapped with a meal time, a tray would, as a matter of course, be brought to your bedroom.

Franzensbad was only a small town, consisting almost entirely of hotels, with a small shopping centre where there were numerous cafés, gift shops and a little cinema which changed its programme very frequently. I discovered an excellent milliner who made me a smart hat (an article difficult to come by elsewhere). A band played outdoors every afternoon and evening whilst the visitors strolled through the parks and woods which extended for miles around. *Vater* and I stayed in our hotel most evenings after dinner. He was glad of the relaxation, and whilst we chatted I knitted Manny a jacket and leggings out of some green Jaeger wool Mu had sent me for a jumper just before the war. One of the hotel lounges was set aside for bridge. There were many enthusiastic players who took the game most seriously, and who would sit playing for hours on end.

Towards the end of our stay *Vater* received a telegram to say that Heinz had been killed in action (on 30 August 1941). It was a blow which we knew came to many homes all over the world but that did not make it any easier for the old man to bear. At first he was too stunned to feel the pain, then gradually it bore in on him. Added to his sorrow he had the responsibility for Heinz's widow who was living in his house and who was expecting a baby in January. This was perhaps a blessing rather than a burden as it was at least a distraction for him.

I travelled back to Barmen with him to collect Manny who had been enjoying himself with his playmate Volker.

Grete, Heinz's wife, was wonderfully brave, so brave that it was even mooted in one tight-lipped quarter that she could never have loved Heinz. She showed an unsuspected strength for so light-hearted a character. The only time she broke down completely while I was there was when she received a parcel containing Heinz's small personal belongings. We were sitting at a table when it was brought in. She opened it gleefully thinking it might be a surprise packet from a friend – then, as she unfolded the wrappings, these intimate reminders of her husband fell into her hands. She did not speak. Her desolation was too deep to find expression in words. Looking up at me, she did not see my face. She saw Heinz standing beside us taking his purse out of his pocket with a familiar gesture. She saw him unclasp the fountain-pen from his breast-pocket and sit down at the desk to write. She saw him take off his spectacles to rub his eyes, polish the lenses, and then put them on again. Covering the things with her hand, her head gradually sank lower over the table as her body was racked with heavy sobbing.

FOURTEEN

During the time that I was away Kurt must have passed through a crisis and overcome some deep-seated problem, for on my return it was immediately noticeable that his attitude towards me had changed, so much so that once again, for a short duration, I felt a new hope for the future. Instead of being an aggravating obstruction I was now a companion. He took an interest in my occupations and discussed many matters with me. There was still a barrier between us, but each one in his own territory was friendly towards the other. He introduced me to the friends with whom he had spent his few hours of recreation during my illness and absence in Franzensbad. He had taken up riding seriously and bought a mare called Weichsel (Vistula). There had been exhilarating rides through the forests, and jolly parties in the evenings; it sounded as if he had come out of his shell at last. Wishing to return their hospitality and hoping to encourage the circle in which he felt at home, I invited all of them to an evening party; but somehow this did not please Kurt. He did not even come down from his study until an hour after the guests arrived. The 'jolly friends' were not jolly in my presence. They were formal and stiff, sitting like dummies in smart evening dress. It could only be concluded that it was I who had this effect on them, because I was the only newcomer, but curiously enough I was the only person who really had a good time. I enjoyed myself, in spite of everything, for the simple reason that I was passionately fond of dancing and had found an expert partner in Rudolf Weiss who, for reasons best known to himself, danced most of the time with me, teaching me the newest complicated steps. This infuriated Kurt and yet I was quite certain that he was not jealous. Maybe I should not have danced with such obvious zest when I saw it displeased my husband, but such a denial is not easy when one has been starved of a favourite pursuit for many years. It would have been just as difficult for me to turn down an expert pianist had one offered to accompany my singing.

After this fiasco we sometimes received invitations to these friends, most of which Kurt refused, and if we did go there was no fun. I suppose I dampened their spirits – anyway I was an outsider again.

It was the same when we invited the nurses from the Clinic. I was unable to draw them out or make them feel we were glad to see them. This was entirely my fault, for Kurt blossomed out on these occasions, knowing exactly how to amuse his staff, although even then he remained remote. But it is the lady of the house who should create the atmosphere of hospitality, and in this case, visiting the wife of their Chief, the nurses, being well brought up, were naturally anything but forward, tentatively waiting for me to set the ball rolling. When speaking English I had long since overcome my ridiculous shyness. The necessity of conversing in a foreign language brought back all the old obstacles to be mastered once more. The worst of it was that I merely gave the impression of being aloof and stuck-up. The nurses were very fond of music and had formed a little choir, singing sometimes for their own amusement, sometimes on the wards, especially at Christmas time. It never occurred to me that they would have been pleased for me to join them, or play the piano for them. I would have been afraid that they might resent the intrusion. After it was too late Kurt pointed out that this would have been a point of contact and a method of co-operation which they would have appreciated. When I remonstrated that I did not play the piano well enough, he replied that any rate I played better than they did.

One of the nurses had an aunt, Frau Dr Schwarz, a *Volksdeutsche* who had been headmistress of the girls' section of the Dürerschule (the grammar school) ever since it had been opened between the wars, while Bromberg was still

Polish. She taught modern languages and, keen to practise English, she invited me to her flat. Thus began a lasting friendship and a series of weekly visits so long as I was in Bromberg. She had a charming study, with one wall lined with books on shelves of light-coloured wood to match her desk and other hand-made furniture. Here we discussed literature, art and every subject under the sun, without noticing the passing of time. After I had known her a little while she asked me if I would give weekly lectures in English to her sixth form. Horrified, I said I could not possibly undertake such a task. I would not know where to begin or what to say . . . She overrode my objections and lack of self-confidence, at the same time making concrete suggestions as to various subjects I might choose to talk about. I finally agreed, but when the time came my mind was a complete blank; there was not one drop of saliva in my mouth, and I could not breathe. All I was conscious of was the thunderous beating of my heart and forty upturned faces waiting for me to begin. In the end it must have been those faces which saved me. They were so eager, so curious, so wondering how much they would understand, that their concentration and intensity of interest helped me to forget my nervousness. I suddenly realized how much this lecture must mean to them, no matter what I spoke about or whether I was as dull as ditchwater. The very fact that I was pure-bred English and standing before them, talking my own language, was sufficient to inspire them as they had never set eyes on anyone of my nationality before, except the prisoners of war.

Once I had started I automatically found myself choosing words they would be able to understand. I spoke slowly and distinctly, my training in diction and voice-production standing me in good stead. It was easy to notice by their puzzled expressions if they were in deep waters. By the end of the lesson they could follow me easily. When the bell rang, Frau Dr Schwarz, who had been listening at the back of the room, came forward to thank me, and with the girls silently standing, we left the room together. As soon as we were in the corridor a roar of excited voices broke loose in the classroom. Later on Frau Dr Schwarz, who enjoyed the complete confidence of her pupils, told me that they were most enthusiastic and that their pleasant surprise at finding how much they could understand proved to be an invaluable encouragement to further study. As I grew more used to it, I enjoyed myself as much as they did, and after a time induced them to talk as well. They soon overcame their shyness and made rapid strides. Keeping them in order was no problem because they were so keen to pick up every syllable that you could hear a pin drop in the silence of concentration. If anybody inadvertently made a noise, the whole class would turn upon the culprit and hiss venomously.

As autumn approached it became evident that Hitler's objective of crushing Russia before the winter descended upon his troops was not to be attained. So confident had he been on this score that the Army was not even equipped with sufficient thick clothing. Stories of chaos and of terrible suffering were brought back from the front. Public appeals were made for skis, fur coats, rugs, boots, woollen underwear and mitts, but before the articles reached their destination thousands of soldiers had died from the cold. Hitler was experiencing his first military setback – or rather standstill. As the year drew to its close few guessed that 1942 would be turning point in the war. Neither did I dream that the gathering of the first storm clouds over Germany would, strangely enough, coincide with a sharp turning point in my personal experiences. Events moved forward inexorably with surprising rapidity.

FIFTEEN

Knowing that Kurt and I did not live in harmony as man and wife I ought perhaps to have been prepared for the next development; nevertheless it came as a profound shock when Kurt brought up the question of divorce. I know now that my strongest emotion was that of fear. I was sitting on the divan in my bedroom one summer evening (in June or early July) with the windows wide open and the breeze was blowing the curtains into the room. Kurt sat opposite me in the old-fashioned, high, wing-backed armchair beside the sewing-table. At the first realization of what he was leading up to I was seized by a violent pain as if I had been suddenly struck in the stomach. The blood rushed to my head, then receded entirely as though I had none left in my body, leaving me icy cold and shivering from head to foot. I had never been really afraid of anything before and did not recognize these symptoms. During and after the air-raid in which we nearly lost our lives, I experienced the identical emotion which I then knew to be fear. As Kurt spoke, my thoughts darted incoherently backwards and forwards, scanning the past and trying to visualize the future *alone*. My first words were: 'And Manny, what about Manny? And what will Mama think?' Kurt said that Manny would naturally stay with me and that it was probably better for him also that we should part, that it was worse for a child if his parents lived together in discord than if they lived peacefully apart. The disappointment that it would cause Mama and my family I could see was also painful to him. He did not wish to make me or them unhappy and he could not bear the thought of giving up Manny. Although outwardly I would be the loser − the odd man out − he was fully aware that he would shoulder many troubles. He went on to say that he hoped, if we were both free to go our own way, our development would not be stunted by constant frustration. He hoped that in the long run, if I were free, I would also be happier than if I remained tied to a man who could never be a true partner.

Very dimly, as yet, the idea of this freedom to lead my own life, unencumbered by the continual effort of trying to fulfil a task for which I was not fitted, made an appeal to me. This was however immediately suffocated by the overwhelming dread of standing alone. How could I face it? Even at that time I must have realized that it was not particularly the loss of a husband that I mourned, for he had been lost long ago. If a woman is treated as a sister, she behaves like one, and eventually, cost what it may, she feels like one. At best I was never more than a half-sister, for during the war the differences of nationality always stood between us and we were separated by vast stretches of 'no-man's land'. I did not greatly mourn the loss of anything so long as I had Manny – neither house, possessions nor position. The house we lived in belong to the town and was let to Kurt while he remained in his job as chief gynaecologist. We would no doubt share our possessions and, given a few rooms, I would soon make them comfortable. As to position – it was always one of Kurt's grievances that I preferred to be 'Frau Sybil Falkenberg' rather than 'the wife of Dr Falkenberg'. No, what I feared was that I would not have sufficient courage to start afresh, to build anew. For nine years I had stood under his influence and for six years I had been sheltered under his roof and protection. In spite of all the gaps in our relationship I had nevertheless had no other serious object in life but to consider his and Manny's interests. I had been completely dependent (much too dependent) upon his advice and decisions, especially since I had been cut off from my family. In all matters concerning Manny, including his feeding and the treatment of his little ailments, I followed Kurt's instructions implicitly. We had the same tastes in our intellectual pursuits. I just could not picture an everyday routine without him. How would it be to drift into the unknown with no firm ground beneath one's feet – no husband, no parents, no home, no motherland? If I had been able to cast a glance over the next few years I could not have taken the plunge. I would never have thought it possible to survive them.

Kurt had already decided to send me to Franzensbad again in July in the hope that the second course of baths would complete the cure. I made the last-minute preparations for the journey automatically as though I were walking in my sleep. Once in Franzensbad I had leisure to regain at least outward composure and came back physically fitter than I had been for many years. Kurt and I arranged for our divorce to take place by mutual agreement. In Germany there was no difficulty at that time in obtaining a divorce by this means. At the court I answered the questions as in a dream. It was all over in a few minutes. The judge squinted and much of my attention was taken up by trying to decide which eye he could see with and whether he was looking at me or not. He was very kind and repeatedly asked me if I was sure I was taking the right step. Each time I answered, 'Yes, I think it is best, provided my son may always be allowed to live with me,' and this was agreed upon. I wonder what would have happened if I had said, 'No, I have changed my mind.'

I had no legal document with regard to alimony and trusted Kurt's promise to provide adequately for us. Up to the time when we fled from the Russians, when he lost his job and was penniless, he gave me an ample allowance which was paid through a banker's order into my new account. Kurt had always been generous and fair in financial matters. When he was still studying and we had little, he shared every penny. When he had plenty, we had a joint banking account from which I could draw whatever I wanted, although I never did so without telling him.

We kept the knowledge of our pending divorce from the public as long as possible, with the result that some peculiar situations arose. For instance, when our dear old Professor Fuchs died, we were invited to the funeral in Danzig and to the memorial service in Posen. We both wanted to go as he had been such a good friend to us, but we did not consider it the appropriate moment to announce that we were in the throes of legal proceedings, so we went and said nothing. When the news of our divorce could eventually no longer be withheld, it burst like a thunderbolt upon the scandal-mongers of Bromberg and set their tongues wagging for months with the most fantastic tales, which were embroidered at every turn until they bore no semblance to the truth.

Our immediate problem of a practical nature was to find somewhere for Manny and me to live. People were not given permission to move from one town to another unless the husband changed his job and in any case I did not want to settle in Berlin or the West, where air-raids were more and more frequent. As a result of the air-raids the housing shortage was becoming acute and the most I could hope for anywhere would be two rooms. For the time being Kurt got permission for Manny and me to move into part of a flat in a house he had annexed as an overflow for his nurses and medical staff. We had two rooms, kitchen and bathroom, which all looked very bare and dismal until I had my things installed. Then everyone was surprised to see the transformation into a cosy little home. I could of course only take a small part of my furniture and left the rest at Kurt's house until I should need it. Dividing up our possessions had proved a painful business, not unaccompanied by unpleasant-ness, which turned out to be entirely irrelevant; in the end we both had to leave everything when the Russians ad-vanced. I furnished the larger room as a dining-sitting-room, where I hung my only picture, the lovely Pasternack water-colour Kurt gave me before we were married. I had no radio. I understood that sets were available if one had something to barter, but as I had nothing, this was out of the question.

Manny had all his toys and belongings, and took everything in his stride without any perturbation. He enjoyed a visit to his daddy once a week, but came back contentedly, as a matter of course.

While I had been in Franzensbad Kurt had caught Valentina red-handed passing some of my precious bottled fruits and vegetables over the garden gate to a friend. I always knew she pinched what she could get hold of, but we had never before been able to prove any theft. There was a nasty scene and Kurt gave her the sack. I was sorry in many ways because she was kind-hearted and genuinely fond of Manny. She wept bitterly when the time came to say goodbye to him. We had no difficulty in finding a new maid, a *Volksdeutsche* called Flora. When I moved out I gave her the choice of coming with Manny and me, or staying with Kurt, and without any hesitation she chose to come with us, although it meant having to sleep out at a friend's as I had no room for her. She served me well and faithfully so long as the Labour Exchange allowed me to employ her. After that they sent her to work for a grocer's wife who had an enormous family, and it was very touching, whenever she came to see us, she brought a jar of jam or some other present she had been given coupon-free from the shop.

We established our daily routine in the two rooms, and surprisingly enough time did not lag, but I was still incapable of making any plans for the future. At first I thought I would like to take up some sort of training and Kurt would have paid for anything I had chosen, but I abandoned the idea because it would have meant leaving Manny, which I could not endure. Then I tried to think of some sort of a job which I could do at home. I called at Professor Haferkorn's in Danzig, with whom I had worked at the Technische Hochschule, only to find that he had been transferred to the foreign broadcasting section in Berlin. His wife gave me his address and I wrote asking if he could give me work by sending translations to do by post. He replied that this would not be possible but that he would be delighted if I would join his staff of interpreters in Berlin, an offer which for obvious reasons I did not accept. The trouble was I really did not know where I wanted to go or what I wanted to do. If it had been possible I would have run away to England long ago but of course Manny and I, as German citizens, were not allowed to leave the country (even if Kurt had agreed to this) so long as we were at war. The only way to pull through was to try to enjoy all the advantages of my position without dwelling on the disadvantages. I had one definite urge, apart from looking after a home and Manny, and that was to start singing again. Immediately after I returned from Franzensbad I made enquiries about a singing teacher and was introduced to Frau Else Daniel, a *Volksdeutsche*, whose husband was a bank manager. They had lived in Poland for many years, between the two World Wars, and before that when it was Germany territory. Frau Daniel became one of my dearest friends and the hours I spent with her are among my happiest memories. From now on, whenever I was in Bromberg, I spent two mornings a week with her, singing and listening to her other pupils. My chief difficulty always was to find somewhere to practise after I left Kurt's house and had no piano.

Frau Daniel had three sons at the front and suffered agonies of apprehension. She was always pessimistic as to the outcome of the war and now events began to justify her forebodings. The year 1942 had started well enough. After checking the Russian winter offensive and defeating a big attack in May, the Germany Army advanced once more, even deeper into the heart of the country. U-boats were operating successfully. In June Rommel made his sensational thrust forward in North Africa. Albert Speer achieved a remarkable rise in war production. The only fly in the ointment so far was the bombing of German towns, which increased in intensity as time went on. By the autumn, when I first met Frau Daniel, the outlook had changed completely.

SIXTEEN

On 23 October Field Marshal Montgomery attacked the German lines at El Alamein. On 8 November Allied troops landed in north-west Africa. But what bore deeper significance for us (because we lived in the east and many relatives of acquaintances were involved) was the encirclement towards the end of November of twenty-two German divisions (330,000 men) at Stalingrad. Although there was now nothing to be gained by it, Hitler persisted in his policy of non-surrender. All through December and January the trapped men, suffering inconceivable hardships through cold, hunger and epidemics, were forced to hold out, until finally Field-Marshal von Paulus, against Hitler's orders, gave himself up to the Russians with the remnant of his forces who had survived. Their anxious relatives could only conjecture at their fate. There were no means of ascertaining who was alive or who was dead. The Russians did not belong to the International Red Cross, and did not (neither then nor at any other time during the war) notify the enemy of the names of their prisoners, who were given no opportunity of communicating with their next of kin. If a German saw a comrade killed, he would naturally report it, but those who were killed or died from wounds and illnesses beyond the enemy lines remain 'missing' to this day, because no proper records were kept. Later, during the German retreats, they rarely had time even to take the identity discs from the bodies in order to report their death, let alone bury them. Many wives and parents clung to the hope, long after the war was over, that their menfolk might one day turn up. Some did, but most of them did not.

The tragedy of Stalingrad hung over us all that winter. It was in every way the most ghastly Christmas I have ever spent in my life. On ordinary working days I could find enough to do and did not feel as lonely as I had expected, but on Sundays and holidays, when everyone was enjoying a rest amidst the family circle, I found no relaxation or comfort. I had not begun to build up any independence and was perpetually seized with restlessness. I drifted from one person to another, from one interest to some new experience – feckless, cold, superficial and lacking in purpose or directive. Except for my affection for Manny there was no warmth within me. This phase lasted a long time.

Manny and my singing were the only real joys. I took Manny to his first pantomime that winter – *The Sleeping Beauty*. He was of course enthralled. Watching the audience was even more entertaining for adults than watching the players. Expressions of joy, disgust or horror flitted across their little faces. There was no blasé criticism; they were so lost in their make-believe world that the whole theatre became the centre of action in which every child felt he was taking part.

Although Manny could busy himself for hours alone, he loved the company of other children. As he was the only child we thought it best to send him to a kindergarten when he was still quite a toddler, in the spring of 1942. He started by going two mornings a week and when we moved to the Nurses' Home he was able to continue there as it was not far away. There were no private schools or private kindergarten in Bromberg. The kindergarten near us where Manny went was run by the National Socialist Welfare Association in a new long, one-storeyed building, surrounded by a nice garden where there were plenty of swings, see-saws, sand-pits and so on. Inside it was fitted out with miniature furniture, tiny low washbasins, numbered pegs, cupboards full of exciting toys and games. The teachers were efficient and extremely kind. Milk (off ration) was served mid-morning and lunch to those who stayed all day. I made Manny a little shoulder bag out of a pocket off my Harris tweed coat, lined with cotton checked material, for a sandwich to be eaten mid-morning. From the first moment he loved school and always looked forward to his visits. He was a good mixer and his love of orderliness made it easy for him to fall in with a regular timetable; indeed he was far too occupied with the many diversions to have time for being naughty. He soon learned to hold his own and was on good terms with his playmates. It was amusing to watch them. At twelve sharp there they would be, dressed in their outdoor clothes, waiting to be collected, like suitcases in a lost property office, until one by one the mothers would come and claim them. For once I was not different. I was a mummy like everybody there and found immediate contact with all the other mummies. We had a common interest which transcended all differences of status or nationality. Merely because I had a child I was accepted without question as one of them. Manny made one special friend with whom he used to play at his home or at ours. We were often invited out to tea together. On the whole I began to find it easier to be sociable, although I was aware that some people only wanted to know me out of curiosity. This caused me, out of sheer bravado, to behave as though I hadn't a care in the world.

Kurt had by this time married again and his wife's former husband, Klaus, who owned an estate near Bromberg, sometimes invited me to his parties.

There was one remarkable party I went to there after we were divorced. When I arrived and saw that the whole company were strangers to me I wondered why Klaus had invited me. Besides myself there were only two other females, one young woman from Berlin who was staying there with her mother (although the mother for some reason was not present that night) and the daughter's friend, a very tense, masculine type. Apparently Klaus was toying with the idea of asking the daughter to marry him. Before dinner, appetizers and drinks were served in the drawing-room. At the dinner table one delicacy after another was put before us and the glasses were filled as soon as they were emptied. As the meal progressed it became evident that in all probability Klaus had asked me there in order to introduce me to one of his friends who was placed next to me at the table. I could imagine Klaus saying '*Vielleicht wäre sie eine Frau für dich! Seh'sie mal an.*' (Perhaps she's the right one for you. Come and have a look at her). We got along quite well together but all the time it seemed as though both he and I were spectators. In spite of the fact that everyone was joining in the fun, there was a queer feeling of waiting for something to happen, of almost pleasurable apprehension, like watching a drama which was exciting but did not affect us personally. I was the only stranger in the party and I could not put my finger on the cause of this perturbation because there were no outward signs to give a clue.

After dinner we broke up into small groups and later the two girls drifted off. I began to think my imagination had been running riot. The men continued to drink and smoke more than was good for them and I went into a smaller drawing-room to listen to one of them who was playing the piano, then, when I could no longer keep my eyes open, I went to bed.

I do not know how long I had been asleep, when I was suddenly awakened by the light from the passage shining through the door where a man stood swaying slightly, staring into my room with glassy, drunken eyes. He lurched forward but said nothing and I waited, calculating the odds rapidly.

I decided to try winning the game by shock tactics. So far I had not stirred and lay with my eyes nearly shut so that he could not see whether I was awake or asleep. As he started to stagger forwards again, I jerked myself bolt upright in bed, struck him on the chest and shouted, 'What do you want?' This abrupt movement startled him and he tottered backwards. Before he could regain his balance I jumped out of bed, swivelled him round and bundled him out of the door, which I then locked firmly this time.

I never discovered whether he had come into my room by

mistake or what his intentions had been. At breakfast he greeted me normally, with no signs of remembering the incident, or if he did, he may not have known that I had been the vixen into whose den he had strayed.

I flopped back into bed, shaken but triumphant. I recalled the queer atmosphere which had hung over us earlier in the evening, then suddenly women's voices raised in anger and fear rang through the house, culminating in piercing screams. My hair stood on end as I listened and wondered what devilish powers had been unleashed. The screams subsided into hysterical sobs and after a considerable time, except for subdued shuffles about the house, all was still.

When I came down the next morning no reference was made to the strange events, and there was not much conversation at the table. Suddenly the daughter's friend, pale and drawn, marched into the breakfast-room. She had her hat and coat on and after gulping down a cup of hot coffee (synthetic, which would do little to calm her nerves) she stalked out without saying a word to anyone. Klaus had evidently ordered the horses for her, because the next moment she drove past the window and was gone.

Everybody relaxed and mopped their brows as though a crisis had passed. They then told me that in the night this girl had tried to murder the other one with a carving knife, and they were afraid she might renew her attacks – hence their relief at her abrupt departure! The mother and daughter had apparently been staying peacefully with Klaus, when suddenly the girl friend had descended upon them in jealous fury, and had demanded that the daughter should return with her to Berlin immediately. This interference naturally enraged Klaus and, whether he cared about the daughter or not, he was determined not to have her whisked away at the demand of her girl friend. A pitched battle therefore ensued between Klaus and the friend, with the mother on Klaus's side. The daughter floundered indecisively between the two of them. On the evening of the party, surrounded by his sympathetic friends, Klaus had felt emboldened, and with them, resolved upon a plot to annoy the unwelcome visitor. They played upon the daughter's indecision, and baited the girl friend until she was so distraught with envy and hatred that she was carried away in a manner that nobody had imagined possible. They paid the penalty of playing with fire.

When I got home to my complacent Flora and my bonny little Manny the crazy party seemed like a fantastic nightmare. Our temporary refuge in the Nurses' Home proved to be of short duration, as the rooms were urgently needed early in the year. However, Frau von Oldenheim invited us to stay with her at Lukowo for a while and this seemed to be the best solution to our housing problem for the time being. All our belongings which we could not take with us were stored in a box room and we set off on the next venture, Flora included, although the Labour Exchange recalled her to Bromberg soon afterwards. Nina von Oldenheim preferred not to be alone in the castle and usually had some friend or other staying with her. Gisela rarely saw any other children than her little brother, so that it was good for her to have a child of her own age in the house sometimes. Now that they were a little older, she and Manny enjoyed each other's company. They loved best of all to be out of doors and when it was fine they spent most of the day with Nina's personal *Kutscher* (coachman) in the stables, in the fields or trundling along on top of a cartload of fodder. They came back filthy, but as happy as sandboys. As a special treat Nina would sometimes take us all for drives in the pony-trap, when we would picnic and play in the woods where there were masses of wild flowers in the spring. We had some unusually warm weather in the middle of March and were even able to sit outdoors and sunbathe.

Nina sometimes had other visitors, one of whom was an astrologer and palmist from Berlin; Nina believed in her occult powers and whenever she thought something important might happen, pleasant or unpleasant, she had her horoscope read. This poor woman had worked herself up to the verge of a nervous breakdown because she foresaw nothing but flames and destruction for Berlin and the rest of Germany. It took her several days to work out a horoscope in detail by means of complicated mathematical calculations. One day she asked me Kurt's and my dates of birth, and immediately said, 'Oh yes, in 1942 your husband was passing through one of the most successful periods of his life, whereas your stars [quoting their names and positions] stood in a most unfavourable relationship to each other, when nothing could fail to go wrong.' She assured me I was not yet through the wilderness and that I had more trouble, perhaps even worse trouble, ahead. I did not believe in these gloomy predictions because it was impossible to conceive any trouble that could be worse than the collapse of all hopes of a happy married life. Neither did I pay any heed at the time to her statement that I would in the future enjoy considerable protection, particularly from my own family.

One day when I was walking down the avenue between the big castle and the little one, I heard the mumbling of many voices approaching and the tramping of many feet. It was a party of British prisoners of war who, I learned later, were to live in the little *Schloss*. I was astonished and rather upset to discover that I could not pick up much of their conversation as they passed by. They spoke with a strong accent of some sort, but I could not imagine where they came from. They were taken off in small groups during the day with German sentries to work on farms in the neighbourhood and seemed quite contented. It was not only their peculiar, inarticulate speech which made it difficult for me to understand them. Once before when Flora, Manny and I went from Bromberg by train into the country during the autumn to look for mushrooms in the pine forests, there had been two smart young British POWs in the same compartment. They were talking quietly together but I could not understand a word they were saying; yet I heard, without any strain, every syllable that the Germans mumbled to each other even while I was trying to listen to the English conversation. Now that I had no radio of my own I never heard an English voice. Near Klaus's estate there was a prison camp for British officers. We passed by sometimes in the trap and I could see them in the distance, always playing football! Once Klaus dropped a remark that some of them had escaped. I wondered what I would do if anyone asked me to help them and was glad that no one ever did, because I had no wish to become involved in such matters. I knew my place was to stand by Manny who needed me more than any one else did.

Nina was in a state of trepidation because the military authorities continually threatened to requisition the big castle. They did in fact take over the guests' wing during 1943, and the rest of the building (except the rooms used by Nina) in 1944 for the Air Force. Manny and I could not, of course, stay permanently at Lukowo, nor could we for ever drift as guests from one place to another. Time passed pleasantly enough amidst those lovely surroundings, but I naturally hankered after a home of my own.

In April I was approached by Frau Linda Petersen, whom I had met at the tennis club, about sub-letting two rooms in their flat. Her husband, Manfred, an architect, with a business in Hamburg as well as in Bromberg, was to be called up and she knew the Housing Department would not allow her to retain all five large rooms, two of which had been used as offices. She preferred to choose her own tenant rather than have the rooms requisitioned and have unknown, perhaps unpleasant, occupants thrust upon her. The flat was on the third floor of a house on the main road. The two rooms at the back, one leading off the other, could easily be separated from the others by boarding up the communicating doors. The house was centrally heated and I would be allowed use of the bathroom, larder, kitchen and gas stove. There was parquet flooring and the wallpaper and paintwork were in

good condition. Large windows overlooked a private courtyard and garden far below where the children could play in
safety. This was as good a proposition as I could expect
under the circumstances. In any case I had no alternative
offer, so I agreed to move in in July when the rooms would
be vacant. In the meantime I accepted an invitation to stay
with *Vater* in Wuppertal-Barmen in May and go with him,
Frieda, Grete, and our three children to the seaside in June.
And this is how I became involved in the first of the war's
'firestorms' – an expression unknown to me until long
afterwards.

SEVENTEEN

Except for a short stay in Wuppertal-Barmen in 1941, this was my first visit to western Germany since the beginning of the war. As usual, it was a relief to get away from the factious borderlands and to come into the heart of the country; not that they had no troubles – in fact they now had more than we had in the east – but particularly when threatened from outside, there was a solidarity and singleness of purpose. The knowledge that they were all in the same boat, and would stick together whatever happened, gave strength to each individual.

Besides the war in general, there were two things which were obviously lowering their vitality; one was the food shortage, and the other the continued air-raids, although the big raids had not yet begun. The food shortage was as yet not desperately acute. There were enough goods in the shops to supply the full complement on the ration cards, but this was just *not* enough. It is easy to go short for a few days or a few weeks without noticing many ill-effects, but when it runs into months, the need accumulates until a permanent state of hunger and enervation ensues. Later on, the shorter the ration became, the worse the need grew, until finally near-starvation level was reached.

At that time, in May 1943, coming straight from the country in the east where we had unlimited supplies of milk, potatoes and vegetables, into a town in an industrial centre in the west, it was remarkable what a difference the deficiency in these foods made to the possibility of varying the menu and still more of satisfying appetites.

In Barmen there was not only no full milk for adults, but potatoes were rationed and vegetables in short supply. As it was impossible to 'fill up' with these commodities, the bread ration also proved inadequate. For breakfast of course during the war there never was anything but bread and a scrape of butter, or a little jam alone if you wanted to save your butter for some other meal, but now there was not even enough bread, in spite of the fact that we had three small children who did not eat their share and that we always ate wholemeal bread, which was the most nourishing and satisfying sort you could buy. If they could get hold of any extra tiny potatoes, we would boil them in their skins overnight, peel them, and then warm them up in a frying pan for breakfast in a minute quantity of fat.

So the cares of the day began for the housekeepers, and it was a constant worry to know how to fill the hungry mouths.

With petrol rationed, *Vater* could no longer take us for joyrides into the country. It was therefore a treat for the children to be bundled into the back of the car and taken round the town on his visits.

Vater, who was over sixty, was beginning to feel the effects of overwork, with so many young doctors absent at the front. He no longer trusted himself to drive in the dark and always hired a taxi.

There were frequent raids on Essen and Düsseldorf. We could hear the bombs thundering down and as we watched the blaze from the top bedroom windows, we shuddered at the thought of the poor devils beneath that inferno.

Most of the Wuppertalers took no notice of the air-raid warnings and rarely went down into their cellars. Grete and I had bedrooms with our babies on the top floor, directly under the roof, with skylights. We decided we could not take the responsibility of leaving the children up there, where there would be little hope of getting them down six flights of stairs to safety in the event of an attack. In this vulnerable position even a splinter would have been sufficient to kill the child in his cot. Therefore, whenever the siren sounded, we lay awake listening. If we heard the planes coming too near or heard the bombs and anti-aircraft guns too distinctly, we would get dressed. Then, with any further signs of approaching danger, we would carry our babies downstairs to the drawing-room on the first floor, where Frieda would usually join us with Volker, and sometimes *Vater*. The maids never stirred. When it got even hotter we took the children down into the cellar, a vaulted stronghold. I always took my handbag with my money, important documents and jewellery wherever I went. We all had our best clothes in a cupboard and in trunks in the cellar.

On my birthday, 29 May 1943, it was like a hot summer's day. They had baked some delicious fruit flans in my honour and as we sat on the balcony for afternoon coffee, we basked in the sunshine. We had been busy packing during the afternoon in preparation for our journey to the seaside on the following day. In the evening after the children had been put to bed, we three daughters-in-law sat finishing the last odd jobs of mending which inevitably crop up when one starts to pack. *Vater* was on night duty at a hospital in the town. Frieda fetched a bottle of wine to celebrate my birth-day, and as we sipped it and talked, we little heeded the passing of time until the siren went, when we saw that it was after midnight. Grete and I were fidgety about the children and we went straight upstairs. Before we reached the top of the house we knew it was already time to bring them down immediately. We had just got them on to the first floor and were already saying we would go into the cellar, so near was the noise of the planes, when we heard the Wuppertal anti-aircraft guns firing, each time nearer and nearer. As I put my hand out to take my tweed coat which was hanging in the hall, the gun on the hill immediately above us cracked out as though it were inside the attic. We all fled with our babies downstairs. I was in front and as I opened the cellar door, there was a terrific explosion, followed by one after another, thundering and crashing all round us as though the devil had broken loose. As Frieda came down the stairs splintered glass from the windows scattered behind her. The electric current had been severed and we only had small torches which we directed at each other with trembling hands to see if we were all there, only to find that the younger maid, who slept on the ground floor next to the kitchen, was missing. The cook volunteered to reconnoitre, but as she crept up the cellar stairs the girl came stumbling down. She had not heard the siren and had been awakened by the window falling across her bed. Still half asleep, she thought there was a frightful storm raging, until she looked through the gap in the wall and saw the bombs exploding everywhere, crumbling the houses like so many packs of cards. The summer-house in the garden was already ablaze and everything was lit up by the burning buildings.

In a short space of time our cellar was crowded with people. We could not think how they had got in because Frieda was sure she had locked the front door and it had not dawned on us that all the windows and doors had crashed in from the blast of the very first bomb next door. Later we learned that the neighbours had been killed instantaneously and the house razed to the ground. Everyone was flashing torches indiscriminately and Frieda automatically cried out 'Licht aus!' Yet the whole town was burning like one enormous bonfire, showing the RAF only too clearly how thoroughly they were carrying out their task! Some of the people who flocked in, came because it was well-known that the cellar was as strongly vaulted as a church crypt. Others brought their wounded, hoping that Vater would help them. But Vater was, of course, not there, and we only had a little emergency first-aid box. They came with fractured limbs, streaming with blood, some of them badly burnt. It was a nightmare. And all the time the bombs were whistling down. Our lungs felt as though they would burst. We could not hear each other speak for the deafening explosions. The children, poor mites, were much too frightened to cry. They sat as quiet as mice, deathly pale and shivering from top to toe in convulsions of horror.

Many of the people arrived in their night clothes. They

had been flung out of their comfortable beds and only had time to snatch a few odds and ends as they rushed underground. I can see now a fat woman trying to squeeze into her corsets, fumbling with shaking fingers at the clasps.

I realized I had not put on my coat in the hall after all and was dressed in a summer blouse and a red skirt made from a swastika flag (the only material available without coupons!). On my feet I only had straw sandals. I wondered if I dared to leave Manny for just one minute while I ran to the other end of the cellar passage where I stored my best black coat and some leather shoes. It was impossible to carry him along with me owing to the congestion. Supposing whilst I was there a bomb fell on Manny, or in between us so that I could not get back to him. It was getting very hot, but I knew if we had to leave the cellar, I would need the coat and particularly the shoes, so I decided I must risk it and pushed my way feverishly between the crowds there and back whilst Frieda took Manny on her lap. The next day I found I was wearing one black shoe and one green one! The smoky air was stifling and we wondered how much longer it would be before we were faced with the alternative of suffocating or going out into unknown dangers. As the bombing abated a little the young maid plucked up courage to slip up to her bedroom near the top of the cellar stairs, to fetch some clothes, but she could not get across to her cupboard. The room was full of fumes and a blazing beam was hanging down from the ceiling. She said the main staircase was also burning from top to bottom. We could not understand how the fire had spread throughout the four-storeyed house so quickly, even if one hundred incendiaries had come through the attic roof. We did not know then that the chief havoc, apart from the explosives, had been caused by the dropping of canisters full of phosphorus which burst into flames as they pierced right through the houses to the ground, leaving a blazing trail throughout their passage. This was a pernicious form of warfare, because it was impossible to extinguish the burning chemical, especially as it caused a major conflagration on all floors simultaneously. In Barmen the whole town was peppered with explosives and showered with phosphorus canisters. There was not a chance of saving any property, even if you had no babies to look after. All efforts were concentrated on saving as many lives as possible.

There was a warden supposed to be in charge of a group of houses and we looked to him for advice. He reported that *Vater*'s main staircase would shortly collapse and the burning wreckage would certainly tumble down the cellar steps. When this happened the heat and fumes would kill any persons who remained in the cellar. By now there were only a few bombs falling and he said it would be best to make for a shelter built by the town authorities in a cellar further down the road which should be safe enough. For some reason (presumably because he feared a panic in the event of our staircase falling in) instead of going out of our cellar door into the street, he led us through the hole in the wall, which had been made according to regulations earlier in the war, into the cellar next door and up into that house. It was pitch dark and the hole was very small, which made it difficult to get through holding Manny in my arms. I was terrified of being trapped alone in that awful narrow passage.

Somehow our two maids were left behind in *Vater*'s cellar, where shortly afterwards the burning staircase did plunge down. They dashed out into the garden, expecting to be forced to climb over the twenty-foot-high wall which surrounded it, but to their surprise there was no wall left, only a pile of rubble. They scrambled over this and, although they saw flames pouring out of the windows of the swimming baths at the back of the house, they ran in there because they did not know where else to go. Grete and about twenty others also eventually found their way in and had to stay there all night as they were cut off by fire in every passageway and exit. In the meantime they tried to keep themselves cool by jumping in and out of the pool and wrapping damp cloths round their heads and bodies, because in spite of the stone flooring, the baths, with everything burning all round, were like a furnace. In the morning some rescue workers tunnelled their way through the debris in the hope of finding survivors and they were then dragged out.

After grovelling through the dark passage in the cellar we came up into the main entrance hall of the house next door, which was flaring up like a matchbox. If the ceiling above us had not been in flames and threatening to crumble on top of us at any minute, we would never have had the courage to go out into the street, because as far as we could see every house was on fire. But it was our only chance, so we darted out, one after the other. I thought I would just follow the people in front. Once outside, however, I could see nobody. Everything was enveloped in thick smoke. I stumbled forward blindly, keeping in the direction of the shelter the man had told us about, to the right. I tried to walk in the middle of the road because tongues of flames were leaping from every window and the trees at the edge of the pavement were also on fire, shedding their blazing branches. The roads were so hot from the burning phosphorus that the tar had melted. Some of the houses were old and built of wood. These were already toppling over into the street. I had covered Manny in a rug made of a felty material so that he could not be scorched by the falling debris. He was now three years nine months old and a big boy for his age. Carrying this heavy weight, it soon seemed as though I must have walked a long way, although I suppose it was not far. Further on the smoke became denser and my path narrower, until finally it was entirely blocked by burning ruins. There was therefore no other course open for me but to retrace my steps. I had no idea where I could find refuge. As I was about to turn I heard a loud crack, then the crashing noise of another house tumbling in flames across the road behind me. I was now cut off from retreat and encircled by fire. I chose the spot where the flames were not so high, only about knee-deep, and made a dash for it – that is to say I walked as fast as I could, handicapped as I was by my precious burden. I do not know how far I stumbled along, nor how long it took me. I was not aware of any pain from the burns on my legs, nor of the sting of the smoke which was in my eyes, nose and throat, slowly choking me, but gradually I was overcome by an appalling fatigue. In spite of fighting against this as hard as I could, I began to sink slowly to the ground, which I knew would mean the end, because our bodies would then be swallowed up in the hungry flames. I said aloud, '*Also doch!*' ('Well, after all'). I had been firmly convinced that I would never be killed in the war by my own countrymen, and here, after all, I was a victim of their destruction. I felt no fear now, only an overwhelming bodily exhaustion, and in my heart the deepest sorrow that Manny's life should be thus nipped in the bud. As my knees gave way I could no longer hold Manny and he tumbled out of my arms. He was still enveloped in the rug excepting that his legs were poking out, and as soon as they reached the flames he screamed in agony, rolling and kicking on the ground before me. Although I was only semi-conscious, his cries pierced my torpor and urged me to one more superhuman effort. I grabbed hold of him and lurched forward through the burning ruins. Suddenly a figure emerged from the smoke which I thought at first must be a phantom. He was covered all over in a queer-looking suit, topped with a gas mask, and glided up to us on what seemed to be a silent motorbike with a side-car. The noise of the engine, of course, was not audible above the cracking and hissing of the fire. I tumbled into the side-car with Manny on top of me. We had not gone far when I caught sight of Frieda and Volker. I shouted to the driver but he did not hear me. By the time I was able to attract his attention we had sped further along the road and had to turn back. For one dreadful minute I was afraid we would not be able to find them again, but the man was in better possession of his wits than I and soon picked them up. He took us down the main road, bumping over the wreckage, in the direction of Elberfeld. All the way, on both sides, what was left of the houses was afire. We were beginning to wonder whether there was any hope of escape, when abruptly all signs of havoc ceased. Along straight lines drawn on a map by the planners of the raid in England, the bombing had begun. Within the area marked by these lines there was total destruction, beyond them no damage at all – a very precise piece of work! On one side of the line was the scene of a distorted nightmare; on the other there was a normal town, where the atmosphere was smoky and where there was unusual activity in the middle of the night, but nevertheless the houses were standing upright. The end of the world had not come after all.

We were taken to the cellar of the new Town Hall where already crowds of frightened people had taken refuge, many of them wounded or suffering from burns, everyone as black as chimney sweeps. As soon as our driver had unloaded us from his side-car, he drove off again in search of more trapped victims. We found a seat on a bench. The Town Hall seemed to be a dumping centre for those who were lucky enough to be rescued, and from there the sick and wounded were being transferred elsewhere for treatment as quickly as possible. Manny was whimpering with pain. Now for the first time I began to feel the burns on my legs. This may sound incredible, but it is true. When I looked at them I saw that they were red and beginning to swell from knee to ankle. On the calves of both legs there were third-degree burns which took six months to heal, and yet up to that moment I had not felt a twinge, nor a prick. If anyone had told me that I could walk through fire and not feel it, I would never have believed them.

It was only complete obsession with the one idea of saving Manny that drove all other thoughts and feelings from my whole being. Logically speaking, it was Manny who saved my life, not vice versa. If he had not been there, without the desperate urge of maternal instincts, I would have collapsed and perished long before our rescuer came. As soon as the crisis had passed and I began to relax, I became increasingly aware of excruciating pain. We had reason to believe that we were now out of danger, but unfortunately there was more trouble ahead before the night was out.

When our turn came, we were loaded into a lorry. Although the bombing had only ceased about half an hour earlier, rescue work appeared to be well organized. It was, however, going forward on rigid lines, no doubt prescribed months in advance, assuming that the adjoining town of Wuppertal-Elberfeld would be attacked at the same time as Wuppertal-Barmen, which was not in fact the case. As we peered through the front of the lorry we saw that we were being carried back into the raging hell. We could hardly believe our eyes. Apparently the standing orders were for a certain number of wounded to be taken to a certain school which was quickly converted into an emergency hospital. These orders were now being carried out blindly, in spite of the fact that the school was in the area of destruction and was itself in flames on the top floors. Nobody had the sense or authority to divert *all* patients to Elberfeld where no bombing had taken place. Out of the safety of the Town Hall we were now brought to this school. Doctors and helpers were working feverishly as patients streamed into the cellars. Their diagnosis was that our legs had been burnt by phosphorus and they put on a dressing soaked in some liquid to prevent the chemical from eating further into the flesh. We were given a bottle of this liquid and cotton wool so that we could dab it on when necessary as the dressing dried up. It eased the pain a little. After some time we were allotted a single bed between the four of us. We were given sedatives and the children were soon asleep. Frieda and I lay wide awake. After what may have been an hour or two we were told we could no longer stay in the school as the fire could not be checked and there was imminent danger of being buried alive when the building caved in. We asked where we should go but nobody could advise us. There were no lorries or ambulances now to carry us away. All means of communication with the outside world were cut off. As we came to the exit leading on to a courtyard we saw that parts of the upper storeys were hurtling down. There was no other safer way out so we had to trust to luck that we could run clear, in between the falling debris. Frieda went first, carrying Volker, and I waited a moment to spread out our chances. Just after she had crossed the courtyard another avalanche came crashing down. I could no longer see her through the smoke but I guessed she would wait opposite the school. I took one deep breath and staggered across with Manny as quickly as I could. We too were favoured by the gods and reached the other side without injury. The school was high up on the hill overlooking the valley. We stood by the railing wondering where to go. As far as we could see there were only flaming ruins and smoke rising into the sky in thick, brown clouds. During the day it had been as warm as in summer, but now it was icy cold. The hot air rose as from an enormous furnace, over a distance of miles, and the cold air came rushing in to take its place, causing whirlwinds and a terrific gale, which swept chimney pots and tottering houses crashing to the ground. Loose bricks were flying down in all directions. We shivered with cold and fright as we beheld this appalling spectacle. Frieda left the children with me while she went to see if she could find some shelter. Later she came back and led me to the cellar of a house near the corner of a street where twenty or thirty people were huddled together. As far as could be judged this cellar stood a chance of remaining intact. Here we waited until about nine or ten the next morning by which time the fires had in the main burnt themselves out. Owing to the pall of smoke overhanging the town it was still dark. No sunshine could break through the dense fumes and dust.

We tried to make our way further up the hill where Kurt's aunt and cousins lived, but the roads were all blocked by smouldering ruins, still red hot. We learned later that half their house had been destroyed, but they had survived. We knew it would be useless trying to get through to Kurt's other aunt and cousins in the centre of the town, where the streets were old and narrow. It was a miracle that this family escaped alive, excepting for poor old Aunt Luise, who was suffocated.

Kurt had some other more distant relatives, *Tante* Magda and her husband, who lived in Wuppertal-Elberfeld, so we decided to try to get there somehow. We were hungry and filthy and we knew she would give us food and temporary refuge. As we scrambled over the ruins we saw men and women digging in an endeavour to recover the bodies of their relatives who were missing. Some people, their limbs crimson and swollen, were wearing only coats or jackets over their night attire, and no shoes. Quite a number were walking about with rags wrapped round their feet. Everyone helped each other and talked without reserve. The calamity which had befallen all alike broke down the normal barriers of convention and revived the ancient tribal impulses to cling together and preserve what remained of the community after fierce attack. Some were weeping beside their dead. Others were dry-eyed in their grief. One poor woman repeated her story to everyone who passed by, as though she were trying to defend her actions. She had had three small children and had been faced with the alternative of carrying two off to safety and leaving the third to die alone, or all four dying together. She had chosen the first course and was filled with remorse about the third poor mite whose cries still rung in her ears. Many people whose clothes had been on fire had jumped into the River Wupper. Those who could not swim had been drowned.

Familiar streets were quite unrecognizable and we made slow progress, picking our way through the ashes and rubble.

When we eventually came to a road which had already been cleared for traffic we were immediately given a lift in a car to Elberfeld. *Tante* Magda welcomed us with open arms, glad to see at least four of us alive. At the same time she wept to see the sad spectacle we presented, covered in sooty grime, our eyelids swollen and red, burns on our hands and faces, besides our bandaged legs, but above all the horrors of the night reflected in our eyes. While she prepared a meal for us we tried to wash some of the dirt off our faces and hands without damaging the tender spots. It was impossible to pass a comb through our hair, it was so matted with soot. My shoes were cutting like knives into my bloated ankles, but I did not dare take them off because I knew if I did I would never get them on again.

Tante Magda asked us to stop a few days with her until we had recovered from the first shock, but we thought it best to push on to Frieda's parents at Bad Godesberg in case the raiders returned to finish off the other half of Wuppertal the next night. (As a matter of fact they did not come until a fortnight later; then they were just as thorough in their work as when they destroyed Barmen, starting exactly along the line where they had left off on 29 May!)

When we sat down to the table, although we thought we were hungry, we could hardly eat a thing, but the hot drinks revived us a little.

Soon afterwards *Vater* turned up. He had escaped unscathed. After working at top speed all night he had only been relieved so that he might search for us. First of all he went to his house, of which only the outer walls remained. Ludicrously, on a hook in the bathroom the children's enamel chamber pot was still hanging, like a monument, and on the marble shelf across the corner of the best dining-room the bust of *Vater* which Kurt had modelled stared down at him in solitary state. This could unfortunately never be retrieved because it was not safe to put pressure on a ladder against the wall.

In the cellar the washing-machine and metal tubs were still too hot to touch. Part of the coke in the furnace-cellar was smouldering. When he saw the end of the passage blocked by the remains of the staircase which had collapsed down the steps, he knew that no human being could have survived down there. As he came out he met the woman who rented the second-floor flat in his house. She told him they had been rescued from the baths where Grete and Bernard had also spent the night, and that they were well and had gone to Grete's elder sister.

Vater stuck a notice on the wall to the effect that he was now going to *Tante* Magda's in case one of us should look there. On many of the ruins you could see this sort of message, which was sometimes the only clue for homecoming soldiers of the whereabouts of their relatives, until bodies (alive and dead) had been traced and properly placed on record.

When *Vater* came we sent telegrams to Max and Kurt who were anxiously awaiting news of us after hearing the report of the raid on the wireless. My people did not know that we were staying in Barmen at the time and on 6 June I was able to send a Red Cross message home: 'Manny, I visit *Vater's*. Air-raid. House burnt down. All saved. Manny I in bed at Frieda's parents, Godesberg, with burns on legs. *Vater* lost everything.' This message did not reach them until 11 September and I received their reply to it on 13 December.

Vater was wonderfully calm, considering he had lost his home and his worldly possessions. He was probably so relieved to know that we were all alive, that nothing else really mattered.

Because no bomb had ever fallen before on the town and because it was the first raid of that intensity as yet experienced in Germany, the population was more than usually unprepared. Lulled into a false sense of security, they did not take the precautions which people in bomb-infested areas were in the habit of taking, and were thus caught unawares.

If everyone had been dressed and in their cellars when the raid started, no doubt many lives would have been saved, but no precautions could have hindered the total destruction of the buildings, so accurate, quick and thorough was the bombing. Not all the fire-brigades in Germany could have extinguished the fires which were started simultaneously throughout the closely packed houses in the valley, most of which had been douched with phosphorus. Even the villas on the top of the hill, each standing in its own grounds, were practically all destroyed. Grete's sister, who lived up there, sat with her baby at the bottom of the garden and watched their house burn down. They at least had open space enough to avoid the toppling ruins and were not caught like rats in a trap.

The news of the disaster in Barmen spread like wild-fire throughout Germany. The dismay and sympathy was such that even the beloved red-tape of officialdom was for once cut. From the highest quarters orders were sent that we were to be given free rail passes, special food and clothing coupons, and every help available. People who had not had time to snatch up their clothes or handbags not only had no money and no ration cards, but also no identity papers – an unheard of state of affairs in Germany where a person does not exist, according to the State, in wartime or in peacetime, unless he can prove that he is registered at a police office. But even this did not shake the lords and underlings of bureaucracy. When we went to Elberfeld station and asked for tickets to Godesberg, which we were prepared to pay for, they would take no money from us, although we did not say we were victims of the raid. Our bandages, tangled hair, blotchy faces, scorched eyebrows, and the wild look in our eyes, were our passwords wherever we went. That morning we could tell at a glance by the expression on people's faces whether they had been through the ordeal or not.

The train was packed and I never knew afterwards how I managed to stand that awful journey, with the pain in my legs getting worse and worse. Every time I moved or anyone brushed past me I could hardly stop myself from screaming.

As we got nearer to Cologne a lot of passengers, out for a trip to the Rhine, joined us. The sun was shining and it must have been a Sunday. They were in a holiday mood. It seemed strange that the world and its pleasures should go on as usual. I could not imagine that I would ever again be capable of enjoying light-hearted amusements.

After being cramped in the train I had the greatest difficulty in walking to Frieda's home. Poor Manny cried every time he put his feet to the ground and had to be carried.

Our arrival created a great commotion in the Holz household. Frieda's father had an undertaker's business. Her mother, whom we called *Tante* Trude, was one of the kindest women in the world. They had another daughter in her teens, and a boy of about eleven. The business and workshops were downstairs and they lived on the first floor in a long-shaped flat which must have been two thrown into one.

Max was given a week's compassionate leave and while he was there, he and Frieda's father motored over to Barmen in his van to collect the things from the cellar before they were stolen as there were, of course, no doors left intact and looting was rampant. They brought the washing machine, the trunks of clothes stored there, bottled fruit and vegetables, and eggs in water-glass which Frieda had been given by her grandmother in the country. When *Tante* Trude came to use them she found they had been hard-boiled by the heat of the fire during the air-raid.

Manny had nasty burns on his ankles and instep, and his screams when *Vater* put new dressings on hurt me even more than my own wounds. My legs were now the same size all down, like balloons, and continuously discharged fluid with a most abominable stench. *Vater* padded them with huge bundles of cotton wool but it always soaked through everything. For some reason, I never knew why, he made light of my burns and said I would be fit to travel to the seaside with him, Frieda and Volker in a week's time. Judging by how I felt and the look of my legs I could not visualize this at all, but knowing he was an experienced doctor, I did not contradict him. Nobody else ever saw my legs unbandaged and they all took it for granted that *Vater*'s prediction would prove correct. In fact they probably thought I was being lazy staying in bed, but I felt so ill I didn't care. It was as much as I could do to wash myself and Manny and hobble along to the dining-room to sit on the couch with my legs up for meals. As soon as I put them to the ground the pain was unbearable. I noticed that Frieda was very embittered about the raid, about the loss of the house and destruction of Barmen, and also I felt that her resentment was directed in particular against me. I wondered whether it was because Manny and I, complete strangers to her parents, were imposing on them, and I asked *Tante* Trude if it would not be better for us to go to a hospital but the dear soul would not hear of it.

By the time they departed for their holiday I had not even reached the worst stages. The first day after *Vater* had gone, when *Tante* Trude's doctor called, she was in the room while he took off the dressings. I shall never forget her face when she saw the huge masses of raw flesh from which lumps of thick yellow putrid skin were hanging in shreds. Poor, dear *Tante* Trude! Through *Vater*'s attitude she was totally unprepared for the revolting sight. She turned green and must have been glad when the doctor asked her to fetch a bowl, which however she held bravely to receive the dead skin as he cut it off. She kept repeating: 'Oh Sybil, I did not know your legs were so bad, I did not know they were so bad.'

By this time Manny was well on the mend and could not be expected to sit still in bed any longer. *Tante* Trude put me in a little room next to the dining-room so that I would not have so far to hobble, and took charge of Manny because she realized there was a constant danger of his bumping into my legs.

Soon after this, however, on about the tenth day, I started to run a high temperature. The doctor did not seem surprised and called it 'wound fever'. I tossed in delirium. Every night I had had ghastly nightmares about the raid, now they haunted me by day as well. When the siren went and I heard the drone of planes I did not know whether it was real or in my dreams. I could eat nothing for days and the only liquid I could keep down was weak tea, which I drank by the pint. The doctor gave me a prescription for some which *Tante* Trude bought at the chemist's.

As soon as I was a little better I began to worry about Manny because he was so terrified of another raid. Before 29 May, as with most children, the siren, the visits to the cellar and sounds of bombing made no worse impression than a villainous film. Now, whenever he heard the siren he turned deathly pale and started to shiver violently from head to foot. We had air-raid warnings practically every day or night, and it proved impossible to comfort him. His burns had healed, so I wrote to Kurt to ask if he considered it wise for Manny to return to him in Bromberg until I was well. He agreed and at the beginning of July, *Tante* Trude asked a Diakoni nurse she knew to take him as far as Berlin, where Hedi, Kurt's new wife, met them. This good nurse would not accept a penny beyond her expenses. *Tante* Trude would also not let me repay her for anything, neither would the doctor take any fees, although I was no longer the wife of a doctor. The awkward part was that there was nothing that one could buy for people as presents.

The doctor said the less I put my feet to the ground the quicker the burns would heal. I thanked God when gradually the pain diminished, at any rate so long as I kept them up. Then only did I begin to feel alive again or take pleasure in anything. It was years before they stopped pricking and hurting badly if I walked or stood for any length of time – standing was much worse than walking – and even now it often feels as though wasps are stinging me, and I cannot bear my legs in the sunshine, or by an open fire. I was awarded the 'Verwundeten Abzeichen', the medal usually given to wounded soldiers, and was granted a state pension of twenty marks a month for life (which I could still draw if I were domiciled in Germany).

We were given lengthy forms to fill in about the extent of our losses in the fire and were paid a proportion of the total value straight away in cash, with promises of further instalments. As the terror-raids ravaged countless towns, the State naturally found it impossible to pay compensation for all the damages. It was the same with clothing coupons, or rather chits. (On each chit the name of the necessary article was written; for instance nightdress, or pair of stockings. We were given chits for two of each article of underclothing, one coat, one dress and one pair of shoes.) Being victims of the first terror-raid, we were comparatively lucky in that we were able to buy the goods for which we were given chits. Later on people were given the chits when they were bombed out (although they were also gradually curtailed) but there were no goods available in the shops.

Nobody but those bombed out (and in 1945, the refugees) were given clothing chits. Everybody else had to manage from now onwards with what they already possessed, except for a very occasional issue of a pair of stockings and in special cases, if you could prove you had none wearable, a pair of shoes made with soles of synthetic material. Sewing cottons and mending silks were also only issued occasionally on coupons with numbers on, which would be made valid when the authorities thought fit, and the number announced in the local paper. Then there would be a terrible scramble in the shops to get the sort you wanted.

Mothers of large families, expectant mothers, the old and infirm were given a special pink card at the discretion of certain doctors which entitled them to jump queues. I was given one of these for over a year and found it a great boon.

At first I was afraid the poor devils behind would raise objections, but they never did. They knew the pink card would not be issued without good reason.

EIGHTEEN

When I finally returned to Bromberg in September and moved into the Petersens' flat, the Labour Exchange allowed me a domestic help three times a week because the wounds had still not healed on my legs and I had to rest them all I could. She was a pleasant Polish girl called Irene.

It was wonderful to have Manny with me again in a little home of our own. We were thrilled to see each other and how he had grown in those two months! He settled down immediately and soon learned that Linda's rooms were not ours and that he must knock before going in to see her. Although we did not lock our doors, we respected each other's privacy as though they were separate establishments. Our common meeting ground was the kitchen, but we never clashed with our cooking arrangements. The main reason why Linda was easy to get on with was that she never made a martyr of herself. At the same time her fairness and independence would not allow her to leave others with more than their share of work or responsibility. She was straightforward and pleasant about the organization of the household. If she undertook to do something, she would do it with a good grace and not make a fuss. If it was not in her province she would leave me to it without interference. Although by no means superficial, she was not forever delving into deep problems, which in the long run is so tiring in everyday life. There was nothing small or niggardly about her character. She had no children of her own, but was passionately fond of them and had an astounding way of managing them. She had her friends and occupations and I had mine. If either of us had visitors we would usually invite each other to join the company. She was gay and sociable, but not many people learned to know her well. It took me a long time to do so, which probably was another reason why we did not quarrel.

At the time I moved into the flat Manfred Petersen was home on leave for a few days before being transferred to the eastern front. He loathed the Army. Everything about it was repugnant to him – the drudgery of the soldier's work, the snobbery of the officers, the discipline, the submersion of separate identities and personalities. He was strongly individualistic, loved his freedom, and was fond of hard work, but only if allowed to use his initiative. Particularly interested in the designing of dwelling houses and flats as quite a young man, with boundless energy, he had soon established himself in Hamburg as a reliable and exacting architect. By birth he was a Berliner and retained the native aptitude for quick-witted repartee – to the dismay or amusement, as the case may be, of his prey. I for one never failed to rise to his bait and for this reason perhaps he enjoyed my company. However, his raillery, although sharp-edged, was not malicious and therefore in spite of our furious arguments there was no ill-feeling.

There were two children in the flat above us, both older than Manny, and two in the flat on the same level in a block adjoining ours at the back, one called Edith and a boy about Manny's age, called Klaus with whom he played most often. This was very convenient because Linda's back door at the end of a long passage leading to the bathroom on the left, opened on to the landing directly opposite Frau Braun's front door. An understanding soon sprang up that the children had only to tap each other's door when in need of company and they would then retire to one flat or the other to play. Manny had as many visitors as he liked, although I could rarely ask them to a meal on our two scanty rations and did not often invite them formally.

I was glad I had no separate flat of my own because, although I enjoyed the advantages of having a home of my own, I was never entirely alone for long. Linda and I did not sit with each other often, but would frequently call in, if we did not meet in the kitchen, and exchange news. Linda told me I could sit in her room and listen to the wireless whenever I liked as I had none of my own. This I often did when she was out and used to switch on very quietly to the English stations. I found the programmes especially prepared for foreign listeners on overseas services not nearly so interesting as the Home services, but this was probably because the psychological effect of listening to the same as everybody else in England made it more enjoyable.

I particularly liked to listen to the news broadcast in England for English listeners, then I would switch over to the German station to compare the reports, but of course I never had a chance to listen in with any regularity. By this time, since the opening of their big attack on 12 July 1943, the Russians were steadily pushing back the Germans, who were never again to take the offensive in a large way on any front. It was not necessary for us in Bromberg to read the newspapers, nor to hear the radio reports, to feel the pressure from the East. We were too near the border to remain unaware of the approaching danger. It was rumoured that air-raids were to be expected and half-hearted preparations were started for civil defence.

Much ado was made of the spectacular rescue of Mussolini by air from his prison high up in the Abruzzi Mountains on 12 September 1943, and Hitler was able for some time to hold the Allies at bay in Italy. But once again all through the winter the losses in Russia hung like a pall over us in the East, depressing everybody and at the same time driving them all the more to reckless frivolity, a state of mind which it was difficult for the increasing numbers of crippled and maimed men, discharged from the front, to appreciate or even to comprehend. The death-roll was greater than ever and more and more were captured, which meant that they would probably never be heard of again.

Linda's parents had lost everything but their lives in the big raids on Hamburg in July 1943, when the block of flats they were living in (which belonged to Manfred) had been destroyed. The fate of her younger brother, who had been among those trapped at Stalingrad, was unknown. Nothing was ever heard of him again.

There were few grounds to look forward with any enthusiasm to a happy Christmas, and yet personally I did not dread it as much as the year before. If I was still lonely, I was at least getting used to the loneliness. Now that Manny was older (he was just four and a quarter) his anticipation of the happiest of all seasons for children was so infectious that I could not fail to share his excitement. One of the chief delights in bringing up a child is the rebirth of past pleasures.

I bought an enormous Christmas tree from a man who was selling them in the street. On Christmas Eve, after I had lit the candles, I rang a bell (in the traditional manner) and Manny came slowly into the room. It was a joy to see his eyes sparkle as he stood beneath the bespangled magic. My homemade toys gave him as much pleasure as the most costly goods in the world.

It was a bitterly cold, long winter as usual. At the end of March there was still thick snow on the ground, but for us, with our cosy central heating, it was easily bearable. Not so for the soldiers in their miserable dugouts. As the Russians pressed forward with their air bases in 1944, the danger of air-raids became imminent. We could not know that even when a year later their tanks had almost encircled the town, they still would not strengthen their attack by bombing Bromberg. As we saw it, there seemed little doubt that the towns in the east would now be erased by the Russians just as the towns in the west were being flattened by British and American bombs.

Manny had not recovered from the shock of the air-raids in Wuppertal. The horror of it remained with him for years and I still wonder what scars it has left on his mind. Even in 1946, in the safety of our English country garden, an expression of abject fear flashed across his face when the fire siren started to howl through the valley.

Fortunately the air-raid warnings we had in Bromberg in the early part of 1944 were mostly at night and he did not hear them. It was difficult to decide whether it was best to disturb his sleep and take him to the cellar, or to risk being caught upstairs in an attack. Unless I heard planes approaching I usually dressed and put Manny's clothes in a bag so that I could leap downstairs with him in any emergency. As far as I knew there were no anti-aircraft guns in or near the town and it would have been easy for planes to sweep in upon us at a low level.

One day when Linda came back from treatment at Kurt's clinic she told me Hedi, his wife, had said Kurt would prefer me to move into the country with Manny, out of danger of bombing, so I went to ask Kurt his opinion. He said he thought it would be advisable. I therefore tried to think where we could go. I made various enquiries which bore no fruit, then Nina von Oldenheim made a suggestion. She could not have us to stay with her as the Army had requisitioned all the habitable guest rooms. She said, however, that the officer in charge, a Herr von Seydel, would let me have a partly furnished room on condition that I acted as housekeeper to him and his soldiers who numbered rarely more than four to six. There would be no payment on either side and we would all have our meals together. A Polish woman in the village could be engaged to do the housework and cooking under my supervision. I had no alternative plan for evacuation and, as this sounded a reasonable proposition, I counted up the advantages which outweighed the disadvantages, and accepted his offer. Manny had always loved staying at Lukowo and he would have Gisela for company. We would be able to get plenty of milk, fruit, vegetables and potatoes in the country. It was June by now and we could enjoy the sunshine and bathing. Added to this, there was the tremendous attraction of the horses.

When the Germans started retreating, in an endeavour to retain at least some of their spoils, they had actually driven the famous *Orloffertraber* (pure-bred trotters) from the heart of Russia to Lukowo. Russian stable hands had come with them (whether willingly or not I could not find out) and they now lived in the little *Schloss* overlooking the dead arm of the Vistula. Herr von Seydel, too old for active service, had been called away from his own estate and put in charge of the stud. The German soldiers working under him were a mixed bag of varying ages, picked from their different stations in life primarily on account of their knowledge of horsebreeding. The faces at our dining table were constantly changing as none of them stayed long. They arrived, usually two of them at a time, hot, weary and filthy dirty, having brought a batch of horses for hundreds of miles across the parched plains of Russia. They then waited in Lukowo for further orders. To them, after their long trek, it was a haven of rest. Some of them had been cut off from civilization for months. They were certainly not hard to please. To sit down to a wholesome meal, decently served at a table covered with a clean cloth and decorated with a bowl of roses was for them the height of domestic luxury. It was a strange thing, but the flowers seemed to make more impression than anything else. At first I put them on the table as a matter of course because there were plenty in the garden. When I noticed what a surprising effect they had I took even greater pains with the decorations and delighted in watching the faces of newcomers as they came into the sparsely furnished little dining-room. Manny was a great favourite. They were always pleased to see a child, who reminded them of their own homes and soon loosened their tongues. Herr von Seydel allowed their wives to join them if he thought they would be stationed there long enough to make it worth while. He presided over this peculiar *ménage* with a jovial, somewhat remote urbanity, and was himself grateful for the simple comforts.

Manny and I had a bed-sitting-room on the first floor

which I made as cosy as possible by bringing odds and ends of furniture from Bromberg. Manny was in his element and spent nearly all his time with the horses; even before breakfast he would hasten to the stables. He knew he was not allowed to disturb me in the mornings until I spoke to him, and I noticed from day to day that he became more and more impatient if I did not officially wake up at the crack of dawn. One morning, after watching me with large impatient eyes, he took the law into his own hands, put on his rompers and crept out of the room. I guessed he was off to the stables and did not stop him. He was much too small to be able to handle the horses and it was surprising that his interest in just watching did not wane. Now and again I would walk down the yard out of curiosity to see what he was doing, and there he would be, standing with his sturdy legs firmly planted apart, his hands clasped behind his back, barefooted and rosy, fascinated by all that was going on. He was on excellent terms with the Russian stable hands, although they could not speak German! If he did not hear me call, a hue and cry would go round from man to man: 'Manny, Manny,' until out he popped from some remote corner.

There were some magnificent animals there, who ran like the wind, with an exquisite grace of movement, their feet barely touching the ground. For racing practice they would be harnessed to extremely lightweight one-man sulkies with two wheels. They had some larger wooden traps for taking passengers, also with two wheels. One day Herr von Seydel offered to take us for a drive in one of these. He was going down to some meadows a mile or two away where the young horses were grazing and the track led us through a large wood. At first the lane was sandy, but as we came nearer the pastures below it was grassy, and full of deep, hard ruts. The wheels did not fit in the ruts so that we were bowled from side to side in an alarming fashion. Now, Herr von Seydel was very large and very fat. I am no featherweight and Manny, for his age, was a heavy load. Suddenly a sharp crack of splitting wood pierced the silence. I ducked, thinking one of the trees was falling on top of us. The next second there was another loud crack and before we realized what was happening the trap, which had snapped off both shafts, jerked backwards. As I was tossed out I caught sight of Manny, rolled up like a little ball, turning two complete somersaults! We landed on long grass and he did not cry. Herr von Seydel had the presence of mind to hang on tight to the reins, and after being dragged and bumped along some distance in the upturned trap, with his feet in the air, he managed to bring the frightened horse to a standstill.

Not long afterwards we set out on another drive with Herr von Seydel. We had hardly gone half a mile when the same thing happened again, only this time we landed on a hard road and Manny was thrown straight into a patch of cow-dung. This was too much for him. As he picked himself up from the stinking mess he cried: 'Oh Mummy, I don't like it! I don't like it!'

Most of the German soldiers who had so far turned up were peasants or farm workers in civilian life. One day two men of a very different type arrived. Their names were Baron von Manheim and Herr von Schindel and they were both Baltic Germans. Baron von Manheim's father had owned estates in the Baltic States and after Hitler sold his country to Russia he had been given land in Poland as compensation. During the Bolshevik Revolution Baron von Manheim, then a young man, had been captured and was to be sent to Siberia. However he managed to jump off the train, and after his escape had to walk hundreds of miles back to safety. In spite of these early troubles he loved the Russians and understood not only their language but their mentality. He said they were the kindest and most hospitable people in the world. He often sat in the evenings with the Russian workers in the little *Schloss*, not in the least disturbed by their smell and their lice and their habit of spitting on the floor. I think he felt more Russian than German. He was not methodical, nor practical. He never worked for pleasure but only when it was necessary to do so. He was generous and soft-hearted and loved to talk long into the night, forgetting the cares of the morrow. He had the Russian weakness for alcohol and when he could get hold of liquor would periodically lapse into a state of prostrate drunkenness for several days at a time. He hated Germany for attacking the Russians, and it may have been his complicated reactions to the war which drove him to drink.

Herr von Schindel had also lived in the Baltic States until 1919, but there was nothing Russian about him, although like all the rest of the Baltic Germans, he looked back on those times with nostalgia.

He had married a German who was the sister-in-law of one of the Professors in the Danzig hospital. Frau von Schindel came to stay at Lukowo and a friendship immediately sprang up between us. She had been a welfare worker and always showed an interest in everybody's problems. While her husband had a quiet, ruminating nature, she was talkative and energetic.

NINETEEN

It was only a few days after Frau von Schindel's arrival that the biggest, entirely unexpected blow fell upon me. During Manny's afternoon rest I sat beneath his window on the lawn because he would not go to sleep with me in the room. One afternoon, before his time was up, a lady appeared round the corner of the *Schloss* and asked if she could speak to me. She was a stranger to me and I wondered, without any apprehension, what she had to say as she did not seem to know how to begin. After much hesitation she said she came on a mission which, although extremely distasteful to her, she had agreed to carry out, knowing that if she did not, some other authority would do so in a far more brutal manner. She explained that she was a social worker from the National Socialist Party Welfare Association, at which I was not at all dismayed, because I knew what good work they did. When she told me her message, it seemed so utterly impossible that I could not believe it was true.

They had received orders from the highest level of an organization not under their control to request me to hand Manny over forthwith to Kurt. If I refused, Manny would be forcibly taken from me, and might be put into a Nazi institution. The only explanation given to them was that this step was necessary on 'world political grounds'. I just laughed. It was so absurd, so fantastic! What had little Manny, who was not yet five years old, to do with world politics? Someone had made a most ridiculous mistake, and we need only make a few investigations to clear the whole matter up. She assured me that unfortunately there was no mistake. Her serious manner sent warning pricks into my heart, which I quickly brushed aside. She had instructions to take Manny back to Bromberg on the next train leaving in half an hour's time and she begged me to go with her as it would be better for him if I did. I agreed to go and said that no doubt Kurt would be able to help us solve the mystery. Whilst we had been talking Manny poked his head out of the window upstairs and asked if he might get up. He came running down and joined us on the rug.

I knew we would have to stay the night in Bromberg in any case, so I packed a small case, told Herr von Seydel and Frau von Schindel the position, and we hurried to the station.

We went straight to Kurt's surgery in the Clinic. The welfare worker came into his consulting room with us and sat quietly listening. Manny was on my lap, and with big eyes, glanced from one to another, trying to understand what the fuss was about, which he gathered must concern him personally.

I explained to Kurt what had happened and asked him if he knew anything about it. No, he said, he knew nothing. He asked the welfare worker the telephone number of her office and spoke to the Chief Organizer. He was kind and polite, but confirmed the instructions, and when Kurt asked him from whom he had received the orders, he advised Kurt not to make further enquiries for fear of stirring up more trouble.

Kurt thought it best to take Manny home with him and see what could be done in the morning. I went to my rooms in Linda's flat. I found her sitting on her sofa reading, and I poured out my grief to her sympathetic ears. By now I felt the noose tightening. It was not a mistake. The fantastic plot was a reality. Unless I could persuade the instigators to rescind their orders I would have to face the calamity. But I could not face it. At the bare thought of it my blood ran cold. No, it must never be.

I tossed and turned all night trying to decide what steps it would be advisable to take. First thing in the morning I went to the Welfare Organization, determined to find out on whose instructions they acted. The Chief pleaded with me to accept the situation and to probe no further into details, otherwise he would not answer for the consequences. He said that his organization had done all they could to prevent the disaster. They had had lengthy correspondence with Danzig and Berlin (he showed me a thick file), but now they could do no more. They had received a telegram from Berlin which was quite final. If they had not acted yesterday the matter would have been peremptorily removed from his hands, and both Manny and I would have been dealt with even more harshly.

Tears streamed down my cheeks as I sat stunned, trying to think what else I could do. The man must have decided that a half-truth is more difficult to bear than a naked fact. After a long silence he said, 'The order came from the Gestapo.' The word struck like a thunderbolt. Recognition of his position and mine was immediate. I thanked him for his kindness in trying to help, and now dry-eyed with fear, I left his office.

Out in the street I cast furtive glances in every direction to see which of these skunks was spying on me. Damnation on Gestapo! Damnation on the whole nation of Germans who allowed a gang of crooks to rise to power and rule with injustice and cruelty! What right had they to break the most sacred relationship between mother and son for the sake of their paltry politics? What had I done to deserve this? I might have made mistakes and I might have many faults, but of one thing I was certain, I had always tried my utmost to be a good mother. This rude parting might have a psychological effect on Manny injurious to his development. At his tender age he needed me more than anybody. Hedi and Kurt might be kind to him but nobody in the world can replace a mother, or the woman who has cared for a child since birth. I saw a vista of endless days and nights, weeks, months and years with no Manny. As I walked along the dreary pavements I sobbed aloud, too miserable to care who saw me.

I took a train back to Lukowo where they were eagerly

awaiting my return, hoping for good news. My dejected appearance, as I walked down the drive without Manny was sufficient answer to the questions written on their faces. They were all very kind and Frau von Schindel offered to take over the housekeeping duties while she was there if I wanted to be free to make more enquiries.

But would I dare 'to make enquiries' at the Gestapo? A trial, an appeal, or enquiries were unheard of in their field of authority. They were outside the jurisdiction of the Law Courts and overruled anybody's decisions when it suited them to do so. So far I had had no personal acquaintance with the Gestapo. We knew they had concentration camps for their enemies and knew they were ruthless in their suppression of Jews, Poles and foreign minorities. Perhaps I was now looked upon as a menacing foreigner? Perhaps Manny's removal was only the preface to my being clapped into a KZ? Would it be safer to lie low and hope for the best? If I was put away, they might never allow me to see Manny again and what good would that do him? And yet how could I accept such a situation without making any attempt at persuading them to reverse their decision? I could not sit back and do nothing about it and felt I must leave no stone unturned. But how could I approach the remote Gestapo Chief? Where were his headquarters? What was his name?

I returned to Bromberg and had no difficulty in finding out that his name was Rux. I then remembered it was he who had quarrelled with the former Chief of Police, Herr von P., because he would not co-operate sufficiently, with the result that Herr von P. was removed from his office. I also remembered that the present Chief of Police, Herr von Salisch, lived nearly opposite Kurt's house and that his wife and I had, as neighbours, been on 'nodding' terms. I rang her up and when I told her my story she could not believe it was true. She promised to try to make an appointment for me with Herr Rux. After I put down the receiver I was again filled with misgivings, wondering whether I was taking the right action. I almost hoped Herr Rux would refuse to see me, but when I heard from Frau von Salisch again, telling me to be at his headquarters at such and such a time and date, I did not dare call it off.

By the time the day arrived I had worked myself up into a terrible state of nerves. I approached the Gestapo building in an agony of apprehension. Just inside on the right there was a porter's room where I boldly announced that I had an appointment with Herr Rux. He asked me my name and after withdrawing from his window for a moment to telephone, he motioned me in. In front of me there were only iron railings, but at that moment they silently swung open. As soon as I had stepped into the passage beyond, they swung back and shut with a loud clang, propelled by the same invisible hand. I felt as though I had stepped into a trap. An armed sentry appeared from nowhere and escorted me down a corridor where there were rows of closed doors along each side. I wondered if they were cells and whether I would ever get out of this awful place unscathed. The clatter of the sentry's boots on the stone floor echoed from end to end. He took me in a lift to the top floor. Here there was no prison-like atmosphere. He knocked on a door and a woman took me to a narrow little waiting-room, no different from a dentist's, with armchairs round a low table strewn with periodicals. Shortly afterwards she led me through her office, where there were several other perfectly normal-looking girls typing and writing, into the dragon's den. But it was not the sort of den I had expected. There may have been invisible microphones, but up here it was like an ordinary office and this was like an ordinary boss's room lined on two sides with files and cupboards, and there at his desk, facing me as I went in, was the boss. He stood up and politely offered me the chair opposite him. If it had not been for his uniform I might have imagined this was any ordinary business appointment. He was a big man with broad shoulders. His eyes, fixed on me with a cold inscrutable stare, were pale blue. I knew he had some small children of his own and I could guess that these same eyes would sparkle when he played with them. But now they were the barrier between Manny and me. I never knew afterwards what I said to him. I only know that I tried with all my might to make him change his mind. He was not angry and he was not rude, but he remained quite firm. He was genuinely surprised that I spoke German so well because he had been told that I had never taken the trouble to learn the language and that I spoke only English to Manny. I always speak German best when I am overwrought, spitting out the consonants, and now my tongue was loosened as it never had been before. But all my persuasion and arguments were in vain. It was like talking to a stone wall. Up till then, there had been one crime which I could never under any circumstances have thought myself capable of – and that was murder. Now I knew what it was like to be overwhelmed with the desire to kill someone. This brute had snatched my child from me. He was the obstacle which must be destroyed. No explanation that the removal of this one man would never set Manny free from the clutches of the vile machinery, and no warning that any such attempt would have fatal consequences, could have penetrated my numbed reasoning powers. If I had had a gun I would have shot him there and then, straight through those cold, blue eyes, with no more compunction than if I had been shooting at a dummy target. I had no gun and he sat immovable. I asked him if he would still keep Manny from me after the war. His answer was: 'No, not if we win the war, and if we don't, we shall not be here to prevent you from having him.'* I remembered this remark when, after the collapse of Germany, I heard that he had fled to his native Austria and subsequently shot himself. It was a relief then to know that it was his finger which had pulled the trigger, not mine.

* Which, I now conjecture, was a sop to me.

I left his office as disconsolate as ever. I stood alone, undefended and helpless. By now it seemed impossible for Germany to win the war, but it might drag on for years if Hitler consolidated his forces within Germany instead of scattering them from the Baltic to the Balkans. If she lost, how would the end come? Would there be any chance of survival? The future was too uncertain to be able to make any plans. Life was short and unpredictable. It was here and now that I needed Manny and the little chap's place was at his mother's side.

There was no hope of getting him back. I must adapt myself to the new situation, but it was hard, so hard that I nearly lost my reason. The worst time was at night. I lay awake for hours in the darkness. If I dropped off to sleep I had terrible nightmares, but none was so terrible as the reality which lurked upon the threshold of consciousness and which could not be dispersed upon wakening. Every morning before I knew what I was doing I automatically glanced to see if Manny was awake – only to be faced with the empty cot.

I could not bear to stay any longer in Lukowo where we had recently been so happy together. Without Manny there was no point in my staying. As it happened Herr von Seydel had just been told that the *Schloss* would shortly be taken over by the Air Force, and that he and the horses were to be removed elsewhere. My position, therefore, would in any case become redundant. They arranged for my belongings to be loaded on to a wagon and thus, early one morning, surrounded by my goods and chattels, accompanied by three stout Russian stable lads, I set off by road for Bromberg. Baron von Manheim produced a little bottle of schnapps for me to give the Russians on arrival which, he assured me, would please them more than anything. If I gave them money there was nothing they could spend it on. It was the first time they had been inside a western 'bourgeois' home and they were as thrilled as Snow White when she found the house of the seven dwarfs, inspecting every novelty with delight. They tried out each armchair in turn, bumping up and down in them – they had never sat in upholstered chairs before. They admired the carpets and the pictures and were very taken with the photographs of Manny. When I produced the schnapps their faces showed that Baron von Manheim had correctly assessed their taste. After exchanging grins and nods – our only method of communication – they departed, leaving behind them the sour smell of sweat and horses.

Back in Bromberg there was nothing for me to do but to mope over my misery. I was too restless to concentrate on reading. Frau Daniel had unfortunately been forced to abandon her singing lessons, as she was not allowed domestic help and had no time to spare. There were few people I could trust. These hard times were the best proof of friendship. Wherever I went I felt I was being watched and informed upon. Now that my eyes were opened I became aware of the spiders who had waited, bursting with 'Schadenfreude' (malicious pleasure), to watch me step into the web. I learned that chance remarks I had made were passed from mouth to mouth with increasing venom. Every action was turned against me. Even little Manny was used as an *agent provocateur*. Guileless words from his lips were pounced upon and, as is always the case with children, he soon took advantage of an easy way to draw attention to himself, spinning fabulous yarns to an audience only too ready to gather 'evidence' against his mother. The fact that he spoke perfect English gave the spiders a high score to begin with, and there would certainly be no difficulty in getting him to show off his knowledge. Even before he could speak either English or German he had been a star turn in this respect, because as a babe in arms he understood both languages equally well, and caused onlookers much amusement. If I said to him, '*Wo ist dein Näschen?*' a chubby finger would touch his nose. If I asked him this in English, the same effect was produced. He would also not be daunted by being asked where his cars were, in German, and then, immediately after, where his toes were, in English, or by any other dodging sequence. Invariably the little finger would move to the appropriate spot as if by clockwork, whilst he beamed with pleasure in anticipation of the consequent applause. He grew up with both languages quite naturally, but alas this was now considered a sin of the first order.

I was allowed to have Manny to see me once a week and that was my red-letter day. Kurt's errand boy, Edmund, usually brought him to my flat straight from the kindergarten before lunch. Sometimes Kurt brought him on his motorbike. I carry a vivid picture of him in my mind's eye, sitting on the petrol tank between Kurt and the handlebars, his fair hair blowing back and his plump cheeks wobbling up and down as he bumped over the oblong stones on the road. As soon as they stopped on the opposite side of the road he would glance up to see if I was waiting at Linda's window; then Kurt would see him across the traffic, and up he would stump, puffing with exertion. On the surface there was nothing to show that Manny was homesick for me. He would come in as a matter of course, full of prattle, just as though he came home to me every day from the kindergarten, except when he had something new to show me when he would burst in, hardly able to contain himself.

Only now and again did he reveal that he was acutely sensitive to the unnatural separation and to the evil powers at work. The first time he came I saw him looking rather wistfully through the window at the children in the courtyard below, no doubt remembering the happy hours he had spent playing there. He did not ask if he might join them – perhaps he dimly realized our time together was short and precious – but after he had had his rest, when I suggested he should go down if he wished I could see he was relieved that I would not be offended. Before I was quite ready with the tea I called him, expecting to give the usual five minutes' warning, but as soon as he heard my voice, he said goodbye to his friends and shot up the stairs. He often played in the courtyard or if it was wet we asked some children in to play; sometimes we went for walks, the favourite direction being down to the River Brahe where we would see barges unloading if we were lucky. Whatever we did, the time passed all too quickly. There were no tears when we parted, except once when he was ill in bed with a cough and I went to see him at his father's house. Kurt, Hedi and Rosemarie (her grown-up daughter, who lived with them) were out, and only Panë, the maid, was in the house, so we had a cosy afternoon in the nursery. When the time came for me to leave, his mouth dropped and tears poured down his cheeks. I said, 'You mustn't cry, Manny, or I shan't be allowed to come again.' As soon as the words were out of my mouth, I could have bitten off my tongue. I had not dreamed they would have such an appalling effect. He certainly stopped crying immediately, but he turned deathly pale and, wide-eyed, betrayed the fear which lurked just beneath his veneer of composure.

One other incident which occurred brought home the turbulent state of insecurity which haunted the child. I knew he went to the kindergarten every morning, and if I was out shopping, before I knew where I was I would find myself turning down the road in that direction, as if drawn by a magnet. There was a high wooden fence round the garden and I could just see over it. If the children were playing outdoors, I could soon pick out Manny and would watch him for a little while. He was always engrossed in the business in hand, but one day, quite unexpectedly, he suddenly looked straight up to where I was standing, some distance away. Even if it had occurred to me that he might spot me, I would not have looked upon it as a serious matter. I would have expected him to wave and smile, or trot up to say, 'Hello.' I was surprised to see him drop his tools at once and rush in a frenzy to the gateway, shouting, 'Mummy, Mummy, Mummy.' When he reached me he flung his arms round my legs and buried his head in my skirts, sobbing as though his heart would break. It took us some time to calm him down, but he finally returned quietly to the sandpit. I never went that way again when I was out in the mornings.

TWENTY

Now that I had no child to look after, I knew I would be forced to do what work the Labour Exchange thought fit. Rather than give an informer the pleasure of pointing out my case, I decided to present myself to them voluntarily. Many stories had reached my ears of their vicious direction of labour, according to which they were supposed to delight in making ladies work as chars in lower-class households where there was a number of small children. I therefore wondered what job would be meted out to me. I waited in a room full of people of all sizes, ages and types, and listened to more tales of inconsiderate bullying, which did not sound reassuring. These officials must be veritable dragons. By the time my turn came I felt very small and timid. I was called into a room where three women were sitting at desks, each interviewing one person. As soon as I was inside I could hear there certainly was no bullying going on, only quiet, reasonable questioning. I stated my position briefly, expecting no active sympathy from a Government department. I noticed the woman was married – perhaps she had children – at any rate she was extremely kind and openly showed her horror at my story. As this was an unusual case, she wished to consult the head of her office and said they would do their best to find me a congenial job. Passing out through the ranks of grumbling gossips I thought again how little one should pay heed to warped hearsay.

A week or two later I received a note from the Labour Exchange asking me to go to the seminary for the training of female school teachers, which was on the outskirts of the town, to be interviewed by the Headmaster about a job as English tutor. He engaged me on the spot and asked me to start work as soon as possible. There was a crying need for teachers as so many men were in the Forces, and the remaining staff were grossly overworked. I was to take one lesson in English conversation per week in each class. He thought it would be a good plan to start by giving lectures as I had done in the grammar school, and then gradually induce the girls to converse. He agreed that I should speak no German throughout the classes and said he would be interested to see how my system worked.

The arrival of '*die Engländerin*' caused a sensation among the staff and pupils. The former were friendly and co-operative and the latter all agog to make their critical observations and to test their knowledge. No matter how good their German tutors were, they loved to hear a native speak and then only were they convinced that they were listening to the correct pronunciation.

We were all just getting into our stride when the Headmaster received a curt telegram from Berlin forbidding him to employ me. There was no explanation and he knew from experience that it would be useless to protest. Was this another sinister shadow cast by the Gestapo, or was the Minister of Education afraid I would pollute the rising generation with too keen an interest in my home country? If they had seen the girls' faces as I talked to them their fears would no doubt have been substantiated!

I left therefore as suddenly as I had come – a ship that passed in the night.

The local Labour Exchange was exasperated, and started to think again how they could make use of my specialized knowledge. The seminary and the grammar school were controlled by Berlin and Danzig officials, so that, although both establishments were in dire need of the help I could give, there was no hope of by-passing the higher ruling. The local Bromberg Education Committee, however, had complete authority over the choice of staff for the *Mittelschule*. The head of the Labour Exchange sounded the Chief Education Officer in Bromberg. He said he was willing to take the responsibility of employing me as a teacher in the *Mittelschule*, which he thought was an excellent idea. I was sent for an interview with the Headmaster, who was even more enthusiastic than the others had been. He went so far as asking me to give an hour a week for conversation in English with his staff. He had spent some time in England and seemed to enjoy recalling his experiences.

The German *Mittelschule* is roughly equivalent to our secondary school. In the German education scheme there is only one type of free school – the *Volkschule* (elementary school). Attendance at the *Volkschule* is compulsory for everyone for four years, starting at six years old (not five), after which a child may stay on there until he is fourteen or fifteen, or he may move either to the *Mittelschule*, or to the equivalent of our grammar school (all of them State schools), according to whether he passes the test and his parents can afford the fees, which are, however, not exorbitant. There are a few privately-owned boarding schools, the pupils of which are mostly children of wealthy parents who live too far from the nearest grammar school, or awkward children, or those from broken-up homes. On the whole they are looked upon as somewhat peculiar.

Now that the Dürerschule (the grammar school) in Bromberg was requisitioned as a hospital by the Army, the *Mittelschule* (the Braesicke Hauptschule, which was opposite Kurt's house) was shared by them both. As schools in Germany normally only have lessons in the morning from eight till one o'clock, it was possible to make a fair arrangement whereby each school had lessons in the mornings one week and in the afternoons the next.

There were about five hundred girls and boys (in separate classes) in this *Mittelschule*, ranging from ten to eighteen, and I taught them all once a week. It was interesting and enjoyable work, but at first extremely exhausting. All the time I was in the classrooms I noticed no fatigue, but when I got home I felt like a deflated balloon and had no energy left. I was as physically tired as if I had been scrubbing floors or beating carpets for hours on end and my mind was a complete blank, so that I would lie on the couch in a panic thinking I would not have the slightest idea what to teach them the next day. I realized why it is necessary for teachers to have long holidays! Every room I went into throughout the first week was a sea of nameless, strange faces. Every class was at varying stages so that I had to feel my way carefully before I could embark on any planned syllabus. I had never stood before a class of boys before. It was very different from talking to girls in their late teens or early twenties, who had already chosen modern languages as one of their special subjects.

There were about thirty or more in each class except in the boys' classes of seventeen- and eighteen-year-olds, where the numbers varied from week to week, and became sadly depleted. If I missed a face and asked where the boy was, the answer was usually that he had been called up or was taking some training course. Almost straight from the school bench they were sent to the eastern front, many of them never to return. There was a desperate spirit of bravado among these boys. The darker the shadow hung over them, the more irresponsible and unmanageable they became. What was the good of swotting if the next classroom was to be the trenches? It seemed ludicrous to make one of these big, naughty fellows sit in the front row by himself, like a small child, after he had misbehaved, when one remembered that he would soon be in a soldier's uniform. But it was sometimes the only way to avoid continual disturbance. They were never rude and took everything in good part. If one of them had been particularly troublesome I would often be followed into the corridor afterwards to be given a shy apology.

The Headmaster was very kind in arranging as far as he could for my periods on duty to be consecutive and, in accordance with my special request, to leave me as long a weekend as possible.

TWENTY-ONE

Ever since I had come back to Bromberg (without Manny) I had spent a good deal of time, nearly every weekend when it was fine, with Linda and Manfred Petersen at their shooting lodge in Domitz, about thirty miles out in the country. These visits and my job helped more than anything else to distract my attention from the void at home.

During the early part of 1944 Manfred had been withdrawn from the eastern front to take a course as NCO near Goslar in the Harz Mountains. There were frequent air-raids over the field where they were exercised by a bullying sergeant-major who would not allow them to take cover. One day planes, flying low, peppered them with bombs so that every one of them was either killed or wounded. Manfred was flung to the ground and when he came to, he found his right elbow joint had been smashed to pieces by a splinter. He spent weeks in agonizing pain at a military hospital while they tried to patch him up and was eventually posted home to attend a Bromberg military clinic as out-patient.

In spite of his impatient temperament, Manfred was very forbearing and quickly adapted himself to the new situation – not, however, without many exasperating struggles. Long before the plaster and cage were removed he started his favourite hobby of shooting by holding the gun with the stiff, horizontal arm and pulling the trigger with the left hand.

Without using a car (which was of course impossible at that time owing to lack of petrol) the only way to get to Manfred's shoot was to travel on a miniature railway as far as Krone, and then, after walking through the town from one station to another, to take a train to a halt called Domitz. From there it was about ten to fifteen minutes' walk to his lodge, a little wooden bungalow with a sun verandah which he had built in a sheltered hollow between a small farm and the forest. As Manfred was unable at first to carry much, Linda and I had to stumble along with rucksacks laden with necessities, and on the return journey (if we were lucky) with part of the spoils from the shoot. We had to fetch water from the farm, where we were able to buy milk, vegetables and potatoes. There was a village school but no proper village, just scattered farm houses. The nearest made-up road was a mile or two down the railway line, and it skirted round the end of a lake where we used to bathe. There was a mill at one end owned by a rogue – a harmless, lovable rogue – called Bäcker. He was a real character, a little man with twinkling blue eyes, always ready with a joke. We never passed by without looking in, on our way to the lake, or to the woods nearby. Sometimes we would wait at the mill in the evening until the moon was up, or after stalking roe deer at dawn we would rouse him by firing a shot outside his bedroom window. There was always a warm welcome, sometimes with schnapps or even real bean coffee – smuggled from some mysterious source. He sold us pure white wheat-flour which was very naughty of him but most acceptable to us. A drink, a pipe, a yarn, and above all shooting, were his main interests. Manfred asked him to keep an eye on the shoot when he was not there and knew very well that he poached – it wouldn't have been Bäcker if he hadn't!

We were sometimes joined by Ilse or Gerhard Krönke, a dentist and his wife, who numbered among my few friends, but there were only four beds, so that our company in the lodge never exceeded that number. Here was a refuge at last from spies, informers and backbiters. I revelled in the peace of the lovely countryside – a peace which was unfortunately all too short-lived.

When in Bromberg I hardly ever went out, except to go to my job, and in the evenings sometimes to the theatre or cinema. Since the attempt to assassinate Hitler on 20 July 1944, and his subsequent reprisals, foreigners and those who associated with them were more than ever mistrusted and maligned. Linda and Manfred were repeatedly warned that they were unwise to harbour me under their roof. In the borderlands we were more vulnerable to foreign influence, therefore more harshly treated than those in the heart of the country.

In the autumn Kurt was called up again into the Air Force and was sent as medical officer in charge of a large camp of women workers on the north coast of Pomerania. Before he left he came to tell me that, in the event of his death, the baby which Hedi had adopted would not in any way alter Manny's financial position as he had taken on no legal responsibility for him. In other words Manny was still his only son and heir.

The grim winter loomed ahead of us as the Russians and Western Allies gradually closed in on all sides. Manfred's brother called unexpectedly one day on his way from the east to the west and gave a vivid description of the appalling suffering of the retreating troops. We were surprised that at this juncture he should be transferred, but the explanation was given when eight days before Christmas the unexpected German attack in the Ardennes was launched. This was of course only a flash in the pan and a waste of energy which should have been used to better purpose. At the time, however, it gave the impression of unforeseen strength. Surely, we thought, Hitler would not embark on an offensive in the west if he were not sure of being able to hold the Russians back. Thus we were lulled into a temporary calm.

We made preparations for Christmas as far as our resources would permit. I bought an enormous Christmas tree for about two shillings as usual, and prepared a feast for Manny's visit. There was a tasty soup, followed by a tender roast duck with red cabbage, and for a sweet a strawberry flan (bottled strawberries and pastry baked with Bäcker's flour) decorated with artificial whipped cream made from cornflour and skimmed milk. I opened bottles of home-made fruit juices.

Bowls of rosy apples stood on the sideboard. Hidden away were various presents to be placed under the tree when the candles were lit. Edmund brought Manny during the morning on Christmas Day. As soon as I opened the front door to let them in I could see something very important was afoot. Before I could open my mouth to welcome them, Manny poured out his news nineteen to the dozen, his face glowing with excitement. 'Mummy, see what Father Christmas has brought me – an engine with coaches and trucks and little railway lines and you have only to turn a key and it runs round all by itself. Look Mummy, Auntie Petersen, look, look!' Edmund unpacked the large parcel he was carrying and with feverish hands they fitted the rails together. Edmund was as thrilled as Manny, and could not tear himself away from it. Manfred and Gerhard Krönke came in to inspect the innovation and spent an hour or two squatting on the floor playing with this toy which never fails to attract males of all ages. It had been amongst some toys sent to Kurt by his kind aunt from her shop before it was destroyed in the air-raid on Wuppertal-Barmen. What made it even more fascinating to Manny was the fact that he had never seen anything like it in his life before and did not even know that such wonderful toys existed.

After the festivities were over there was more bad news. The attack in the west was repulsed. Large numbers of German soldiers were encircled, among them Manfred's brother. It was whispered that even more had given themselves up voluntarily.

Permits for civilians to travel by rail were only granted under exceptional circumstances. Nevertheless as the threatening shadow of our giant neighbour drew ever closer many people who had no ties in Bromberg managed to slip away into Germany. I would have tried to do the same myself if Manny had not been there and I had had no job. I asked Hedi if she would not consider taking the children further from the frontier zone, but she said Kurt had told her to stay and not to panic. The population became divided into three groups – those who feared the worst and did their best to take precautions; those who accused such persons of panicking and would not listen to any warnings; and lastly the Poles who could do nothing but bide their time whatever happened, although none of them relished occupation by the Russians any more than by the Germans. (Some Poles had optimistically been learning English!)

Manfred could not leave Bromberg because he had not been discharged from the Army and had orders to stay where he was until his medical treatment was finished. If he disobeyed these orders he ran the risk of being shot as a deserter. Linda, apart from her job, did not of course want to leave without Manfred.

We therefore had no alternative but to wait. I transferred my money from the local Bromberg bank into the General Post Office, as I reckoned that in the event of evacuation I would be able to draw on the latter wherever I was. If Germany collapsed completely the Post Office would probably be the last savings bank to become bankrupt.

I made enquiries from the Welfare Office whether any arrangements were being made for the evacuation of children if the worst came to the worst. 'Oh yes!' they assured me, 'there is no reason to worry or panic. Firstly, there will be no need to evacuate; and secondly, if it does become necessary, preparations have been made to meet every contingency.' At the same time rumours were spread that Russia was amassing vast forces all along the line from the Baltic to the Carpathians in preparation of an overwhelming attack. Who was one to believe? Wherever we went, whatever we did, we felt the muzzle of a pistol at our backs.

In spite of the fact that our thoughts and conversation had centred on the one topic for so long – the possibility of a breakthrough the lines by the Russians – when it happened, disaster struck us so suddenly that we were taken completely unawares.

TWENTY-TWO

On 12 January 1945 Marshal Zhukov opened his attack with 180 divisions. By the end of January they were only a hundred miles from Berlin. In March the United States and British Armies crossed the Rhine. By the middle of April there was only a narrow strip of about a hundred miles between the two fronts. The 'invincible' German Army had collapsed like a pack of cards.

The Russians made their major thrust forward on the northern border in the direction of Bromberg and reached us within a week. Königsberg on the other hand (which is on a longitude a hundred miles further east than Bromberg) did not fall until 9 April. (Danzig was in German hands until towards the end of March.)

Once the offensive had been launched, therefore, we hardly had time to look round before the Russians were on our doorstep. I rang Hedi every day to ask if she was not leaving with the children. No, Kurt had told her on the telephone not to leave unless orders were given for the town to be officially evacuated, which according to confirmation he had from Berlin would be in plenty of time. I went daily to the Welfare Office, but they had been given the same information as Kurt from the Berlin authorities. Because the Nazi Chiefs did not want to own to failure, thousands of lives were sacrificed for the sake of their prestige. Most of those who perished on the ghastly trek from the east could have been saved if measures had been taken sooner to have them evacuated. It was not the fault of the Welfare Organization, who were supposed to carry out the evacuation arrangements of women and children, and had indeed made efficient preparations; it was the fault of the chiefs of departments in the Government who ignored all warnings given to them either by the Army or civilian officials. No amount of careful or elaborate planning could be put into action at such short notice. It was not until refugees from Thorn (a town only thirty miles east of Bromberg) were already swarming through our streets that the order to evacuate Bromberg was given. Even then we never knew whether the instructions came from Berlin or whether the local officials had finally taken the responsibility into their own hands. The day before, the Headmasters of my school and of the seminary, where Linda worked, had closed down to leave the pupils a free hand. The Gestapo had already packed up and gone, before the women and children received notice to go! What heroes!

Manfred had been told to go to Danzig to fetch his discharge papers from the Army. He arrived back to find us in a state of extreme alarm because Linda had spoken to some people in the street from Thorn who said that it was already encircled by the Russians. Manfred gave me a wooden box about two foot square and said: 'Pack it full of anything you like. I have two more for ourselves and I'm going to try to put them on rail to Hamburg.' He was gone for hours and returned exhausted. 'I've been all this time running from one office to another trying to persuade them that the boxes contained important documents and architectural designs which must be preserved at all costs! But I've done it at last!' We bid those boxes tender farewell and never thought we would see them again.

In the meantime Hedi rang me up (at about four in the afternoon) and said: 'A welfare officer has just called and given me a permit to travel with the children on a special coach leaving from the centre of the town at midnight. She didn't know what our destination will be, but Kurt has told me to make our way to his camp in Pomerania where he can find some sort of accommodation for us.'

Now that I knew Manny was leaving I could at last try to make plans to go myself. Only women with children were being given evacuation chits for transport. Everyone else had to get away as best they could. A brewer called Hermann

Winzel, who had the finest horses in Bromberg, had offered to take Manfred and Linda, also another family, on one of his wagons. Manfred understood that there would be room for me, which was a great relief, because I did not know anyone else who could take me, neither did I know where I should go, until Linda and Manfred asked me to go with them to their home-town of Hamburg, for which I am forever grateful to them.

I did not want to say goodbye to Manny and make a scene. Hedi told me she was putting him to bed straight after tea and arranged for me to go and see him, when he was asleep. I went round during the evening and tiptoed into the nursery. Blissfully unconscious of the approaching danger, the two children lay peacefully in their cots, rosy-cheeked, their chubby hands resting on their pillows. Hedi's adopted baby looked a dear little chap, about six months old. Manny was a giant beside him.

The room was the same as when I had furnished it four years previously, so full of hope in setting up our new home – the familiar hand-woven linen curtains with coloured borders, the gay carpet, and hanging round the wall above Manny's bed the painted wooden figures from his favourite fairy stories. There was not a sound to be heard in the house but their gentle breathing. Outside someone passed beneath the window, their footsteps muffled by the snow. A horse trotted down the road drawing a sledge. After the tinkling of the bell was lost in the distance all was quiet. For a moment time stood still.

I do not know how long I stayed drinking the silence in such precious company. A thousand doubts flashed through my mind as I watched the sleeping children. Now I would not have Manny's weekly visit to look forward to. We would be hundreds of miles apart – if ever we reached our proposed destinations alive. Would we both come through the ordeals which lay ahead of us? Supposing we died of cold and hunger on the way? Supposing Manny disappeared into the

18. Myself and Manny, 27 December 1939.

19. Kurt and Manny at home in Bromberg, October 1940.

20. Bromberg before the war. Later on, there would be very little traffic on the River Brahe.

21. Manny in 1943.

22. A residential quarter of Wuppertal-Barmen showing bomb damage after the raid of 29/30 May 1943.

23. Throughout Germany, bombed-out families left messages on the ruins of their homes or shops, Wuppertal-Barmen, 1943.

24. Manny and myself just before the Gestapo took him from me.

Left 25. My singing teacher in Bromberg, Frau Else Daniel.

Above 26. Linda and Manfred Peterson after he was wounded, at Zoppot, near Danzig, August 1944.

Left 27. Linda Petersen at the shoot which her husband rented at Domitz, near Bromberg.

28. 'I could see nothing, far and wide, but broken bricks, dust and ashes,' Hamburg, 1945.

29. Fire has burnt out most of these typical five-storied residential blocks leaving outside walls standing, Hamburg, 1945.

30. I rented a room in Frau Seelig's house, Hamburg. Due to tireless efforts of the Seeligs' extinguishing the incendiary bombs, it was the only house in the street that escaped destruction.

31. The traditional children's lantern procession every autumn in Hamburg.

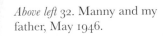

Above left 32. Manny and my father, May 1946.

Above 33. We stayed with my brother in Scotland, summer 1947.

Below left 34. Manny during his first term at Christ's Hospital, Horsham, 1951.

night and I never saw or heard of him again? Supposing we did not get away in time and were deported to Siberia where Manny, if he survived the hardships, would grow up a nameless orphan? Soon the serenity of the night-nursery must be disturbed and the children rudely awakened to prepare for the flight. How much longer would this cruel war last? When the end came would Manny and I be reunited, or were we doomed never again to live together in peace and security?

In a trance I returned to my flat and tried to finish packing as much as I thought I could carry. But my thoughts kept straying to the nursery and it was difficult to concentrate. Faced with such a limited choice, it was still more difficult to decide what was really essential. In the afternoon I had already started to divide my portable belongings into two categories: (1) things I would like to take with me; and (2) things which were irreplaceable or immediately necessary for the journey. The second category was easier to pick out than the first – money, identity papers, post office book, legal documents, jewellery, photographs of my immediate relatives and of Manny ranging from two days old onwards, six silver teaspoons which had belonged to my great-great-grandmother, and so on. These I packed in my rucksack so that they would not leave my person. I then filled it up with the most concentrated foodstuffs in my possession.

The other things which I would *like* to take with me littered the bed and floor and would have filled six cabin trunks. I went through them over and over again, each time eliminating masses of articles which were dear to me, but not really necessary. Still the piles remained too big. I could never hope to be able to carry more than one large suitcase besides the rucksack. I gradually weeded the articles out until I could squeeze the remainder into the bulging suitcase. Then I allowed myself one other package – my music-case with a few favourite song albums.

Manfred told me to tie an eiderdown, blankets and sheets

into a bundle to be carried into the wagon, where they could be used as a mattress and a warm covering.

Last of all I dressed for the part. I put on three sets of underclothes, a thick skirt over my riding breeches, a blouse under a thick pullover, a costume jacket (the skirt of which I tucked into the flap of my rucksack with a coat and my travelling rug) and over all this my fur coat. I wore boots, and on my head a woollen scarf tied turban fashion, pulled well down over the ears. By the time I had finished I felt and no doubt looked like a stuffed pig. These layers of garments, besides serving as a protection against the severe cold, were intended to assure a change of clothing in case our luggage was lost.

After Linda and I had had a full dress rehearsal, we peeled off some of the outer coverings and waited for the arrival of Winzel. In the meantime Gerhard Krönke had come round, also hoping to be taken on the wagon. He had sent his wife and children the week before to their other house somewhere east of Berlin. It was now well after midnight and I sighed with relief that Manny would be safely on his journey. We tried to eat what was left in our larder to give ourselves a good start, but found we could not swallow a morsel. Even the luscious flans I had made from my best bottled fruits for Manny's visit, which had been planned for the next day, remained almost untouched. Linda had baked an extravagant cake as a final treat, which at any other time would have been gobbled up. Even this could not tempt us. We had already drunk what little there was left in Manfred's cellar. Gerhard brought a bottle of Cognac which we were glad to consume to give us warmth and to soothe our nerves.

The clock moved slowly as we waited impatiently. The first time Manfred had rung up Winzel to ask what time he was coming, he seemed in no hurry to move, as though he were trying to drink his brewery dry before he left. This was not very reassuring. The next time he was busy loading the wagon with food and fodder. The third time (an hour or two later) he was still loading the wagon. The fourth time, Manfred got no reply, so we guessed he had set off. But still he did not turn up. He had gone to the Weiss family first and stowed Käte, her children and luggage into one corner. Käte's husband, Rudolf, was the head of the railway repair workshops at Bromberg and was one of the last to leave the town. He and the other railway officials, in spite of tremendous odds, saved a great part of the population and continued their rescue work after the Army, Police and other authorities had left.

When at last the front door bell rang, a shock ran through us as though the executioner had come to fetch us to the gallows. Then everything happened very quickly. Within a few minutes the course of events swerved abruptly in an unexpected direction. As in many a crisis (before and since) my actions were determined by circumstances beyond my control.

Hermann Winzel's figure loomed even taller and larger than usual in the shadow of the landing. The part of his face which was visible between the mufflers was ashen grey. On the way he had heard disconcerting rumours that Bromberg was almost surrounded by Russian tanks, and he was seized with an urgent (but belated) desire to push off as soon as possible. We needed no prompting and immediately started to put on our coats. As I walked into my room to fetch the bundle of bedclothes, I heard Winzel say to Manfred: 'There's no room for Sybil and Gerhard. I can only take you and Linda.' I stood motionless with fright as the portent of his remark penetrated my stunned senses. After all this suspense, were we now to be abandoned at the last minute? Manfred's reaction was violent. He flared into a rage. 'We men can't run away like cowards and leave Sybil behind. If you haven't enough room for us all, you take her in my place, and Gerhard and I will get away as best we can.'

'No, you must come with us; Gerhard can have Weichsel and a dog-cart and can take Sybil with him.' (The very same mare, our old friend Weichsel, whom Winzel had bought from Kurt.)

Manfred stormed, 'I wouldn't dream of going with you in a covered wagon whilst we leave a woman to drive in an open dog-cart. Put her in the wagon with the other women and children, and I'll drive with Gerhard.'

'No!' Winzel was adamant. But so was Manfred. Linda and I hovered in the background wondering what the outcome would be as the two men became more and more heated. With everybody's patience already strained to the utmost and knowing that delay might ruin our chances of escape, this unexpected clash was almost more than we could bear. When I said, 'It's all right, Manfred, I will go with Gerhard' (not with much conviction I fear), Manfred snapped, 'You be quiet. I'll settle this.'

It is impossible to say how long the argument would have continued, or how it would have ended, if it had not been interrupted by the ringing of the telephone bell, which startled us all into silence. Linda ran to take the receiver off, but could hardly speak, her teeth were chattering so violently. The call was for me. I looked at the clock as I crossed the room – 4.30 a.m. – whoever could be ringing me at this time, when everybody I knew was well away from the town? My heart leaped with apprehension when I heard Hedi's distraught voice. 'Oh Sybil, thank God you have not gone yet! We are still here in Bromberg.' Between her sobs she told me she had been at the coach centre and at the station all night with the children, but there had not been the faintest chance of getting near either a coach or a train. Thousands of women and children were surging in masses inside and outside the station and there was no organized system of evacuation in the few vehicles available. 'We couldn't even get anywhere near the station. We've been waiting for hours in the cold, being pushed, and shoved and trodden on, and now we've come home. We couldn't stand it any longer. Oh Sybil, what am I to do?' As I listened to her story, tears streamed down my cheeks. Manny was still in danger. Was there no way out? 'Rosemarie has been helping me, but now she can do no more. She is expecting her fiancé to take her away in his car now at any moment.' (He was an officer in the Cavalry Regiment stationed in Bromberg.) 'Panë does not want to leave Bromberg, and in any case she is ill. Everybody else I know has left. I can't cope with the two children and the luggage all alone, and I don't know what to do next nor how to get away. Will you come and help me?'

I said I would come round at once.

Our sad plight at least settled the dispute between Winzel and Manfred. Winzel still would not take Gerhard, but told him he might fetch Weichsel from the brewery and the best cart he could find. I feared for Gerhard, a bad asthmatic, driving three hundred miles through the intense cold on slippery roads. But dear Weichsel ran like the wind with her light burden and brought him safely to his family. It was a miracle. With winged feet she overtook every vehicle on the road, hundreds of which were fatally stranded in the snow, with their horses lame. Their occupants had to continue the trek on foot and many perished by the wayside, particularly women with small children and old people. Weichsel, showing her true mettle, arrived exhausted, but sound in every limb.

I had to leave my bundle of bedclothes, but Linda and Manfred offered to take my suitcase with them to Hamburg. If I had tried to carry that as well as my rucksack, I would not have been much help with the children. In any case there was plenty of room for it in the wagon, and who knew how Hedi and I were going to travel? Possibly not at all. The Petersens tried to cheer me up and told me to make my way to their house in Hamburg and meet them there. I could see they were wondering, as I was, whether I would ever get so far. It was all so fantastic, so unreal. It was best to concentrate on the practical problems of the immediate future and not to probe too deeply into ultimate issues. Hamburg seemed a very long way off.

I shut the door of my rooms quickly without casting a glance at the pictures and familiar objects I treasured. A last glimpse into a coffin does not bring back the dead – the memory of the living face remains vivid for ever.

We left the flat together and I followed the others into a side street where Winzel's wagon was waiting. There was a thick fog and in the darkness, even standing near enough to touch it, the cart was only visible in vague outlines. It was very large, drawn by the strongest horses from the brewery, and was covered with thick tarpaulin, supported on posts. A dim figure was standing at one end to receive and stow away the luggage. Linda and Manfred clambered in and disappeared under the cover. At the click of the driver's tongue the horses lurched forwards, and slowly, creaking under its heavy load, the caravan moved off. Their voices echoed through the silent night: '*Aufwiedersehen*, Sybil! *Lebewohl*! *Lebewohl*, Sybil!' until they turned the bend and were out of hearing. I hastened down the deserted street. Now I had no more protection and would have to rely on my own resources. All thoughts of the past, of loneliness and despair were thrust behind me. I had no idea what I was going to do. All I knew was that I would move heaven and earth to get Manny away. The prospect of determined action was exceedingly comforting.

In the meantime Hedi had given the children hot drinks and had been rapidly reorganizing her luggage, as she had found two cases and a rucksack were too cumbersome. She was trying to pick out the more essential items to fit into one suitcase and a rucksack.

Hedi had no petrol to use Kurt's car so we decided our only hope of getting away would be by rail. Although we knew there were thousands waiting at the station we had no alternative but to set out once more to join the crowds.

Panë appeared to say goodbye. She looked ill and was as

frightened of the Russians as we were. The Poles stood between the devil and the deep blue sea, sandwiched between their two enemies. When Panë came into the hall, little Pinkie, my beloved cat, slunk through the half-open door, rushed forward and made one leap onto my chest, licking my ears, purring and talking to me. She knew we were going away for good and was pleading with me to take her with us. Finally, I had to wrench her from my coat and shut her in the dining-room so that she would not follow us into the street. I could hear her miauling pitifully until we were outside the house. This was far worse than abandoning my inanimate treasures.

Hedi pushed the pram (which used to be Manny's the same one that I had bought in Danzig for his first Christmas). Uwe, her adopted baby, was almost invisible inside, smothered in coats and rugs, with the suitcase balanced on top. The roads and pavements were covered with frozen snow, like glass. Hedi's legs skidded in all directions as she clung to the handlebars. I pulled Manny along on his sledge and landed flat in the road several times, which caused hysterical amusement, especially to Manny. His chuckle was so infectious that we all laughed till the tears rolled down our cheeks. It was a relief to laugh because it gave vent to some of our pent-up emotions. In the end we did not know whether we were laughing or crying. Anybody watching us would have thought we were a merry little party out on a spree – perhaps a trifle eccentric starting off so early in the morning, long before daylight.

The crowds at the station had barely diminished, and it was no good attempting to push our way through. We talked to a few people and found that many of them had been given chits from the Welfare Organization, without which, they said, nobody was let through the barriers. Hedi had lost her coach chit in the scrum, and as there was in any case no chance of getting near the barrier for hours (if at all) she said she would go back to the Welfare Organization Office to ask for another chit for the train. I waited with the children and luggage. The situation seemed desperate and yet, as I stood there, suddenly a stream of hope descended upon me. I say 'descended upon me', because I could feel it entering my being from without. It was not engendered from within. I had no grounds whatever to be hopeful, so much so that I fought against it, telling myself that it was ridiculous to lead oneself into a fool's paradise, subsequently to meet with even more bitter disappointment. And yet, against all reason, this uncanny feeling persisted. From that moment onwards, although the outlook was apparently as black as could be, I knew we would escape. Was this telepathy? Was it the combined thoughts and prayers of my friends and relatives which travelled across land and sea to give me strength and serenity?

I was standing outside the crowd in a side street, to the left as you face the station. Whilst I waited for Hedi, patiently this time, I noticed that every now and again one or two people coming from the town, some pushing prams, went along this road and turned in through a small wooden gateway on the right. They walked with no hesitation as though they knew where they were going, and none of them came back.

After about half an hour Hedi returned from a wasted journey. The Welfare Office was open, but deserted.

I asked her to wait with the children while I explored beyond the mysterious gateway through which the people had disappeared. I pushed it open cautiously for fear that some irate official on the other side might bark at me, but no one was there. I followed the path which, unguarded, led straight on to a platform thronging with dim figures. I hurried back to impart my sensational news to Hedi. We feared that those who had entered so easily by this back gate must have had special passes. Perhaps they were the wives of the railway workers. Anyway, passes or no passes, it was worth trying. At the worst no harm could be done. At best we might be able to bluff our way through. I led the party, with Manny holding my hand, and tried to look self-confident as though we had special passes from Hitler himself. We met no obstructions. No sooner were we on the platform than a train glided slowly alongside. In the confusion which followed, our gate-crashing passed unnoticed. Everybody was frantic to get on the train. We did not know whether it was going to halt or not, but it did, and miraculously, as it pulled up we found ourselves directly opposite the door of a cattle truck. This meant that we could take the pram with us which would have been impossible in any ordinary compartment; in fact if some sort of a door had not stopped very near us we would never have got on the train at all. I left the sledge on the platform. Pushing Manny and the suitcase in front of me, I turned at the truck door to help lift the pram. The surging masses behind Hedi heaved her and the pram forward. Before we knew where we were, we had been pushed into the furthest corner of the van, which within a few seconds was full of prams. More and more kept squeezing in. The rest of the train was evidently already packed, judging by the cries and wails of those who were rushing madly up and down the platform in a vain endeavour to find room.

We had hardly recovered from surprise at our remarkable stroke of luck before the train crept out of the station and we were soon in the open country, the faint light of dawn shimmering on the snow. Thus began a journey which was to last over thirty hours.

TWENTY-THREE

A normal fast train from Bromberg to Berlin took about five and a quarter hours. By the time we left Bromberg, however, the direct route had already been cut off by the Russians and we had to make a wide detour northwards. Besides this, all lines were congested with train-loads of wounded soldiers as well as civilian refugees. The first transit camp carefully prepared by the Welfare Organization at Vandsburg, where we were supposed to be given hot food and drinks, was evacuated before we left Bromberg.

We had nothing to eat except what we had brought with us and the only drink we were given was a small quantity of cold water, which we had to keep for the babies. This water was a godsend, because by that time everyone had run out of milk. Hedi had brought a tin of baby food from the Clinic which only needed to be mixed with water. We warmed the bottle as best we could over the flame of a candle I had packed in my rucksack. A kind woman next to us gave Manny a cup full of bottled strawberries and juice to quench his thirst. We had nothing but our luggage to sit on. The only alternative to this crouched position was to stand. Outside the temperature varied between 4 degrees below zero centigrade in the daytime to 22 degrees below zero at night. There was no heating in the train, which must have been dug out of a museum, it was so ancient. There were only four tiny windows high up on the walls of our truck which did not open and it was much too cold to leave the door open. There was no sanitation and no possibility of leaving the train. Screws of newspaper (while our supplies lasted) were passed from one to another to be cast out of the door. After that the floor had to be used as a lavatory. The stench of the babies' dirty nappies was overpowering.

Little Uwe was an adorable baby, and really very good,

considering his routine had been disturbed. He had his naps and his bottles, and in between he sat up in his pram and surveyed the peculiar scene before him with obvious enjoyment, gurgling and chuckling to himself. He thought it was a grand picnic to wake up and find Mummy on the spot all the time. Manny also thought everything was great fun. We had not told him why we were leaving home so hurriedly, and to him it was just one of those odd things grown-ups sometimes decide to do. My presence gave him an added feeling of security. Most of the day he was perched up high on the upturned suitcase so that he could see through the window. At night Hedi and I took it in turns to nurse him on our laps because there was no room for him (or us) to lie down anywhere else. This, the second sleepless night, was the most trying of all. Our stiff, cold limbs ached with the weight of him as we crouched on our rucksacks, especially as our legs had to be bent up in such a small space. We thought the night would never end. Worst of all, the train hardly seemed to be making any progress. All day and all night, if we moved at all, it was at a very slow pace. Sometimes we halted for hours on open stretches of land. Even if we were near a station nobody dared to leave the train in case it suddenly moved on without them. But we could not complain. Bitterly cold as it was, we were lucky to be sheltered by wooden walls and a roof. Some of the trains which passed us, full of wounded soldiers, had open trucks. The motionless bodies were lying wrapped in rugs and they must certainly have been frozen to death.

When dawn of the second day broke, we still could not make out where we were. The unbroken stretches of snow gave no clue. Farmers were milking their cows. We could hear them clattering churns. I could imagine the homely smell of the cattle-shed and the cosy fire in the kitchen where the farmer's wife would be brewing hot synthetic coffee for breakfast. What a fortune we would have given for just one sip by the warmth of her fireside! Cramped in the corner, with no possibility of movement or relaxation, the cold seemed to penetrate into the very marrow of our bones. Whenever I have felt cold since, the memory of that dreadful journey has returned with such clarity as to produce the peculiar psychological effect of living through those times again.

As the morning dragged on, signs of physical and nervous strain became increasingly apparent. The children were still as good as gold. We wrapped them up well. They had food, sleep and their mummies, so that their main needs were provided for. Some women were apathetic with weariness. Some tried to preserve a superficial cheerfulness. One woman slowly went mad under our eyes. Every now and again the silence was broken by a torrent of gibberish, followed by raucous, uncontrolled laughter. At shorter and shorter intervals this uncanny performance was repeated until we felt we must all scream like lunatics.

If only we could get up and walk about for ten minutes, away from the stench and the tension, we thought we might revive. Our food supplies were getting low. We had nothing to drink. Just as we were wondering how much longer we could hold out we noticed that we were now passing more and more houses, as though we were on the outskirts of a large town, and truly we were. Oh, what joy when Hedi recognized it to be Berlin! Surely we would soon draw up at a station. Hedi's sister Alma lived in Berlin and we hoped her flat would be a temporary refuge. We powdered our grimy faces and combed our straggling hair in an attempt to look presentable. But still we steamed slowly on, with long halts every few minutes. Then we halted and moved no more. Our train stood in the middle of rows of railway lines. Either side there were four or five tracks where there was considerable traffic. How much longer were we to stop there? About a hundred yards further down there was a station. Even if we dared to risk crossing the busy lines, how were we to get out of the truck unless everyone else got out first? We waited and pondered over what best we could do until our patience was exhausted. We decided that by hook or by crook we *must* get out and we *must* cross those busy lines. To this day I do not know how we scrambled over the top of everybody and over the prams to get to the door. People were helpful and passed the case and Manny over their heads. Then I climbed over and between us we heaved up the pram, followed by Hedi. I took a three-foot leap down to the ground. My worst fear now was that the train would move on before the others could get out, but I need not have worried – when we looked back afterwards we saw that the engine had been taken away and there was no knowing how long the train would thus be marooned, with warmth and food so near at hand and yet tantalizingly out of reach. We heard later that after standing there all day the train moved out of Berlin southwards to a refugee camp, by which time there were several further cases of insanity, not to mention bodily ailments.

After we had collected our wits a little and waited for a few trains to roar past, we made a dash across the lines as best we could with the children, luggage and pram. We could not see far up nor down, and might have been trapped between two expresses, but again our good luck held. Once we were on the side, we had only to keep close to the bank and were soon at the station. Here the railway officials were most understanding and helpful. We had no tickets but they let us pass. Our train was only one of many stranded in Berlin, causing the authorities consternation, and no doubt its arrival near the station had raised a considerable amount of speculation and controversy amongst the staff, who looked at us as though we had landed from the moon.

The railway officials were the only people we met in Berlin who remotely envisaged the catastrophe which was taking place with lightning speed in the east. The ever-rising tide of refugees and wounded soldiers sweeping into the city, of which we were but the harbingers, could not long be hidden from them. The process of distribution and further despatch was a major problem which they already realized would become more and more acute as the Russians advanced and trainloads of homeless people piled up on top of one another.

Except for the railwaymen, nobody we met in Berlin had heard that the German defences in the east had collapsed. As far as they knew, the ghost trains which had drifted into their city might have been wagonloads of prisoners – if they noticed them at all – as practically none of the passengers got out. There had been reports and rumours of the Russian attack, but the Berliners still suffered under the delusion that the frontiers of the Greater Reich would be held at all costs.

We met with sour disapproval from the smug petit bourgeoisie. In Berlin at that time refugees were looked upon as scaremongers who, by evacuating the border towns unnecessarily, were lowering morale amongst citizens and the Army. Perhaps Berliners were influenced by official orders to defend every town to the last man. Perhaps it was wishful thinking that made them regard all unpleasant rumours with suspicion. Whatever it was, within a short time, faced with bitter reality, they were soon to change their views. It is ironical that from the day we were given a cold reception in Berlin, up to the present, hundreds and thousands of refugees have swarmed into the city every week!

As we struggled up the steps from the station respectable stodgers passed us by with their noses in the air. The first soldier who came along took one glance at us and immediately gave us a hand with the pram, then ran back to the bottom of the steps to fetch the suitcase. He knew the suffering and hardships of battle and recognized the misery of our plight. Time and again it was the ordinary soldier who stepped in to help, always bright and willing.

Apart from short rations, Berlin did not yet know the meaning of real war. They had had air-raids, much worse than London ever experienced, but still only a scratch in comparison with the wholesale destruction of the city by bombing which was yet to come, followed by the Russian attack and occupation. In the end they were in a worse position than anybody else because for them there was no escape and they faced the challenge with great courage.

Hedi and I made our way to the nearest suburban railway station. On the platform there, who should I run into but Kurt's old friend Frau Niemann. Her husband had been killed and she had married again. She had just fled from Schneidemühl where the trains had run in nearly packed out, but still took only a little over the normal time to reach Berlin. Schneidemühl is about seventy miles further west than Bromberg and the direct route to Berlin had not yet been cut off by the Russians. Our conversation took place hurriedly. I did not know whether Kurt had told her that we were divorced. I had Manny by the hand and was just wondering whether I should introduce Hedi and how I could briefly explain our peculiar position, when our train came in. She was going in the opposite direction. I shook hands and jumped into the nearest carriage, and that was the last I ever saw of her.

There were no unoccupied seats in the compartment, so Hedi and I rested our aching backs by lodging the rucksacks against the wall to take off the main weight. Some passengers, seated comfortably, looked at us over the top of their newspapers and mumbled something about 'panic-stricken women'. To us the word 'panic' was now like a red rag to a bull. Our faces flamed with anger. We opened our mouths to shout abuse at them, then as we caught each other's eye, we shut them again simultaneously with a feeling of futility. What was the good of entering into a brawl? We could never explain all that we had seen and experienced. They would learn soon enough when the Russians were on their doorstep and the tanks rolled through their streets.

Only those who had friends or relatives in the east were beginning to become alarmed at the thought of a possible breakthrough. When Alma, Hedi's sister, opened her front door, realization of the portent of our arrival gradually spread across her face as she surveyed the full sum of our worldly possessions grouped around us. '*Mein Gott! Es ist also doch so weit.* The Russians are coming.' She knew Hedi would not be there otherwise. Her surprise changed to relief that Hedi was safe. I was introduced. Without stopping to enquire why I was with Hedi she welcomed us all with open arms. Oh, how warm and snug it was in her room!

While we were taking off some of our layers of clothing and having a wash, she heated a soup which she had ready cooked, and prepared the best meal she could at short notice on her one ration. Simple as it was, I have never relished a meal so much in my life before or since. Afterwards Alma and Hedi went to the Food Office, shopping and to telephone to Kurt, while I cleared up and washed the nappies. After Uwe had finished his snooze, when his next meal was due, he became restless and started grumbling. I had nearly finished the washing so I asked Manny if he would mind playing with Uwe for a little while to keep him quiet until I was ready. He said in a confidential manner: 'I don't mind for a *little* while.'

Hedi had managed to contact Kurt who told her to take the children to join him in Pomerania after they had rested sufficiently. I planned to travel from Berlin to Hamburg the next day. It was no good thinking of taking Manny with me, because however much or little trouble it might stir up, I did not know how or where I would find shelter. The Petersens' house was let to somebody else and in any case had been badly damaged in the terror air-raids.

Tired out, we all went to bed early and slept like logs. It was wonderful to wake up in the morning to find Manny lying beside me.

Hedi had not been successful in getting emergency ration cards from the local Food Office, so I went out in the morning to another address they had given her and spent the whole morning being sent from one place to another, having to queue each time - and all to no purpose. Normally emergency ration cards were issued from your home town and could be renewed, but of course we had no chance to arrange this before leaving Bromberg. Refugees were not supposed to stay in Berlin, and nothing had yet been arranged for those travelling independently to other parts of Germany. If you did not register with the Police you got no ration cards. But you were not allowed to register with the Police until you had been given permission from the Housing Department to stay in the town. As this was not forthcoming, no amount of cajoling was any use.

I left Berlin that afternoon. The longer I stayed with Manny, the harder it would be to part company again. He looked very glum when I told him I must go, but he did not cry. His face showed that he was trying hard to grapple with emotions which he could not comprehend but which had a profoundly disturbing effect.

It was dark by the time I boarded the train. There were crowds on the platform, but I managed to get a seat. I preferred to travel at night, even if it was more tiring, because I wanted to have the daylight before me on arrival in Hamburg to look for temporary accommodation. I imagined Manfred and Linda would be there by now and would have found shelter somewhere.

We were packed like sardines in the train and it was fairly warm, but we had a restless journey in our compartment because one poor woman had gone crazy. Funnily enough she came from Bromberg too. She tried to steal handbags, luggage, gloves – anything she could lay her hands on – and mumbled to herself all the time. As soon as you dozed off you felt a gentle tug at one of your belongings which startled you into wakefulness. Her husband and daughter explained that she had been perfectly normal when they left home. They wondered whether she would ever recover her sanity.

TWENTY-FOUR

As we steamed into Hamburg Hauptbahnhof the jagged ruins of the town rose stark and eerie against the chill light of dawn. Was this the ghost of the city I had visited ten years ago when I had witnessed that memorable performance of *Die Walküre*? Had Wotan in reality encircled Brünhilde with consuming fire? The town itself was now the stage where scenes were enacted more dramatic than could ever be devised by any playwright.

It seemed impossible to believe that so many human beings could still exist in these shattered houses, still less survive the bombing which had, eighteen months previously, reduced the second largest German city to a vast pile of rubble. But communal life was not broken. The survivors had crawled out of their cellars, buried their dead if they could find the corpses, and started afresh. Much reconstruction had already been done. A few streets, with their rows of new shop-windows, appeared to be normal until you looked more closely and noticed that above and behind the bright façade there were gaping walls hiding the burnt-out interior. Some buildings had been repaired on the lower floors, whilst the walls of the top storeys projected above like fantastic monuments. Many large areas were so completely devastated that repairs were out of the question. As I travelled down the Wandsbeker Chaussee by tram (the main thoroughfare northwards) except for little shacks scattered along the side of the road, which the shopkeepers had erected to replace their once prosperous stores, I could see nothing, far and wide, but broken bricks, dust and ashes.

I had been advised to get out at the Wandsbekerchausseebahnhof. There I asked the way to Manfred's house. It was in a small street which had once had fair-sized detached houses on each side, with pretty gardens. Not being as closely packed as the blocks of flats and larger buildings nearer the centre of the town, some of them had escaped total destruction. The first two houses on the right, the second of which was Manfred's, looked presentable but were not yet habitable. Down the rest of that side, except for the last house, only clumps of ruins showed where the villas had stood. On the left there were a few houses standing further down the road.

I prowled round Manfred's house but found no signs of occupation. I thought they must be staying with friends and had no doubt left a message for me with some neighbours. I walked down the road to see if anybody was about. The nearest house had been blown to pieces. The next one also, and I was just passing on when I saw a boy of about thirteen beating a carpet in the garden. I asked him if he knew where I could find Herr and Frau Petersen. 'Oh no! They live in Bromberg and we haven't seen them for a long time.' I said, 'I have just come from Bromberg, and the Petersens left before me. We had to leave because the Russians were encircling the town. I thought the Petersens would be here by now.'

As he listened to my explanation, his eyes grew wider and wider with surprise. 'No,' he said, 'they haven't turned up yet. They would be sure to have come along if they had. Just a moment, please. I will call mother.' He darted off into the ruins. Surely, I thought, they cannot be living in that heap of crushed masonry! But yes indeed! As I drew nearer and made a closer inspection, I saw that what had been the garage next to the house had been repaired and converted into a small bungalow. Frau Lippert appeared and asked me in. The garage was divided by a partition. The children (two daughters and the boy) slept on one side in bunks. Father and Mother Lippert slept in the other compartment which was also used as a dining-sitting-room. At one end there was an all-purpose stove, and somewhere at the back there was a pantry. Thus, in this humble dwelling, one of Hamburg's wealthiest merchants was housed with his family, only too thankful to have survived the terror-raids and to have a roof over their heads.

Tired and cold as I was, it seemed wonderfully cosy to be enveloped in Frau Lippert's hospitality. Before I could look round she had brought biscuits and real tea made from the last packet received from her elder son who had been called up early in the war. This was a great favour and I let the delectable drink slip slowly over my tongue.

Frau Lippert was interested to hear the latest news of the Petersens and of the position on the eastern frontier. The Petersens had not been there, but she wondered whether they had gone straight to Manfred's parents. She knew the address and told me roughly the direction. It could not be far. I started off again and took a tram to what was supposed to be the nearest stop. There I enquired the way but nobody had ever heard of the street. Eventually I found a person who could tell me *exactly* where to go. I optimistically fol- lowed his instructions, but got lost in a maze of what looked like shacks erected on allotments in which people were living. Here again nobody had heard of such a street. I worked my way up the hill back to the main road and started hunting afresh on the other side. I roamed the district for hours, being sent from one place to another by stray people who said they knew *exactly* where the road was, each one telling me to go in the opposite direction. I began to wonder whether it really existed. If only I had had a map I would have walked straight there without anybody's help.

Later on, when I became familiar with every twist and turn, it seemed ridiculous that I had had such difficulty in discovering the house, but at the time it was like a bad dream, dodging to and fro between the ruins, with my destination always just out of reach, besides which I was half frozen and feeling very ill.

When at last I read the name on the corner of the road, I could hardly believe my eyes. It was not surprising that the place was unknown to many local inhabitants because it was a tiny cul-de-sac. Originally there had only been one house on each side. Now, further down on the left, there were also two bungalows built by people bombed out during the big raids. The further one belonged to Manfred's father. Here I again received a warm welcome. They knew all about me and were greatly relieved to hear that Manfred and Linda had left Bromberg. Manfred's mother had died when he was quite young and this Frau Petersen was his father's second wife. She threw her arms round me, then rushed into the living-room to pass on the good news. They wanted to hear every detail about the last days in Bromberg, and as Manfred and Linda had left before me, they were certain that they must soon turn up.

Frau Petersen gave me a hot meal for which I was more than grateful. It is not until you are destitute, after prolonged exposure to the bitter cold, that you realize how soothing hot food and drinks can be to the human body. What is normally taken for granted becomes the greatest comfort and generates energy to a remarkable degree. By now it was nearly dark and Herr Petersen insisted on going back with me by tram to the main station to fetch my rucksack which I had left there, whilst Frau Petersen looked out for somewhere for me to sleep.

The house near the Petersens, beyond the other bungalow, belonged to Herr and Frau Hahn. They had two sons in the Army and one daughter at home. Frau Petersen asked them if they could put me up, which they agreed to do, although it was only a small house with two rooms and kitchen downstairs, and two bedrooms and bathroom upstairs. With the housing shortage becoming ever more acute, it was unlikely that they would be allowed the four rooms for themselves, even if they wished to keep at least one of them free for their sons' return. In any case they were very kind people, always ready to do a good turn. I was given the daughter's room and she moved into the little dressing-room adjoining the parents' bedroom. What a comfort to be in a cosy, warm bed again!

The next day I was sitting with Frau Petersen in the afternoon when Manfred burst in. Needless to say there was great rejoicing. He had an amazing story to tell. He always had! As we listened to him we laughed until we cried, and then we could not stop crying because everything seemed so hopeless.

'We drove between herds of cows, pigs and weeping human beings, in the direction of Danzig, towards Vandsburg. As we passed the Bromberg Police Station we saw that it was being set on fire. Winzel's driver was a Pole, and Winzel and I held a gun pointed at each side of him. It was terribly cold, about 30 degrees centigrade below freezing point. There was a tarpaulin over the van and the floor was covered with straw, but from hour to hour it seemed to grow harder and harder. In the early hours of the morning, with the sun shining brightly on the thick hoar-frost, we pulled up because the horses had lost their shoes. Then we discovered that they could not draw the van any further because there were about a thousand bottles of frozen mineral water carefully hidden under the straw. This was of course calculated by the Poles to prevent us from getting away! After we had thrown the bottles overboard we continued our trek in the procession of animals and vehicles. The refugees had to get out and push the carts up all the hills as the horses could not draw them up the slippery tracks. So our progress was very slow, but eventually with the greatest difficulty we reached Vandsburg in the evening. The town was full to overflowing and we slept on the floor in an inn. Then we wanted to open our first tin of preserved venison. But – oh horror! – they were your tins, and were all filled with pickled gherkins! In my haste I had grabbed them from the wrong shelves in the cellar store-cupboard.

'The next day the horses could go no further as they were snowblind. So there we were, landed in Vandsburg, and not a soul could let us have any horses or take us with them, because they all had enough troubles of their own to cope with. Late in the evening, Winzel, Käte, Linda and I had noticed several wagons of ammunition in a railway siding, which however were not attached to an engine and were patrolled by a strong guard of two soldiers who had orders to defend the train. Our two ladies made friends with the soldiers who, hoping to enjoy a pleasant diversion, told them to wait there as they were expecting a locomotive to run in for the train some time during the night. When the ladies then divulged the fact that they were accompanied by some menfolk, the guards changed their tune. Ah well, Winzel had a demijohn of pure alcohol and one hundredweight of sugar which we gave to the soldiers, trusting the locomotive would turn up. Then they said they would take us too. We waited for the engine until three o'clock the next morning. In the distance we saw two lights on the line, but they did not come nearer. In the meantime Russian tanks had advanced into the outskirts of the village and were shooting all round, at our ammunition train too.

'To our dismay the evacuation of the military hospital now took place. The men who could walk were given a blanket each and were crammed into an empty lime wagon, which was put in between two ammunition trucks. About ten severely wounded men were brought into our wagon, some of whom had only one arm, freshly amputated limbs, bandaged with paper serviettes. We managed to pull our wounded through, but ninety per cent of those in the lime wagon were frozen to death. At the last minute the locomotive arrived and, under fire from the Russians all the time, it was coupled on and slowly shunted to and fro until we were on the right line for Schneidemühl. Now, we thought, we're off! But every five minutes the train halted. The whole day long we kept stopping, moving a little, then stopping again. We did not arrive in Schneidemühl until the evening – normally only a two-hour journey.

'Schneidemühl was just as packed with refugees as all the other stations. We had dosed our wounded with pure alcohol on the way. When Linda wanted to fetch some hot coffee for them, an SA Leader came up to her and bellowed, "Why are you running away in a panic? There's nothing going on." Whereupon I bellowed: "You had better have a look at my wife's backside; she's got a Russian's monogram on it!" All the wounded men swore at the fellow terribly and wished they could have beaten him up.

'So finally we arrived in Frankfurt-an-der-Oder. From there most of the evacuees were sent down to the Sudetenland so that they would have to go through it all over again when the Russians advanced further. We, however, travelled in an empty beer lorry to Berlin, where we were comparatively lucky to be squashed like sardines into a train leaving for Hamburg. The next day the station was blown to pieces in an air-raid because an ammunition train had been left there by mistake.'

With the arrival of Manfred and Linda I thought everything would now turn out all right. I would surely not be deported from Hamburg into a refugee camp, to sleep on sacks amongst hundreds of strangers, and to eat with them from a communal cauldron – the usual fate of the homeless. Those like me who could not be housed with relatives were supposed to go to the appropriate centre for the intake of refugees from their area (which was, for Bromberg, somewhere in Silesia I believe). The bureaucrats dealing with these matters on paper did their best to get me there. It was the same vicious circle that I had encountered in Berlin, only still worse, because there I had only wanted emergency ration cards for a short period, whereas here I wanted permission to live in the town. Besides preferring to stay near my friends, I thought that when Germany finally collapsed, Hamburg – the biggest seaport – would certainly be occupied by the

English. In my ignorance I was naïve enough to imagine that my troubles would then be at an end!

Permission was only given to a refugee to stay in Hamburg on two grounds: if he had near relatives who would let him live with them; or if he had a job which was considered sufficiently important to justify his retention. These were hard and fast rules and no amount of persuasion would induce anybody to make an exception. As all my relatives, near and distant, were in England, there remained for me only the second alternative. But whatever job could I find which would be passed as being important enough to satisfy the authorities? To crown everything, I was so ill that I was finally incapable of using my brain to any useful purpose, let alone get about to make enquiries. Frau Hahn sent for her doctor who diagnosed acute inflammation of various internal organs, and ordered me to bed until further orders. The cold had penetrated the weakest spots. So there I was – with no ration cards, helpless, and no good to anyone, in fact nothing but a burden. The enforced inactivity was a torment to me, especially at a time when so much depended on energetic resourcefulness.

The Petersens were staying with friends right the other side of Hamburg in Blankenese (about one and a half hours' tram and train journey away) and Linda was also ill from the effects of the journey. The full responsibility therefore fell on poor Manfred's shoulders. He had endless battles with countless officials before he finally got permission for me to stay in Hamburg – but this permission was dependent on whether I was accepted for the job he had found for me in a factory owned by an old friend of his, Herr Wolf, the brother of the friend they were staying with in Blankenese. To the Housing Department Manfred had managed to make this job sound of vital importance – in fact he gave the impression that I, and I alone, could fill the gap! The personnel manager in the factory was indeed finding it difficult to entice suitable candidates for the post, which entailed helping at the first-

aid station and with the welfare work. He needed an educated woman with some experience in nursing, but there was
apparently nobody of the right type forthcoming who was
prepared to clock in at seven o'clock in the morning in a
god-forsaken area on the outskirts of the town and to trail
round still more god-forsaken areas, mostly on foot, in search
of sick workers' homes. The Hamburg ladies were no doubt
able to find more congenial employment nearer home. Nevertheless, in spite of Manfred's magnificent praise of my personality and abilities, the personnel manager would, naturally,
not engage anyone introduced by the boss himself without
first of all interviewing the applicant. Here was the rub,
because the doctor would not hear of my getting up, still less
going out. It was an awkward position. Both he and Frau
Hahn had been kindness itself and were doing all they could
to get me well quickly. It would therefore be mean to risk
having a relapse as a result of going out in the cold too soon.
On the other hand, Manfred had talked himself hoarse and
run holes in his soles to find me the job. Finally he was able
to postpone the interview for another week. Then, still against
the doctor's orders, I braved the elements.

By the time we got to the factory my knees were shaking
and my teeth chattering with weakness and apprehension.
Manfred was a tower of strength. He said he would try to do
most of the talking and on no account was I to let out that I
was English. Even if the personnel manager did not object to
this himself, the Labour Exchange might have different
views on the subject. Anyway I had long since decided that
the one advantage of our sudden flight from Bromberg was
the possibility it gave me to 'go under' in a town where
nobody knew me. The Gestapo in Bromberg had been much
too occupied in saving their own skins to find time to post
out reports to other districts and they did not in any case
know the proposed destination of their suspects. I was therefore constantly on the alert amongst strangers, so as not to
give the game away. On the other hand it was a tremendous

relief at last to be free of the spying and informing. There was altogether a very different atmosphere in Hamburg in comparison with the cramped depravity in Bromberg. The Hamburgers had to a great extent retained their cosmopolitan broad-minded outlook.

It was a reassuring interview, not, however, without its pitfalls. My qualifications (if I may call them such) sounded to me hopelessly meagre – attendance at Red Cross lectures and in the theatre at major and minor operations, six years married to a gynaecologist, and a practical knowledge of baby welfare. That was all, but he seemed satisfied. When he asked me, '*Wo kommen Sie her?*' I knew he meant, 'What part do you come from?' in other words, 'What is your native town?' – quite a usual question in Germany. I answered, 'From Bromberg,' and appeased my conscience by remembering that it *could* mean, 'Where have you *just* come from?' He asked me how old I was and, 'Are you used to finding your way about strange places?' 'Oh yes, that will present no difficulty!' I said nothing about Manny, because I was scared to divulge the fact that the Gestapo had removed him from my care. He gave me the job without any hesitation. The salary offered was reasonable, but whatever it had been I would not have quibbled. A secretary was called in to take down particulars and it was agreed that I should start work as soon as I was well enough. Back at the Hahns', after receiving congratulations, I flung myself into bed, exhausted, but in a happier state of mind.

The Hahns most generously allowed me to stay with them and would never accept a penny for rent.

Linda and Manfred were still living with their friends in Blankenese. They met with many more difficulties than anticipated before they were allowed to proceed with repairs to their house. While they had been in Bromberg, it had been rented to a businessman who had not lived there since the bomb damage of 1943. At the same time he doggedly stuck to his claim as a tenant and did his best to prevent

Manfred from moving in himself. The man had certainly saved the house from complete destruction by fire for which Manfred was grateful. Nevertheless he had lived quite happily somewhere else ever since the raid, and now that Manfred had no permanent abode, he naturally wanted to move into his own empty house and start work again. If Manfred had broken into the house under the pretext of carrying out repairs, under these peculiar circumstances, it would have been a criminal offence. He had therefore to wage more battles with more officials before he finally got permission to occupy the two rooms and kitchen on the ground floor, and the basement as offices. He was then able to start having this part of the house made habitable.

The house on the corner next door to the Petersens was also being repaired, and the owner, Herr Schnur, agreed to let a fair-sized, partly-furnished room to me as soon as it was ready. This was a hope for the future, although how long the builders would take to complete the work it was impossible to predict.

TWENTY-FIVE

In the meantime I started work at Wolf's. As usual, at the outset I was assailed with agonies of doubt as to whether I would be capable of coping with the job. It was Herr Hahn's detailed map of Hamburg which helped me more than anything. Such rarities were of course long since unobtainable in shops. He let me take it with me wherever I went and would give me advice as to the best routes to take. In order to arrive at the factory by seven I had to leave the house before six o'clock. It was pitch dark and bitterly cold, with snow still on the ground. As the crow flies it was not much more than three miles. By walking through by-roads it was possible to find a fairly direct way, but to get there by any other means except by car, it meant a zig-zag journey by tram, train and tram, with two changes, followed by ten minutes' walk.

The factory was surrounded by high walls. I walked through the gates with a stream of workmen (dressed in their usual short overjackets and peaked caps) and felt like a new girl going to school for the first time. A porter from the enquiry office at the entrance took me to the first-aid station. The original factory buildings had been bombed flat and had been replaced by temporary erections mostly only one storey high. I was shown into a room which was obviously the surgery, equipped with numerous instruments. Leading off this was an inner sanctum with a writing desk, chairs, files and cupboards. Both rooms had windows running along one side beneath the ceiling. The building was raised from ground level and the windows were too high for anybody to be able to see in from outside.

The full-time staff consisted of a fully-trained nurse, a male orderly and a Russian doctor. They worked under a German doctor who came once or twice a week. Besides myself there was one other married woman who helped part-time with the visiting.

The nurse, Schwester von Dohlen, was a fresh, fair-haired girl, very pleasant to work with. The orderly had been with the firm since its inception and knew each workman by name. He and the nurse did most of the routine work and writing. The Russian doctor was a sweet old boy; unfortunately he could not speak a word of any language but Russian so that our communications were confined to signs and grimaces. He greeted us each morning with a handshake and a low bow, whilst his eyes and face glowed momentarily with a friendly smile. When there was work to be done he did it quietly and efficiently. The men seemed to have confidence in him. At other times he stood staring rather sadly through the window, perhaps thinking of his home and his family.

Herr Wolf was a self-made man who ran his factory on up-to-date lines and enjoyed the reputation of being a just and considerate employer. A number of the men had been working for him ever since he started in a modest way. Now, in spite of wealth and power, he had remained unspoiled and still had the welfare of his workers at heart.

Most of the day I was out visiting the sick in their homes. If a man had not come to work for three days and had sent no word or doctor's certificate, I had to go and find out what had happened; or if a man had been ill for some time, I had to go to see what progress he was making, and find out if he was having proper care and treatment. I was handed a list of names and addresses in the morning by a man on the personnel officer's staff. He had (like Manfred) one stiff elbow, wounded in the war. He gave me forms, one of which I had to fill in for each visit, giving detailed information such as the nature of the man's illness, name of his doctor, the date of his last certificate, which I was to be sure to examine carefully, who was looking after him, also a description of his home circumstances and the general appearance of the patient.

I was afraid that the intrusion of a stranger into their homes, asking personal questions, might be resented. On the contrary, without exception wherever I went the people were friendly. This was no doubt a compliment to the tact of my predecessors and to the general benevolence of the administration of the factory. It was at once obvious that I was stepping into a service which had been running as efficiently as the well-oiled machinery in the workshops.

No, the people made no difficulties. The worst part of the job proved to be the search for their homes. Under normal circumstances this would have been easy with the aid of Herr Hahn's map; but to begin with, owing to fuel shortage, all trams and local trains ceased running from about 10.30 a.m. till 4 p.m., which meant that I could travel to any district before 10.30, and after that I had to walk. This was no joke, because Hamburg is a large city. Even while the trams were running, I often had to walk miles because some men lived quite a distance from any form of transport. As far as possible I was given addresses for each day which were not too spread out. Also if there was a visit to be made fairly near Wandsbek the clerk would tell me to go there in the afternoon and then go straight home, or he would sometimes give me some addresses overnight to look up on my way to the factory in the morning in order to save a double journey.

Once I had successfully reached the vicinity of the home I was looking for, my difficulties were still by no means at an end. On the map it would look simple enough. In practice it was a different matter. I often got off the tram at the appropriate stop only to find no side streets visible at all beneath the rubble – nothing but a sea of broken bricks. Here and there a few paths were cleared between them, but had they once been roads? There were no signposts, no numbers, nothing to go by. Some washing might be seen fluttering like a flag above the ruins, which pointed to the presence of a human habitation. More often than not the paths led to a solitary cellar where some family was housed. It might be the one I wanted, or it might not. The only way to find out was to go and see. This meant many fruitless searches before I finally tracked my man down.

Another difficult type of place to find was the little hut on allotments which had once been used as a tool-shed, now converted into a dwelling. These would have amusing names, but there might be dozens of huts in one area and it needed a strong sense of humour to enjoy the jokes when one after another round each corner the wrong names popped out on the doors. At the end of a tiring day when I could not find the one I wanted I wished 'Mum's Paradise', 'The Refuge from the Storm', 'The Better 'ole' and all the 'Cosicots' and 'Cosinooks' at the bottom of the sea.

However derelict their dwellings may have been, they were always clean and tidy inside. My opinion of the Hamburg workman's wife went up in leaps and bounds. If they could get hold of any broken-down shanty or cellar they set about making as comfortable a home as circumstances would permit.

We were having frequent air-raids night and day. Often when I was sent to enquire why a man had not been to work for three days and had sent no word, I found him and his wife still rummaging in the remains of what had been their home. Sometimes I found the man had been killed, or sometimes that his wife and children had been the victims. These were the most difficult visits.

One day I was given an address to call at in a street near the Reeperbahn (the amusement centre once famous throughout the world to sailors). This district had been bombed badly over and over again. I could not find the house, nor the street, although I circled round and round where it should have been according to the map, clambering over the debris in the hope of finding a clue. None of the people I met could help me until at last by chance I ran across a neighbour of my man.

'Oh yes, Miss, four nights ago it was, we all took the kids round to the shelter when the siren went and we were only just in time. We were still in the entrance when the bombs came down. When we came out there was nothing left of our homes. They was only temporary anyway in the ruins, but now we haven't got nowhere else to go so we've been allowed to live in the shelter for the time being.

'No, we was none of us killed because we was all in the shelter. Wonderful places them shelters. But when's this bloody war going to end, that's what I'd like to know? Some says we're going to join up with the English to keep the Russians out. If they're not darn quick the Russians'll be here in Hamburg before anybody gets a look in. They're a tough lot them Russians, tough as nails they are. My boy what was wounded out there says they live on bark from trees and grass and roots when they can't get nothing to eat. Ah! they're a rum lot! They say it isn't safe for a woman to show herself in the streets where them Russians come along, and they say it isn't safe at home either. They break into the houses and knock the men over the head and rape the women and girls.

'My old man's brother's wife, she was bringing her kids away and she was waiting for a train when a crowd of Russians overtook them. She was on the platform and there was no getting away from them. They flung her on the ground and some of them held her down and the others raped her, one after the other, about a dozen of them, in front of the kids and everyone. She was that bad afterwards she had to be taken to hospital. She's still that bad she can't get over it. They say lots of them have got diseases, and think of all the little bastards what's coming! They say you can have them taken away at the hospital if you can prove you've been raped and got witnesses. Not so easy though is it? Lummy Miss, we don't want nothing like that here in Hamburg, do we?

'I don't know what to make of it. One day they tell you

over the wireless we're going to win the war with these wonderful new weapons and wot not. Next day somebody tells me the Führer is going to scorch the whole earth because no one's fit to live on it! Then somebody else says the English'll get here first, but there won't be none of us alive to see it after they've done their bombing! Ah well, while there's life there's hope, as the saying goes.

'Herr Schmidt? You'll find him at home in the shelter just round the corner to the right then sharp left. You can't miss it, it's the only building in the whole street what's standing. Cheerio, Miss, cheerio!'

After I had recovered my breath from listening to this commentary on current events I made my way, as directed, to the shelter. It was the oblong-shaped sort, above ground, cleverly constructed to resist the bomb explosions. As a shelter against air-raids it was admirably equipped. As a communal home for hundreds of people for which it was now being used, it was totally inadequate and they lived under deplorable conditions. There was no daylight of course and, as far as I could make out, very little fresh air. The little cubicles, originally intended as rest rooms, were occupied by families, at least four people in each one. There was only just enough room for four bunks, one on top of the other on each side, with a narrow gangway in between. There were rows and rows of these cubicles. The partitions between them did not reach to the ceiling and there were only curtains in front of the entrances. The place stank of human bodies and used-up air. No amount of personal cleanliness could counteract the obvious results of having crowds huddled together day and night in this stuffy atmosphere.

In spite of these drawbacks, the inhabitants were cheerful in a passive way because they felt safe. No bombs had yet been known to damage this type of shelter. Each night, therefore, they could enjoy the luxury of undisturbed sleep. They were provided with a hot vegetable broth once a day and otherwise eked their rations out as best they could in cold foods. None of them had anything more to lose now. That their lives had so far been spared was a miracle for which they were profoundly thankful. They were all struck down to the same level and after the war was over they hoped to make a new start. Shortly after a calamity the spirits of the survivors often rose to a degree which was out of proportion to the circumstances, and subsequently sagged when the situation did not improve as quickly as anticipated.

My man was in a cubicle with his wife and another couple. While running to the shelter his wife had been hit by a falling wall but was not seriously injured. He would be able to return to work the next day. It was a rule of the firm that compassionate leave for three days be granted to men who had been bombed out, and this was extended in some cases.

While I was talking to him the siren went, so I waited until the all-clear sounded, thankful to be in a safe spot for once. As the people thronged in from outside I realized why the air was as thick as mud, for this must have happened every time there was an air-raid warning. They squashed into every nook and cranny. When it was full to capacity the door was slammed shut. Many had to be turned away and I knew how desperate they would be feeling.

More often than not I was caught far from any shelter during the daytime raids. Sometimes I would be walking through the ruins with not a soul in sight. Then I would cringe against a piece of wall and hope for the best. One blow would have brought the already tottering brickwork showering upon my head, but somehow there seemed at least some protection against splinters. If I had been buried alive (or dead) on the spot no one would have known where to look for me when it was discovered that I was missing. My corpse would have provided food for the rats which slipped in and out of the holes and crevices undisturbed by my presence or by the crashing of the bombs. Since the terror raids of 1943 it had been impossible to combat the plague of rats. The stretches of uninhabited ruins were ideal breeding grounds which, deeply hidden, withstood the feeble onslaught of man. These conditions prevailed until the rubble was removed after the war. Standing alone during the raids watching these revolting creatures running about, it seemed as though I must be the only human being alive on earth. Sometimes in a panic that was stronger than the fear of the bombs I would run and run until at last I found inhabited buildings.

If I got a chance, I took refuge in a shelter but it was so unpleasant that each time I swore I would never go in one again – although of course I invariably did when it came to the point. Some of them were like round towers above ground. Inside you went up and up on a gradual slope in a wide spiral passage. Nearest to the centre wall there were wooden benches, but I was never early enough to get a seat. There was always a long queue at the entrance and usually the bombs were falling before I got in. Slowly the spiral filled with people pressed close together. Those at the bottom shouted impatiently to the more fortunate ones higher up, telling them to move on more quickly. Then just as you thought you were going to be pulped into jelly, the warden's voice rang out, 'Full up – no more,' followed by cries of despair from the people left outside, cut short by the clang of the door. The longer the raid lasted, the more unbearable it became inside the dimly-lit low-pitched passage. There was hardly enough air to breathe. We heard nothing, but if an explosive hit the shelter there was a dull vibration and it rocked in an alarming manner. There was always the thought – supposing a bomb penetrated into these seething masses, what an infernal havoc would result.

At the factory during air-raids we all had to go into cellars, which looked reasonably safe. In between visiting I had to be on duty in the first-aid station. Besides illnesses there were the usual accidents, such as cuts, bruises, abrasions, burns and crushed limbs, to be dealt with. There were frequently patients who had minute particles of metal in their eyes for which the nurse had an effective treatment. Unless there happened to be a rush on, there was nothing for me to do but fetch and carry, and pass the necessary instruments.

If it could be arranged, I tried to be at the factory at lunch time, otherwise I had no hot meal and no midday break. Eating a sandwich alone amongst the ruins in the cold was not much relaxation! Meals in restaurants were just a waste of precious rations. There was a canteen at the factory where they served up a wholesome hot-pot with very little meat in it, but certainly as much as the number of coupons they asked for, added to which (thrown in, coupon free) there was a good helping of potatoes and vegetables, which were rationed and in short supply. We lined up to fetch the soup-plate full of steaming stew. The kitchen visible through the serving hatch looked well-equipped and clean. Again I was embarrassed at first about joining the workmen – quite unnecessarily. I thought they might look askance at the newcomer in a fur coat (it was the only winter coat I possessed so I had to wear it every day). But no, they took my presence as a matter of course. They made room for me at one end of the long, narrow tables, and drew me into their general conversation. A skilled workman was as important as a skilled nurse or draughtsman or salesman. Each took his place side by side, indispensable and complementary to one another. All the men, whatever their jobs, were intelligent, clean and kind. Here of all places, where I had expected to be a misfit, I never felt like a fish out of water. When trying to reason this out I decided that it was not *I* who had changed or taken a conscious active part in adapting myself to the situation. I had applied for the job for the selfish reason that I wanted to stay in Hamburg, not because I felt called to do the work. No, they accepted me because, like them, I had a job to tackle.

Like the majority of Germans, they enjoyed hard work,

and when there was gradually less and less to do, owing to lack of materials, they were genuinely depressed – not only because it was obvious that they might soon be out of a job. Herr Wolf kept as many men employed for as long as he could, but eventually he had to close down. No doubt he helped those who had worked for him for many years as much as possible. The others, such as myself, were given the sack.

Now that the chaos and pending total collapse of industry and transport were causing widespread unemployment, the Labour Exchange no longer forced people to work; on the contrary, there were not nearly enough jobs to go round, so that they were at their wits' end to place the people on their books who really needed wages to support their families. Thus, again through circumstances beyond my control, I was set free. I had enough money in the Post Office to keep me for years at the standard of living to which we had now been reduced. My job at Wolf's had served its purpose – I was allowed to stay in Hamburg. I had enjoyed the work and the insight it gave me into factory life. But it had been tiring, especially as the effects of under-nourishment were daily becoming more noticeable. I was therefore not sorry to conserve the little energy I had on merely continuing to exist.

Whilst I was still working at the factory I had moved from Frau Hahn's to the Schnurs' house next door to the Petersens'. The large room I had been promised had not yet been renovated, but the builders had finished work in one small room on the first floor which Herr Schnur said I could have until the other one was ready. The roof was watertight; there was water and drainage in the bathroom and lavatory; but that was as far as it went. The rest of the house was in a terrible state, including the kitchen. There was no light and no heating. Fortunately it was now springtime, and Linda offered to let me cook on the stove in her cellar – what little cooking it was possible to do – so I decided it was best to move in, especially as Frau Hahn was expecting her son home any day, and my room would be needed.

I had arrived in Hamburg with nothing but what I stood up in and the contents of a rucksack. When I came to pack I was astonished to find what a conglomeration of articles I had collected. Frau Hahn had given me odds and ends, and, with the object of setting up house again, I had scoured the shops to find as many utensils as I could. They were shoddy goods which I would previously have rejected, but we considered ourselves lucky to be able to buy anything at all. Once again (as after the terror-raid on Wuppertal-Barmen) I benefited from the fact that we were the first to suffer from a major calamity. Coming from the towns on the eastern frontier which were the first to be attacked, we were the forerunners of a vast movement of the population, but before the administrators in the west had realized to what extent they were to be overwhelmed by the influx of eastern Germans, we had already been issued with coupons for bare necessities. Not only were we given priority with regard to coupons, but in the first few weeks it was possible, with perseverance, to ferret out a shop here and there which could supply some of the items. Later on, as the millions of homeless streamed in and as production gradually came to a standstill, all reserves came to an end, excepting for goods carefully hidden by manufacturers and shopkeepers for the purpose of black-market racketeering.

TWENTY-SIX

All this time, of course, I worried about Manny. I had received three letters from Kurt since Hedi, Manny and Uwe had joined him in Pomerania following our flight from Bromberg. The first one was written on 2 February 1945 to say they had arrived safely and that he had managed to find temporary accommodation for them. He explained that all his post was censored and that it was impossible, owing to the present situation, to write to me regularly. For the time being it would be in the best interests of the child not to communicate with him, but he would let me know if there was anything particular to report or give me any change of address.

On 16 March Kurt wrote again and enclosed a page of scribbles and drawings by Manny which became one of my most precious possessions. He said Manny was at that time well except that the damp weather was not suiting him.

On 14 April he wrote once more to tell me that Hedi and the children, together with all refugees from East and West Prussia with no more than a few hours' notice had had to leave to make room for evacuees from East Pomerania. Their destination was unknown. All he had gathered was that the receiving district for East and West Prussian refugees was supposed to be Thuringen. He had told Hedi to write to me direct as soon as she was settled somewhere. He had himself just received orders to leave shortly and did not know how much longer he would remain there. 'We have heard that Hamburg is at present having particularly heavy air-raids and I hope you are all right. This war can't last much longer now.'

After that I heard no more from either Kurt or Hedi for nearly five months. I did not know where they were or whether they and Manny were alive or dead. I only knew that if they were alive they must be somewhere where it was impossible for them to communicate with me, which was not consoling because this could only mean that they had not been able to escape to the west.

Those months of suspense seemed like years. The strange thing was that so long as nothing else upset me I could keep a stiff upper lip, and yet as soon as I was worried or hurt about any other matter (which normally would hardly have affected me at all) I was overcome with grief about Manny. Alone in my room I cried my heart out, not about whatever it was that had originally distressed me, but about Manny's dangerous position.

Every morning when I woke up I wondered whether the day would bring me news of him. Frau Hahn was very sympathetic and would have taken Manny into her house had he arrived whilst I was staying there. I rented the room at the Schnurs' house only on condition that he should be allowed to join me if he turned up.

The small room into which I moved at first until the larger one was ready was hardly big enough to swing a cat in, but big enough for my scanty belongings. The Hahns lent me a pushcart to move my goods the mile or so from their house to the Schnurs' (the sort of cart which the carpenter or painter uses to transport his tools and equipment over short distances). To my surprise this was bulging with oddments by the time I had finished packing. There were jars and cans which I had had given me, a frying pan, a saucepan, a coffee pot, two plates, two mugs, a broom and pan, a pail – in fact I could have written quite a long inventory! During normal times I would have felt highly self-conscious pushing a hand-cart full of junk through the select streets of Hamburg-Wandsbek, but now I thought nothing of it and such a spectacle was taken as a matter of course. I had not gone far down the road when the air-raid alarm sounded. I thought it was not worth going back, so I pushed on. Before long the planes were overhead. I left my cart unguarded in the road and dashed for cover in the milkman's cellar just as the bombs started to crash down. Needless to say I was the first out of the cellar as soon as the danger had passed to make sure that no one ran off with my cartload.

Added to these goods – oh miracle of miracles! – the wooden boxes, which Manfred had sent off from Bromberg by rail, arrived at his friend's place at Rahlstedt on the outskirts of Hamburg. They had taken months to get there and we had never expected to see them again. Then (I suppose it was in March) Herr Klein rang to say that *one* box had just arrived. *Which* box was it? That was the burning question. Manfred hastened to Rahlstedt and returned rejoicing for themselves, grieving for me, to say it was one of theirs. The next day exactly the same thing happened again – again it was one of *their* boxes. Some time elapsed and we heard no more so that I gave up hope of getting mine – but at last it came after all! Opening it in Herr Klein's cellar it seemed like a magic box, full of surprises. It had been packed in haste and so much had happened since that I had forgotten what it contained. On top was my little green eiderdown – what a godsend! There were three sheets, two pillow-slips, tea towels, a linen tablecloth and napkins, a few knives, forks and spoons, a large sharp knife (what a treasure!), little enamel trays, lace mats, shoes, and look! a black coat and a silk dress, a pullover, underwear, two books and an album of Wolf's *Lieder*. As I dragged each article out it was like meeting a long-lost friend. It was amazing how much I had stuffed into the little box. Excepting for the things we needed urgently, such as bedding, we left most of the contents in Rahlstedt for the time being where there were not so many air-raids as in Hamburg.

Soon after we arrived in Hamburg Manfred had managed to find a shop where they sold beds on coupons, and he had also bought one for me – with plain wooden slats at each end, very rickety, and with a mattress as hard as wood – nevertheless a bed of sorts. He had also bought two cottony grey rugs for each of us. Now, with my eiderdown, I was very comfortable.

Frau Schnur lent me two chairs and a round table, also a wardrobe and chest of drawers, but the latter had to be kept in another room for the time being owing to lack of space in mine.

The builders were proceeding slowly with the work in the Schnurs' house. While I was working at the factory I left long before the men arrived in the mornings, so the foreman was given a key to the front door. I did not realize this and the first day that I did not have to get up so early, I was surprised to be awakened by footsteps and to see a man's head peering round the corner at me. Judging by the sheepish look on his face the Nosy Parker was even more taken aback to see an occupant than I was by his intrusion, and hastily withdrew. There was as yet no door to my bedroom, so I now thought it best to forfeit one of the rugs and hang it over the opening!

I did not mind living in the house alone except when there were night air-raids. I was then afraid I might not hear the warning and be caught unawares. Also the three choices open to me were not very inviting. One was to stay in bed, the other to go into the Schnurs' cellar alone, or thirdly I could run out through the two gardens into the Petersens', who always unlocked the side door ready for me to slip in. When the planes were near I usually finished up by bolting over to them. We would then listen to the wireless report until the raiders had either passed over, or started bombing near enough to make us dive into the cellar. Deep in the bowels of the earth somewhere in or near Hamburg there was a man who made a running commentary on the radio of the progress of the planes and their action, reading from sensitive instruments. If you could listen in you therefore knew exactly who was catching it worst. Some people kept a radio in the cellar. Needless to say ribald remarks would be made when the voice calmly announced that bombs were now falling in *your* district as though it were news to you, whilst in fact you could hardly hear what he was saying for the noise of the explosives! All the same, we grew fond of the voice. It was the same one, night or day, always on the spot when we were in trouble, and there was something reassuring about his quiet efficiency.

In their own homes everybody evolved different methods of calming their nerves as best they could during raids. Some liked to lie flat on their backs, others flat on their stomachs. Frau Hahn always knelt on the floor and buried her head in a cushion on a chair as though she were saying her prayers. Herr Hahn stood about on the alert. I shall never forget him rushing into the cellar one night clad only in his underpants because he had stayed in bed too long, and was only just dressing when the bombs rattled down all round us. Their cellar was quite cosy as they had it full of surplus furniture. Linda and Manfred, of course, had no surplus furniture, so we had to sit on a bath tub.

About once a week Linda heated water in her copper and invited me to a bath in the wash-cellar, which was a great luxury, because it was impossible now to heat water by gas or electricity. Each household was rationed to use only a small number of units per month. If, when the meter was read, the allotted amount had been exceeded, the supply would be cut off from the main until the 'overdraft' had been worked off. To avoid this drastic punishment it was necessary to be extremely economical. There was just enough for lighting, but practically none left over for cooking, heating or ironing.

After the factory closed down I missed the midday hot-pot. Linda and I were registered at the same greengrocers, but unfortunately our numbers were wide apart so that we could not buy both our lots of potatoes on the same day to avoid both of us queueing. The numbers due for rations were written up each day in the shop window, just as for fish. It was necessary to keep a sharp look-out when your number was approaching, which was not often, because if you missed the right day, you had to wait until your turn came round again. If you did not join the queue and went later in the day you might find everything sold out and the shop shut.

As we arrived in Hamburg in the middle of the winter, we had been unable to buy a store of winter potatoes. We had no bottled vegetables, mushrooms or fruit. Worst of all, we missed the happy shooting expeditions which had kept our larders supplied with meat. The bread ration, supplemented by Bäcker's wheat flour, had been ample as a side-line in Bromberg. Now that it was one of the basic foods, the two or three slices a day went nowhere. Once we stooped to laying a snare for rabbits, but only succeeded in trapping a starving dog instead. I had nothing to barter with and no business or private connections.

Breakfast consisted of one slice of bread with a scraping of butter or jam and a cup of hot synthetic coffee. Lunch varied between:

1 A hot soup or stew made from vegetables (usually swedes) or an ounce of meat or bone,

2 A potato fried with $\frac{1}{4}$ oz. of diced fat bacon,

3 Cabbage cut into fine strips and boiled quickly, in very little water,

4 Once in four weeks a little macaroni,

5 Once in three or four weeks a little piece of fish,

6 Once in three or four weeks pea soup with pickled cabbage.

If you went without skimmed milk in your coffee, these delectable dishes could be followed every other day or so by a little blancmange or custard.

For tea the white-bread coupons would provide one roll a day (and leave a little over for wheat flour to thicken sauces, etc.). The roll would be served with the inevitable cup of synthetic coffee.

Supper had to be a cold meal because there was only sufficient fuel to cook once a day. There would be a slice or two of bread, perhaps a wafer-slice of cold sausage or a wafer-slice of cheese, or a scraping of lard if available (melted down with diced onion, apple and marjoram if available). Potato salad was a rare treat (boiling skimmed milk poured on to the hot slices seasoned with pepper, salt and vinegar, and left to cool); when this could be accompanied by a hot Frankfurter sausage, it was a dream come true. Proper mayonnaise could not be made or bought. Such luxuries as eggs or milk-powder were not on the market, neither rationed nor unrationed, and egg-powder was only issued very rarely and then in the minutest quantities.

This was, of course, the winter menu. In the summer there were more vegetables, salads and fruits to give variety.

After a few weeks in Hamburg I had reached a state of perpetual hunger, which increased in intensity as time went on. I ate anything I could get hold of. On the whole I kept well, except that some internal organs ceased to function properly and that I had to battle against fatigue and depression.

I lay in bed late in the mornings to conserve energy. In any case what was the point of getting up early?

Practically every night since January I had dreamt of my mother so vividly that, on waking up, it was difficult to realize she was not near. This puzzled me, and although the dreams were not unpleasant, I could not help wondering whether she was in trouble. Linda and Manfred tried to console me by saying it was only a coincidence that I had dreamt of her once or twice, and then I had let it prey on my mind. The last Red Cross message to come through, written on 18 July 1944, received in Bromberg on 1 December, said all were well at home. At the beginning of January 1945 I had posted some new photos of Manny to Baron von Langen in Sweden (which eventually arrived in England) but since our flight to the west it had been impossible to send any further communications either through the Red Cross or otherwise. I had not consciously been worried about my people any longer. After all, they were winning the war now. There was no fear of air-raids or an invasion, only a few rockets, or flying bombs. It was therefore strange that my subconscious mind should, night after night, return to my mother in particular. I fought against what I thought might be a neurotic illusion which caused the recurrence of the dreams. Towards the middle of April they ceased – as a result, I thought, of my determined efforts to be sensible. When finally news came from home after the war, my sister told me that the progress of Mama's complaint (Parkinson's Disease), from which she had been suffering for forty odd years, had suddenly become much more rapid in the New Year, and she had died on 19 April 1945.

In the spring Manfred dug up his lawn and sowed potatoes and vegetables. He got permission from the friends who had been bombed out next door to dig up their garden also. They gave me the use of part of it, and I produced a good crop of peas and dwarf beans. Manfred even tried growing tobacco, with considerable success. He ordered fifty plants from a nurseryman he knew in Rahlstedt which he asked me to bring back with me as I happened to be going to Herr Klein's to fetch some things from my box. We thought they would only be small plants, but when I called to collect them, the gardener said they could only be transplanted if a good deal of soil were left on the roots. I was already laden with a heavy rucksack and now I had to carry a box which seemed to weigh a ton by the time I had walked the considerable distance to the station, and again from Wandsbekerchaussee station to the Petersens'. When I finally arrived, staggering under my burden, they greeted me with hoots of mirth. At first I resented their *Schadenfreude*, until I had cooled down sufficiently to be able to appreciate the joke. However, when the tobacco was gathered, I felt no compunction in enjoying a share in the harvest. Manfred dried and treated the leaves with meticulous care, according to a recipe given to him by a friend. When he at last pronounced them done to a turn, they still had to be cut into the thinnest of shreds, which was no easy task. The leaves, pressed tightly into chunks, were so tough that it was necessary to sharpen the knife very frequently and the job soon made our hands ache. The chopping-board was passed round and round the table, each taking a short turn, followed by a rest, until the tin was filled, after which we could sit back and puff our home-made cigarettes for a brief period in bland contentment. The tobacco was mild and had quite a pleasant flavour, much better than the atrocious cigarettes sold on ration (only a few per adult per week). Another difficulty was to come by cigarette papers in which to roll the tobacco. These were much sought after and as rare as gold.

I had never before been what could be termed a smoker, although I enjoyed a cigarette sometimes when in company. Now that I was always hungry, I developed a craving to smoke. A cigarette seemed to dispel the empty feeling in the stomach for a short time. Later on, as soon as I had enough to eat, the craving passed, although it took a great effort finally to break myself of the habit altogether.

TWENTY-SEVEN

Our needs, fears and worries increased in number and intensity as the German state toppled ever nearer towards complete destruction. Within a few months, with the Allies advancing on all sides, town-dwellers were reduced from a finely organized community to primitive cave-dwellers. The veneer of civilization was stripped off. Streets became more and more deserted. Only a few women, children and old or wounded men were to be seen. Rabbits hopped across the roads from one derelict patch to another. Rats crept swiftly beneath the rubble.

Our immediate question in Hamburg was whether the town would be defended or not. Hitler had repeatedly given orders for every town, every village and every house to be defended to the last man. Many people in responsible positions had been peremptorily shot for disobeying these orders. Would Karl Kaufmann, the Gauleiter of Hamburg, risk his life to save ours? It depended no doubt on the amount of support he could count on from his underlings, and whether Hitler's fanatic followers in the town could be kept under control until the occupation was completed. We were to reap advantage from the fact that Hamburg had never been a hotbed of Nazism, but so far there was no clue as to which course Kaufmann would steer. He had taken the precaution of storing quantities of food within the city in case we should be cut off from incoming supplies. He now divided these provisions between the population. Each person was allowed one 2-lb. loaf of bread, a little chunk of fat bacon and about ½ lb. of smoked sausage over and above the usual ration. We were advised to keep this extra windfall 'for an emergency'. What sort of an emergency could this mean? Were we supposed to hold out on this whilst the town was being peacefully occupied, or did it mean that this was the last food we would ever eat?

As the English closed in upon us, the suspense became almost unbearable. The noose was pulled so tight that we felt stifled. Would it be released or was the final overpowering tug still to come? We held our breath and waited. The heart of the city stopped beating.

At last on 1 May it was announced that the town was not to be defended. '*Die Stadt Hamburg wird aufgegeben!*'

Oh, thank God! We shall live to see the end of the fighting after all. No more suspense! No more air-raids! Every night will be undisturbed! The Russians will not come. Occupation by the English won't be so bad. This awful war will soon be over. The relief was at first so great that everybody relaxed into a state of false optimism. The full implications of the unconditional surrender of all German armed forces, which took place six days later, were only gradually realized.

I thought, ingenuously, that I would now be 'liberated', that I would be allowed to write to my people and go home to visit them, then return to find Manny with the aid of the Allies; means of communication, even the possibility of travelling between the east and west, would be opened up. I would not have long to wait now. Alas! Disillusionment was soon to come.

We were ordered to stay indoors whilst the occupation of the town was taking place. Anyone seen outdoors would be shot. For several days we were shut in and saw nobody. I slunk like a criminal from Schnur's house to the Petersens' and back again after dark. When the radio station was taken over it was the familiar voice of the air-raid reports who spoke to us for the last time. This voice had been near us all in times of danger, within our very homes. Now the invisible link was to be severed. We could visualize the armed guard waiting behind his back as, with a catch in his throat, he bid us goodbye.

With the total collapse of Germany, Linda and Manfred, like many others, were struck low with despondency and temporarily stunned. However, as soon as they had recovered from the initial depression, with typical energy, they began to sum up the situation as far as was possible. For the time being Manfred had sufficient funds to live on. When these were exhausted their chance of survival would rest on what decision the occupation powers might take with regard to the rebuilding of Hamburg. Even if only a few permits were granted, Manfred might get enough work to eke out an existence as he had a well-established business. People for whom he had planned houses which had since been destroyed would come to him again as soon as they had permission to build. Manfred, with his customary flight of fancy, was optimistic enough to hope that he might be allowed to rebuild the block of flats which he had owned. Linda and I immediately poured scorn on this idea, amidst roars of contemptuous laughter. At that time we could not foresee the tug-of-war between the West and Russia which was soon to take place over Germany's dead body, making it dangerous for the Western Allies to leave their Zones weak and vulnerable. Within five years Manfred had built those flats, and many more besides.

After the occupation had been completed and we were allowed into the streets again, everything was at a standstill.

It was strange to observe my fellow-countrymen while I was, so to speak, in disguise. It was like being a peeping Tom. Soldiers were only allowed to speak to civilians on necessary business and they led an entirely separate existence. Uniform was a dividing line. Those in uniform were the conquerors. Those not in uniform were the conquered, the underlings, the scum of the earth. Being a civilian, whether I liked it or not I was automatically herded amongst the Germans, the underlings. I therefore inevitably formed my opinions of all regulations according to the German point of view.

My first plan was somehow to let my parents know that I was alive and in Hamburg. I went to the nearest military quarters in Wandsbek and enquired about the possibility of sending my address. The young man I spoke to was polite and friendly, but said that officially nothing could be done until the Red Cross set up an office in Hamburg perhaps in a few weeks', perhaps in a few months' time. The Army had orders not to send any messages for civilians. I pleaded that I did not wish to send a message, only my address. What was to prevent him personally from writing to anybody in England? Letters were censored and he obviously had considerable misgivings. He would not promise anything, but said he would see what he could do. I gave him my address and that of my parents, and awaited developments. Time passed, but nothing happened. I had no idea what my people could do if they received my address, but I thought they would somehow find a way of letting me know they had got it. I began to wonder whether the young man had not dared to write. Still there were no official means of communication. One day as I was walking towards the Lombardsbrücke I saw two or three Tommies waiting under the large tree by the roadside. I could easily stand near them without suspicion as though I was waiting to cross the road. I hastily scribbled the two names and addresses on a slip of paper and decided to try my luck again. I spoke to the man nearest to me who showed no signs of fearing detection, only utter surprise at hearing an English voice coming from a civilian mouth. He said he would send the address to my parents. I naturally did not ask the name of this man or of the other one I had spoken to in Wandsbek, so I never discovered which one wrote. It was a Lance Corporal Duckworth who took the sporting chance and relieved my people of their anxiety. He even told them he would have tried to contact me in Wandsbek had he not been posted to another part of Germany. It was not until the beginning of June 1945 that an opportunity arose for my people to send me a message.

In the meantime I had also been hoping against hope that I would receive some news of Manny, either from Kurt or

Hedi, but I was to be kept much longer in suspense. Until I had heard from home or about Manny, I was too restless to feel any inclination to tie myself down to a job. However, as the days and weeks went by with no sign from anybody, I decided it would be better to have a regular occupation and to earn some money.

The large room in the Schnurs' house had been renovated and I had moved into it, and could also now use the kitchen. The rest of the rooms were being repaired and I was still the sole occupant of the house. There was very little for me to do, and the situation in general was extremely depressing. As far as was possible the occupation troops in Hamburg behaved decently to the Germans. It is, however, natural and inevitable that a defeated people should be treated ignominiously. The fact that I was British-born did not make my position any less unpleasant as no discrimination was made with regard to civilians. The policy of non-fraternization encouraged contempt of the natives amongst the arrogant elements in the Army. House-to-house searches for arms, and still worse, requisition of property for the use of the English, aroused bitterness. Not even the home was secure from intrusion or confiscation. Soldiers were not allowed out unarmed, and seeing them walk along with their rifles slung over their shoulders, even when off duty, invariably made us laugh. At the same time it provoked a childish perversity. I longed to make a loud bang, or jump unexpectedly from a hidden retreat. Manfred had no time to fetch his guns from the shooting lodge before we left Bromberg, otherwise he would now have been faced with the alternative of giving them up or of keeping them secretly on penalty of death if they were discovered. If Manfred had had a gun I know we would have been sorely tempted to let off a volley of shots in some sequestered spot, just to startle the English and see them run!

Not only German homes, but also German cafés or restaurants were out of bounds for the soldiers, and needless to say we, the lowly civilians, were not allowed into theirs. They were given separate second-class reserved carriages on the Stadtbahn (district railway) with upholstered seats, which were nearly always practically empty. We on the other hand were packed like sardines into the third-class carriages with no upholstered seats. The position was not improved when gradually more and more Tommies travelled in our carriages, for reasons which we were unable to ascertain. We wondered whether it was because they preferred to be among the jostling crowds of men, women and children, rather than in the solitary grandeur of their own superior compartments.

Towards the end of May I received a surprise visit from Rosemarie, Hedi's daughter. She came to enquire whether I had any news of her mother. She had left Bromberg, as arranged, with her fiancé by car and they had called on Kurt and Hedi after that, but had not heard from them since the beginning of April. She had nothing outstanding to relate except that she had taken Manny's precious engine with her to Pomerania and he had been almost more thrilled than when Father Christmas had brought it in the first place.

Rosemarie was surprised that I had not yet secured a swell job with the British. In her temperamental way she said: 'If I were in your position, I would be the Queen of Hamburg by now!' She had, by coincidence, been born in England. On the strength of this she was thinking of applying for British nationality and to this end had already penetrated into the Displaced Persons Department at the Atlantic Hotel (now temporarily used as offices by the British). She said they had a number of German men and women working there as interpreters and secretaries. As I had already decided to look for a job, I thought I might as well try my luck there.

Not long after Rosemarie's visit I walked into the spacious hall of the Atlantic Hotel and on enquiring where I could find the DP Office, I was told the number of the room, was swept to the appropriate floor in the lift, and then left to my own devices. In answer to my tap on the door a lieutenant appeared and I asked him if they needed an English-German interpreter-secretary or knew of anybody who did. He was astonished to hear my English voice so I briefly explained the circumstances. He told me to wait in another room while he retired, obviously to report to his seniors. In the room I was shown into, sitting at a desk with a typewriter near the door, was one of the most striking young girls I had seen for a long time. She was fairly small but well proportioned, and was wearing a vividly coloured cotton dirndl dress. Her face was as bright and charming as her dress, with no trace of bored sophistication. From the first moment I liked her and, as it turned out, the attraction was mutual for Hedwig Widegreen became one of my best friends. What struck me immediately about her was her vivacity, although she hardly spoke a word whilst I waited in that room. Later she told me that she was most struck with what she called 'my fine musical voice'! Another silent spectator was a pleasant-looking man in his twenties. The main conversation was carried on by another young woman, sitting near the window, who was also attractive, but not in a way that appealed to me so much, although I found her good company. She was tall, dark and elegant, and extremely self-possessed.

I had barely time to sum up the three of them before I was called in to an interview with Captain Tomlinson, the head of the department. He was standing at a large desk with a lieutenant on each side. I was asked to sit on a sofa opposite them and after a short informal conversation in which he enquired a few details about my qualifications, he asked me whether I could start work there and then that afternoon! I suspect that even if I had been a poor shorthand-typist it would not have altered his decision to engage me. The fact that I spoke perfect English, and obviously must have at least a working knowledge of German, was sufficient recommendation. For my part, I thought he would be a pleasant person to work for and I hoped the job would prove interesting. I was not keen, however, to stay that afternoon, as it was my birthday, so I arranged to start work the next morning.

As I walked up the street afterwards, I chuckled to myself at the casual way in which everything had taken place – such a contrast to the business-like methods of the Germans, who would have wanted references and my *'Lebenslauf'* (life story), and a signed agreement as to conditions and hours of work, holidays, salary, and so on. I suddenly realized that none of these matters had been touched upon by Captain Tomlinson or by me!

Later on I discovered I was to receive my pay not from the British, but from an office in the town that received money from the German State for these purposes, as the Germans were responsible for occupation costs. There were various grades of pay and I was given the maximum salary for the highest grade female secretary-interpreter. This, after various deductions for insurance, tax, etc., amounted at that time to about 250 RM per month. I paid 50 RM rent and about 16 RM on fares per month, so that there was ample surplus.

For my birthday present Linda invited me to supper and promised I would for once be able to eat until I had had sufficient. To this end she had taken great pains to buy food at fantastic prices on the black market.

From that evening onwards, 29 May 1945, I was never really famished again because I was given a substantial midday meal from the English canteen every day, but it took four weeks before all my bodily functions returned to normal working order.

TWENTY-EIGHT

Starting the new job marked the beginning of a new phase in more ways than one. It was the first time for eight years that I had come into daily contact with English people and it was the first time in my life that I had had contact with anything or anybody pertaining to the Army.

I did not have to wait many weeks before the next step was prepared for me. One evening when I got back to Wandsbek, as soon as I saw Linda, I knew something exciting had happened. She said: 'A Captain Brown has called and asked for you. He left no message excepting to say that he had been sent through the Red Cross and would like you to call and see him in the Town Majors' office in Standard House tomorrow at ten o'clock.' We were all agog. Who could this mysterious Captain Brown be? I hardly dared whisper to myself that he *might* bring a message from home, but Linda was quite sure it must be so. I had given Linda's address because I knew she would always be there and could contact me, whereas I might have to change my lodgings for some reason. Therefore what other English person could possibly know her address unless he was sent through my relatives? I was burning to see him.

It seemed a long while to wait until the morning, but at last the appointed hour drew near. The Town Major soon relieved me of all suspense by saying his sister, who was in charge of the Red Cross office at his home town of East Grinstead, had asked him to look me up. My people had sent messages to me all through the war via Miss Brown and had now taken her my address in Hamburg which they had received from Mr Duckworth. Officially there were no means of sending messages yet, but Miss Brown was delighted that she was able to help through her brother who, she knew, would co-operate, thus bringing her work for one correspondent to a successful conclusion. I was completely overwhelmed by the good news, the extraordinary coincidence and by Captain Brown's sympathetic attitude. I told him I had never mentioned our divorce in my Red Cross messages, nor the fact that Manny had been taken from me. How could I have bluntly transmitted such news in twenty-five words? In any case what was the good of worrying them with my troubles so long as they could do nothing about it? We decided, however, that now a full report should be made, so Captain Brown offered to write details and let me know their reply. Then he asked: 'I suppose you don't want to change your job? I badly need a secretary-interpreter.' I jumped at this opportunity because Captain Tomlinson had been transferred elsewhere and work had slackened off in our department so that I was thoroughly bored. Captain Brown went straight away to ask our officer in charge if he would release me, and having settled the matter amicably, told me I could start work for him in the Town Major's office the next day.

One of the biggest advantages of the job was the safeguard it gave to the house where I lived. Soon after I started work for Captain Brown, Herr Schnur, my landlord, dropped a bombshell by saying I would have to move back into the tiny box room, as he intended putting someone else into the big room, which he had always promised *I* could retain. When I reminded him of this promise he said, 'Times have changed, the Housing Department say that the small room is large enough for one person.' I said, 'I am now working for the Town Major and I can easily get official permission to keep the big room, as I am expecting my son to return, in fact my presence will protect your house from being requisitioned.' I would not have minded so much moving into the box room myself, but I was determined not to stay where I could not accommodate Manny at a moment's notice. Supposing Manny arrived and I had no lodging to offer him? As usual, however, something happened which steered the course for me. Linda mentioned my plight to Frau Lippert, the friendly neighbour who gave me a warm welcome the first day I arrived in Hamburg. That afternoon another neighbour, Frau Seelig, visited Frau Lippert and told her she was very worried because some English officers had stopped outside her garden fence in the morning and had eyed the house with great interest. Frau Lippert said, 'Frau Falkenberg is looking for a room for herself and her son if he turns up, and wherever she lives the house will not be requisitioned, because she works for the Town Major.' This set Frau Seelig thinking. By the time I came back from work that evening she and her husband had left a message with Linda asking me to call to talk it over. As I walked up the drive I took a good look at the house and was favourably impressed. It was large and well-built, surrounded by a good-sized garden. Herr and Frau Seelig were exceptionally nice people. He was one of the top dogs in the corn trade and was a typical example of the honest, reliable Hamburg merchant.

In spite of their wealth there was nothing ostentatious about the house. Good taste and quality of workmanship were apparent throughout. Frau Seelig was vivacious, impulsive and extremely warm-hearted. I felt immediately that we would be good friends. She explained, 'We have our full quota as far as the German Housing Department is concerned (one person per room, not counting the office) excepting one empty room which we are allowed to keep for our three sons who are prisoners of war; the youngest, who is with the English, is expected home any day now; the second is in Italy, and the eldest missing in Russia. There are seven of us here already and we cannot be compelled to take anyone else, but we live in constant fear that the house will be requisitioned by the English as it is one of the few undamaged properties in this district. We were so happy to have saved it and would be broken-hearted if our sons came back from the war to find we had no home for them. If you would care to take our sons' room we would be pleased to have you and if your son comes, we could let him sleep in a little dressing-room adjoining our bedroom. You could then sit in your room in the evenings without disturbing him. You need bring no furniture and I would provide the bedding. My maid would clean your room. We can empty part of a cupboard for you to use in the kitchen and some shelves in the cellar. I can promise you that we would do everything possible to make you comfortable.'

Needless to say I did not hesitate to accept this offer. The Housing Department naturally agreed to the proposal and I moved in the next evening.

Captain Brown had left Hamburg by now, so I asked my new boss, Major Holcombe, if an index card might be filed for Herr Seelig's house marked 'Reserved for the Town Major'. He kindly agreed and gave instructions for this to be done. I thought that by this means any application for the house would be refused at the outset, because the index cards were always consulted before further enquiries were made. We had a lot of cards marked for properties which for some reason or another were considered worthy of protection.

To my horror, on returning the very next evening I was met by a frenzied Frau Seelig, her eyes red with weeping. On the front door was the fatal requisition label! I could hardly believe my own eyes and assured Frau Seelig there must be some misunderstanding. 'Oh no, it is true, it is true! They came this morning, the officers I saw looking at the house from the road a few days ago. They had no interpreter and could speak no German. I tried to explain the situation to them, that you live here, but I could not make them understand. They looked over the house, pasted the label on the door and then left without saying a word. Now we shall be turned out. Our sons will come and find strangers in their home. Oh, what can we do? *Please*, Frau Falkenberg, can you help us?' We all spent a night of agonizing unrest and doubt, and I was never so glad to get to my job as I was the next morning. I went straight to the index cards. Yes, there it was

– a new card made out for our house, requisitioned for an officers' mess! Permission had already been given and instructions for eviction were being prepared. Where was the original card? I hunted through the trays and eventually found it, shoved in out of alphabetical order. I rushed to Major Holcombe to ask if he could help. He was most understanding and said he would do his best. Later on in the morning he came to tell me that all would be well, the house was being relinquished and alternative accommodation had been found. Nevertheless I did not feel safe for days, fearing that some mortal might slip up again during the process of derequisitioning the property, but the machinery worked '*wie am Schnürchen*', without a hitch.

Major Holcombe advised me to type out a notice in English and in German stating that the house was reserved for the Town Major. He signed this over the official stamp and told me to stick it on the front door. With this precious document I then returned in triumph and tore off the hateful requisition label. We put the typed notice on the inside door in case it got spoilt by the rain.

Thus the situation was saved and, although numerous other officers came from time to time to inspect the house with a view to requisitioning it, they never dared to penetrate beyond the notice on the front door. This label also mightily impressed the German Housing Department officials who came on routine inspections.

It was a great relief to feel secure in a comfortable house. All the same we could not help thinking of the poor devils who had been turned out instead of us. We had been so near the brink of disaster ourselves that I was even more sorry now for the families which were being evicted every day in some part of the town. The knowledge that they were a defeated people who had been misled, or had brought ruin on the nation through their own violent deeds, did not make it any more pleasant to witness their punishment, especially as it was the women and children who suffered most.

Considering that nobody was allowed more than one room, I could not have been more comfortable anywhere in Hamburg, nor in a more friendly household. I can honestly say that in spite of our numbers and various ages, I never had a cross word or the suspicion of a difference with any of them. We all went our own ways without interfering with each other. I used Frau Seelig's kitchen and, as they had their main meal at midday when I was out, this presented no difficulty.

They allotted me a delightful corner of the garden where I could sit undisturbed. An oblong niche was cut out of a high hedge in which there was gay garden furniture for my use only. On hot summer evenings I always had my supper in the garden and had a good bask in the sunshine on Sundays. The day on which the ban on fraternizing was raised was gloriously hot and sunny. It must have been a Saturday or a Sunday because I had invited Hedwig Widegreen and Reg (my friends in the DP Department) to tea. We lay on the lawn talking lazily or dozing, and Reg told us there would soon be a surprise announcement on the radio. He and Hedwig had arrived in Wandsbek by the same train, pretending not to know each other, and Reg had walked behind her down the street. He was determined to be the first to take advantage of the lifting of the ban, and when they left he strutted off with her arm in arm. That evening the streets were full of English soldiers and German girls who had previously only dared to meet surreptitiously after dark in parks or in German houses.

In our house there were three mothers, each with a son missing, not knowing whether he was alive or dead. (Frau Seelig had news of two of her sons). It is strange how the instinctive prediction of each mother proved to be correct. Frau Stiebel, although she hoped each day as much as we did for some miracle, had all along in her heart been convinced that she would never see her son again. In my case there was more hope because my son had not been in so much danger as the soldiers in the East. Although sometimes for days I would be in utter despair, the glimmer of optimism always returned. Frau Seelig was sure all her sons would come home – and they did.

The first to turn up was Günther, the youngest, a boy still in his teens. There followed weeks of anxiety with no news for any of us. Trainloads of returning prisoners of war rolled through Hamburg bringing relief and happiness to other parents, but not to us. There was not even a message from a passing comrade.

Then at last one day the Seeligs' eldest son, Herbert, walked into the house, but he had altered so much that no one recognized him at first. He had been in a camp in Siberia, and in spite of the fact that a motherly woman in Berlin had carried him into her home from the street, where he had collapsed from exhaustion, and had fed him for a fortnight, he was still emaciated. The hair of two or three weeks' growth on his head stood out in spikes. The skin on his face was greenish-yellow, sagging over hollow cheeks. He had a little pot-belly, and the rest of his body was nothing but skin and bones. His digestive organs were ruined. Poor Frau Seelig laughed and cried simultaneously with the pleasure of his return and the pain of his illness. Very gradually, very carefully she tried to bring his diet back to normal.

Kurt Seelig, the third son, was not released until after I had left Germany.

A branch of the British Red Cross was eventually opened in Hamburg and Major Holcombe was good enough to take me along to enquire about the possibility of finding relatives in the Eastern zone. Unfortunately they were unable to make any suggestions at all. A little while later a German office was set up where all persons seeking relatives could register their names and addresses and the names of those whom they wished to contact. These were then sent to a central department who tried to link up the people with each other. I made enquiries there and they registered my name and address, but said that so far they had no communication with the Russian zone, except by chance word of mouth through refugees.

There was of course no postal service between the Eastern and Western zones, so there was nothing further I could do for the time being but wait.

TWENTY-NINE

It cannot have been many Sunday mornings after Herbert's appearance that Linda burst into my room with the news that Kurt had turned up at her house and was on his way round to see me. She had taken a short cut through the gardens to prepare me for the surprise. My first question of course was: 'And Manny, where is he?'

'He is in Hamburg-Rainbeck where Kurt, Hedi and her mother are staying.' It seemed almost too good to be true. But sure enough, I only just had time to fling the blankets and eiderdown on my bed (which was having its weekly airing), before I saw Kurt coming up the garden path. He looked gaunt, weary and sad. In the ten or eleven months since I had seen him he had changed remarkably and I realized how badly he had been hit by the collapse of Germany and the loss of his position and property. On his face were the clear signs of mental suffering and physical strain.

He said Manny was all right. He had not brought him, nor even told him he was coming to look for me, in case he found I was no longer alive.

Briefly he recounted their experiences.

'The camp in Pomerania was closed down after Hedi, her mother (Oma) and Manny left, and I was able to join them. We hoped to come to Hamburg then, but there was no transport and it was impossible to get away quickly enough. The Russians overtook us while we were walking on the road leading to Rostock. We hid in a ditch on the edge of a wood as the tanks roared past, shooting at everybody within range. Before I was rounded up as a prisoner of war I got permission for Oma, Hedi and Manny to stay in the hospital at Rostock for a day or two. After a rest there they made their way westwards on foot, accepting any sort of a lift which they were lucky enough to be offered. Sometimes it would only be a little way in a cart. Sometimes they would walk for days with no lift at all. They had to beg for food and lodgings and thought themselves fortunate if they were given a crust of bread and a glass of milk in a barn with straw to sleep on.'

Kurt had not mentioned Baby Uwe so I asked how they had managed to feed him. 'Uwe died whilst we were being overtaken by the Russians. He had twisted intestines and we were unable to reach a hospital in time for him to have an operation, which would have saved his life.'

So dear little Uwe was dead. I remembered how good he had been in the cattle truck when we left Bromberg, and could see his sweet round face beaming with pleasure at the sight of his bottle. I remembered how Manny had played with him on the sofa in Berlin, bouncing him sky-high.

Uwe's death was a terrible shock to them all, including Manny. Months later he was still brooding over it, because one day, without any previous conversation on the subject, he said to me, 'He was lying quietly in his pram and I didn't know he was dead.' When I asked, 'Who do you mean, darling?' he said, 'Uwe. Then they told me he was dead and they carried him away and buried him.' Hedi told me Manny was so upset that he could not stop crying for hours. Uwe was one of the dearest babies that ever lived and Manny loved him as if he had been his own brother.

'The Russians tried to stop all German refugees from leaving the Eastern zone,' Kurt continued, 'so Oma and Hedi pretended they were making their way to Hamburg in order to return to their native South America. They always speak Spanish together anyway, and whenever Russian offi- cials approached them they made out that they did not know much German. Manny had to be coached to answer, when interrogated, that Hedi was his mother and that his father was dead. I managed to get released from the Russian prison camp by temporarily producing signs of severe illness, and finally, with more luck than good judgment, escaped across the frontier.' Kurt went on, 'Hedi, Oma and Manny arrived in Hamburg a short time before I did and went to some friends of hers where we had arranged to meet. On the way she had been obliged gradually to discard most of their belongings because she was too weak to carry them. Everything I possessed, except what I stand up in, was taken from me in the Russian prison camp. My securities and insurances are worthless. The deposits I had in the Bromberg bank cannot be claimed. I have no job, no money, no instruments and no home. My only assets are knowledge and experience. However, if I can get official permission to stay in the British zone, I shall make an application to be allowed to start a practice, when it may be possible to obtain a loan for the purchase of necessary instruments. The outlook is not encouraging, but so far we are still alive, which is something to be thankful for. Manny is fairly well now, except that he suffers from diarrhoea, which so far I have been unable to cure. In Pomerania he had asthma and bronchitis, and only just escaped a mastoid. Neighbours have been very kind in giving us clothes for him which Oma is mending or cutting down to size.'

Kurt suggested that Manny should come to live with me now, and go to stay with him about once in every three months after he got settled. This seemed reasonable enough to me. My people in England had from the outset persistently urged that I should return to England straight away, *without* Manny, and then have him sent over if and when he was found. My refusal to do this met with their strong disapproval, but nothing and nobody would have induced me to leave Germany without Manny.

Now that he was safely in Hamburg, although I told Kurt my people would welcome us at home, I could not bring myself to suggest that we should go to England. Until Kurt turned up that morning neither of us had been able to formulate any definite plans about Manny because neither of us knew whether the other still existed, nor in what circumstances they were placed. It was impossible for me, still less for Kurt, to make far-reaching decisions of this nature on the spur of the moment. Besides which it went strongly against the grain for *me* to suggest that he should part with his only child – maybe for good. In any case it would be no light matter for him to determine that his son should be brought up in a foreign country. If, after due consideration, Kurt came to the conclusion that it would be best for Manny to go to England, I knew he would make the sacrifice, but then the suggestion would come from him, which would be much better for the child, because it would be sure proof that his parents were not in conflict on such an important subject. I knew Manny would suffer if we had a dispute and for this reason I wanted to avoid trouble with Kurt at all costs. I knew his temperament well enough to realize that he would need time to work out the problem quietly in his own mind. Until this process had taken place he would be incapable of passing an opinion. Manny would not benefit from any over-hasty action or any attempt to force irrevocable decisions, and I must wait once more.

When my people at home heard the good news of Manny's safe arrival in Hamburg, but that no plans had as yet been made for our immediate repatriation, there was considerable bitterness. They did not understand my position now any better than they had understood it before when I said I would wait in Germany until I had found my son. It was again impossible to explain the intricacies of the situation in letters which were supposed to be written by a third party (who was more or less a stranger to me and a complete stranger to them) and which were also liable to be read by the censor. My English friends in Hamburg who took the risk of breaking the regulations out of kindness to me by forwarding my letters, would naturally be punished if the censor became suspicious and discovered their crime. Everything therefore had to be veiled in somewhat vague terms. Steeped in the security of England, my people could not begin to visualize the complications of my official status as a German subject.

For my part, on that Sunday morning, my cup of happiness was full enough for the time being. Manny was alive and he would be shortly coming to live with me. That was sufficient so far – the future would take care of itself.

Kurt suggested that Manny should spend his birthday in Rainbeck and move to his new quarters with me the day after, 7 September.

Our conversation during the morning was interrupted by an unexpected phone call. I ran downstairs to Herr Seelig's office and a familiar voice answered.

'Hullo Sybil, this is Max. I am a prisoner of war on my ship. We have just docked in Hamburg and are allowed out on parole.'

The very morning that Kurt appeared out of the blue, so did his brother. I had not seen or heard of either of them since March, neither did they know each other's whereabouts. It was ironical that I, of all people, should be the connecting link for the family. Through Max, Kurt was also able to hear news of his father who had taken over a practice in the French zone, where Frieda (Max's wife) had joined him with Volker and his little sister.

Max was on the high seas when the war finished and had been kept on the ship ever since. Some time previously, while in the Navy, he had passed his finals as a doctor and as soon as he was free he proposed to join his father, who badly needed help. The work in the country practice was much too strenuous for the old man and Max was hoping that on compassionate grounds his release would be speeded up.

I left the two brothers busily talking whilst I prepared as good a meal as I could muster at short notice. I slipped round to tell Linda and Manfred my news and they invited Max and me to tea as Kurt was leaving in the early afternoon.

We four then went for a walk in the cool of the evening,

after which Max returned to his prison-ship. Shortly afterwards he was transferred elsewhere and then allowed to go home, so that I did not see him again.

All the inhabitants of the house rejoiced with me that Manny was found and was soon to move in, and Frau Seelig helped me to make the necessary preparations. She went with me to the Labour Exchange where she knew the head of the domestic department, and asked her to send me a suitable young girl to look after Manny during the daytime.

About a week before Manny was due to move, Kurt came to see me again. He had been considering carefully the possibilities for Manny's future, having regard to his own position and mine, and the international situation. Kurt's fate was undecided. The outlook for Germany was increasingly grim. Food supplies were diminishing and the already half-starved population, who could not afford black-market prices and had nothing to barter, were faced with a winter of even more severe hardships. Fuel was practically unobtainable. Those who survived the winter could not expect improved conditions in the following year, nor for many years to come. There was no security, no opportunity for advancement.

In England we hoped there would be a good home waiting for us, everything that a child needs, stability and freedom. As a British citizen the doors of the world would be open to him. Kurt therefore suggested that I should apply for repatriation for Manny and myself forthwith, and that we should then put in our claim for British nationality.

Thus once again, without taking any active steps, a clear path lay before me, indicating a major change, which was to affect Manny and myself for the rest of our lives.

As yet no civilians of German nationality had been repatriated to England and I was told that there were long waiting lists. The information I gave had to be checked. The formal consent of my father to give us a home and to pay our fares over had to be sent to the Home Office in London. When the hundreds of applications had been sifted out and the deserving ones eventually approved, there was still the question of obtaining passages in a troopship. The date of our departure could, therefore, not even be roughly estimated. Under the circumstances, in case there was a long delay, I thought it best to continue working just the same, as Kurt was unable to give me financial assistance. Manny was now six years old, and we decided to send him to the local elementary school.

The great day of his arrival at last drew near. Kurt had promised to bring him in time for tea and I had a spread of luxuries ready which I had been given for the occasion or had made from ingredients saved up during the preceding weeks. The timely arrival of a wonderful parcel from home (through a devious course) contributed largely to the display. The table was decorated with brightly-coloured flowers from the garden and candles were burning in attractive candlesticks, lent to me by Frau Seelig, which added a festive touch.

I was ready long before the appointed time, waiting at the window to see him approach. At last Kurt's head appeared, just visible above the hedge, and a few seconds later he opened the gate to let Manny pass through. In the seven and a half months since I had last seen him he had hardly grown at all. His usually fat, rosy cheeks were deathly pale and pinched. He was thin all over, except for a little pot belly. Before they reached the front door I had leapt down the stairs and run into the garden. I picked Manny up and raised him high in the air. At that moment everybody from the house appeared to welcome him and in a flash we were surrounded by sympathetic well-wishers. Several of us were laughing and crying at the same time. Manny was too bewildered to show much excitement; in fact it seemed as though he had become dulled through subjection to so many new impressions – most of them unpleasant – and to the ever-changing surroundings over the past months. I was more than ever thankful to be in a position to give him a home in a nice house, where he could at last settle down quietly until our final move to England.

Having never been parted from Manny before for any length of time, I did not know what his reactions would be or whether he would feel strange to be with me again, but there was no need for any misgivings on this score. Once we were in my room he behaved exactly as though he had only been out to tea or away for a day or so. He was bursting to show me his new possessions which had to be unpacked immediately. There were a few old toys which his friends in Rainbeck had passed on to him as parting gifts – fabulous treasures in his eyes, especially a wooden aeroplane about twelve inches from wing to wing. It was pathetic to see what an interest such a small boy also took in his newly-acquired clothes, not as a little girl would do, because she liked finery, but simply because he had become fully aware of the value of such articles. Only a few weeks before he had been a ragged, destitute child, begging for food and shelter. Now he had toys (such as they were) and two complete changes of clothing, including pyjamas, and – his trump card – a *Lodenmantel* (a raincoat with a hood), which he pulled out of the suitcase with a quick smiling gesture, like a conjuror producing an unexpected rabbit out of a hat. Nothing was new, but thanks to Oma, all the garments were neat and presentable. My bed was strewn with his things.

The unpacking completed, he found time to explore the room. His eyes nearly popped out of his head at the sight of the food and we soon sat down to a good tuck-in. I was horrified to see how hungry he was. We could not stop him gobbling, until I eventually had to remove the plates for fear that he would make himself sick. Kurt told me that he was still suffering from stomach disorder and diarrhoea, which had not been improved by his eating a large lump of yeast picked up in the bakehouse belonging to the father of one of his friends.

It was clear that Manny had passed through a very bad patch, the effects of which it was difficult to assess straight away – in fact the lack of nutrition necessary for bone formation did not manifest itself until six months after we had been in England. It was surprising, though, how quickly he lost the pinched look. When Kurt came to see him a fortnight later his cheeks were already plump and his pot belly was dwindling fast. I was fortunately in a position to feed him well as I had lunch out and Linda offered to give him a good meal every day, so that he could have nearly all my rations, besides his own, for breakfast and supper. English friends gave him chocolate. Besides parcels from home, now that we were on the list of those applying for repatriation, I also received a large carton of tinned foods each month from the Canadian Red Cross. During the summer fruit and vegetables were more plentiful. Frau Seelig had a quince tree opposite the kitchen window from which she allowed me to pick as much fruit as I liked. It was delicious mixed with a small quantity of apple (instead of in the customary reversed proportions). I bottled several pumpkins (cut into small cubes) in sugar, vinegar and water in large earthenware jars. The first time Manny saw pineapple chunks in England he thought it was pumpkin as it looks just the same. I also pickled runner beans in earthenware jars as glass screw-top bottles were unobtainable.

When I had more bread coupons than we needed for current use I bought *Knäckebrot*, a sort of Ryvita, which I stored in case there was a shortage of bread or potatoes later on.

Manny soon became very attached to *Tante* Seelig whose kindness we shall never forget. Having had three sons of her own she was most understanding, and even lent Manny precious toys, such as beautiful model yachts which he floated by the hour in the bath. She often gave him presents too from her store of pre-war treasures. When Saint Nikolaus came overnight he left a bright red boot filled with sweets in front of Manny's door, also a snowman and a glittering little snow-covered house, both used to this day as money-boxes.

Manny had instructions to come to my bedroom each morning as quietly as he could when he woke up. Frau Seelig told me that if she kept her eyes shut he crept through their bedroom without a word or a sound. If she opened them he went to her bedside and gave her a kiss. When I felt lazy and pretended to be asleep he slipped silently into my bed or got dressed, according to how he felt inclined, otherwise there would be a continuous running commentary on all his activities. On the rare occasions when I went out for the whole evening Frau Seelig was always willing to put him to bed.

Another of Manny's favourites in the house was Frau Seelig's maid, Ilse. Whilst I was getting the breakfast he invariably disappeared into the cellar where he discovered she would at that time be cleaning shoes. She was very fond of him and they always enjoyed each other's company.

At first Manny did not get on well with his lessons. Linda was wonderfully patient and spent an hour or more every afternoon helping him. As there were so few teachers and only a limited number of classrooms available, the younger children did not have a full morning's lessons and were given homework instead. It seemed as though Manny could not get the hang of it, and then suddenly, for no apparent reason, the penny dropped, and he mastered his phonetics and sums. From that day on he picked up everything quickly with little effort. Within two months he could read anything we put before him (even if he did not understand it) and spell correctly from dictation.

He, of course, loved being read to. Kurt gave him a book of Grimm's fairy stories, and the promise of hearing one of these before going to bed was sufficient to put a prompt end to all other games. The stories I told him about my home and relatives were equally interesting to him but he found it difficult to distinguish between fiction and reality.

Since Manny had been taken away from me he had forgotten every word of English. However, he quickly learned to understand simple, everyday conversation, but nothing would induce him to speak English himself. I hoped he would pick it up as soon as he found that no one at home understood German, but I was a little worried because one of my Army friends thought he would be seriously handicapped if he could not speak the language from the outset. He also thought Manny's German manners, such as the polite bow when he shook hands, would cause derision. As it turned out these misgivings proved unfounded, for he soon adapted himself to new conditions. When my friend met us in London three months after our departure from Germany, he was flabbergasted at being confronted by a small boy speaking and behaving as if he had lived in England all his life. Only a slightly rolled 'r' was still noticeable. But it is a fact that the quick change was only superficial, because for many years he had difficulty in expressing himself in writing, and suffered severe drawbacks in his lessons through the switch-over from German to English.

Although I always spoke English to him in Hamburg when we were alone, this was, of course, only for a short time in the mornings and evenings, as I was away at my job all day. Even at the weekends he naturally spent most of the day playing with his numerous friends in the neighbourhood. The ruins which surrounded us on all sides may have looked depressing to grown-ups, but for children, who could not remember the houses as they had stood originally, the numerous secret passages and hide-outs were wonderful haunts for adventurous games. Manny and his chums were hardly ever visible when they were playing, although they were never far away. When I wanted Manny to come in I had just to walk round the gardens or into the street calling his name as loudly as I could until he made an appearance.

In the autumn it is a custom in Hamburg for children to

walk in a procession through the town after dark carrying
coloured lanterns held on long sticks and singing:

> *Laterne, Laterne,*
> *Sonne, Mond und Sterne,*
> *Lösche aus das Licht,*
> *Lösche aus das Licht,*
> *Aber nur meine liebe Laterne nicht!*
> *Meine Laterne ist so schön,*
> *Da kann man 'mit spazieren gehn,*
> *In den grünen Wald,*
> *Wo die Büchse knallt.*

Manny was all agog to join them. Frau Seelig gave him
three beautiful lanterns and we set off one evening with a
party of about twenty in all. The excitement of the children
was infectious and there was something strangely fascinating
about this expedition. Every now and again we would see
other groups of lanterns bobbing along in the distance and
hear the treble voices ringing through the night air like an
echo to our own song. When we arrived at the level-crossing
we had to wait for a long train to pass. It was packed with
Germans returning from prisoner-of-war camps. As each
carriage came along we could see the men's faces light up
suddenly as they caught sight of the gay lanterns. They
sprang to the windows, cheering and waving until they were
out of sight. A few weeks later I happened to talk to a man
who told me that his first welcome home from the war had
been from a lantern procession at a railway crossing, and I
wondered whether it had been our little group. He said he
and his comrades had been overcome with emotion at the
sight of the familiar scene which stirred up memories of their
own childhood and brought them to the realization that
their homecoming was now a fact, not a vague dream.

THIRTY

As we passed from October into November with still no sign of our permit for repatriation, I began to fear that there was little chance of getting home before Christmas. The English Consul-General in Hamburg, who knew the Town Majors, was most helpful and gave me the reference number of my application and an address in London where he said it might be possible to persuade the officials to expedite the issue of the papers if someone could call there personally. I passed this information on to my people and it was no doubt owing to Mu's visit there with her husband that our permit (picked out of hundreds of applications) was amongst the first to be granted. Immediately it came through the Consul-General telephoned the good news to me and told me to call on him as soon as possible. I was given time off and went over to him straight away. Everything was in order but he could not say how long we would have to wait for a passage. It must have been towards the end of November or the beginning of December. The RTO told me he would do his best to get us home for Christmas, but could make no promises, and asked me to call again in three days' time. When I went back he said he had been able to book passages for us to leave Hamburg on 13 December. This news was immediately telegraphed to my people.

A period of feverish activity followed, winding up my business and personal connections, arranging what was to happen to the goods and money I could not take with me, trying to buy or barter for various things I needed for the journey. Frau Seelig had introduced me to one of the best fashion salons in Hamburg, Madame Pauly, who had designed as many clothes for me as I could obtain coupons for. (Civilians working for English authorities were given special clothing chits.) Another friend's neighbour, who was a dressmaker, made a jacket and trousers for Manny out of one of my grey rugs. Silk stockings, obtained through the office, were swopped for a thick canvas bag with leather corners. In return for introducing the Town Majors to a leather merchant and a shoemaker, I was allowed to buy some leather with which I had four handbags, a suitcase and a pair of shoes made.

Nobody knew how much money I would be allowed to take with me, as apparently no regulations had as yet been issued. First of all we were told it would only be one pound. My father had already sent a cheque for twenty-six pounds to London for our fares to England, but the tickets only took us as far as the port of entry, which was Hull. The pound would of course not nearly cover our train fares from Hull to Sussex, so this meant another SOS to my people. Mu replied that she would meet us in Hull and had booked rooms there for the night at the Station Hotel.

Another question was how much luggage we would be allowed to take. Here again nobody had the slightest idea, but it was presumed that we should only reckon on a very limited amount. On one of my visits to the RTO I met a young woman who said she had so many trunks that she knew they would never let her take them all. I remarked that I had a few possessions but no trunk to take them in. She immediately offered to lend me a small cabin trunk which, on my arrival in England, I could forward to an address she gave me. She was a complete stranger, but neither of us doubted that the other would keep her word. The empty trunk duly arrived at my home in Wandsbek and proved a godsend, as the suitcase would have been quite inadequate.

It was a relief to know that we would soon be stepping into a new life, free from the fear of cold and hunger, but I felt desperately sorry for those I was leaving behind, faced with the dreaded winter. Avenues of trees gradually disappeared, as night after night they were hacked down for firewood. Nearly all the offices and houses were only equipped with central heating, which was useless owing to lack of fuel; consequently people wore coats and mufflers all day indoors and went to bed early in the evening in an effort to get warm and to save their ration of electricity for more pressing needs. Most households managed to rig up some sort of a stove in one room which was lit when fuel could be obtained.

A few days before the date fixed for our departure Manny developed a cough and his temperature rose alarmingly. I called in the doctor who had attended me when I was ill on my arrival in Hamburg and who had also come to Manny several weeks previously when he had had chicken-pox. This doctor had for some reason been knocked off the register, probably because he had been a Party member, and he was still awaiting the result of his appeal. As I knew him to be an extremely efficient and hardworking doctor, who had always done his duty towards his fellow men, and particularly as he had been so kind to me when I was ill – a refugee with no resources – I had no intention of going to a stranger. He had been the family doctor and a close friend of the Seeligs for many years and came to my help immediately. He said Manny had an attack of bronchitis and that there could be no question of his being well enough to undertake the long journey by 13 December. Needless to say this was a great disappointment, especially as it was now improbable that we would be able to get home before Christmas. It entailed more hectic telegrams all round. The RTO was once again most helpful and after all managed to book us passages on a boat leaving Cuxhaven on 21 December. We kept our fingers crossed, hoping that Manny would be all right by then.

Before we realized it, 21 December was upon us. Manny was in a whirl of excitement, especially as he was able to take all his toys this time. He packed the dilapidated relics into the new canvas bag and this was more precious to him than all the rest of the luggage.

We had to be at Altona Bahnhof at about 9 p.m., I think. I know it was long after dark. There were no taxis, of course, so I accepted the offer of one of the Town Majors to take us to the station in his jeep. When he came to fetch us the house was full of neighbours and Manny's school friends who had flocked in to say goodbye. He did not understand German and the jabbering multitude must have presented rather a strange spectacle to him. With the luggage in the back and Manny and me perched in front, we drove off amidst a chorus of '*Lebewohl* Sybil, *Lebewohl* Manny!' Nobody called '*Aufwiedersehen*', as though we were driving off to the moon and would never return. Linda and Manfred and several others came to the station to see us off. I had had such a rush to make my final arrangements that I still could not realize we were really leaving. It was not until the train slowly pulled out of the station and the familiar faces of my friends grew smaller and smaller that the inevitability of the parting struck home. Would I ever see them again? Would they survive the winter? How long would we have to wait before we could correspond? Even so, would we ever be able to describe our new experiences in a changing world? We had been through thick and thin together during the war and understood each reaction to the shifting circumstances. Now our paths diverged.

Manny was oblivious to any farewell pangs. In spite of the late hour he was wide awake and enjoying himself to the full. There were only five civilians on the crowded military train and he was the only child. Consequently everybody made a fuss of him, brought him fruit and sweets, and tried to understand his unceasing flow of questions in German. He seemed far too excited to realize that everybody round him was now speaking English, or if he did, this may have contributed to the sense of being the central figure in a fairy story. We were indeed transported into a strange dream-world. Instead of having to rush up and down, laden with baggage, in a vain endeavour to find a seat, we were conducted straight to a reserved compartment. Our trunk and large case were whisked away by invisible hands straight into our cabin on the boat. Everything possible was arranged for our convenience. As soon as we arrived in Cuxhaven, we were escorted to a brilliantly lit dining hall, decorated with balloons, flags, garlands and fir branches, where we were invited to partake of a banquet served by flunkeys, right and left. In sombre retrospect I realize it was quite an ordinary supper – but to us that night everything was tinged with the magic of novelty. I had not had a coupon-free meal in a restaurant since before the war. Manny had never been inside a restaurant, because far more nourishing meals could be concocted at home for fewer food coupons. At one end a man was icing an enormous cake in the form of a ship about five feet long. It was perfect in every detail. I had to tear Manny away from watching this fascinating operation because a car was waiting to take us to a hotel. Our boat was held up in the fog, but I was told to keep myself in readiness as it was hoped that we would be able to embark within a few hours. We would be called by means of a loudspeaker in the corner of our bedroom. I put Manny to bed and lay on top of mine, fully dressed, in case they did not allow us much time to get ready. I guessed Manny would have to be carried if we went in the middle of the night because he would be doped with heavy sleep. It was already well after midnight. I dozed on and off. Dawn broke, but still we were not called – in fact the whole of that day we had to wait in the hotel. We were not allowed out even for a little stroll, in case a message should come through from the harbour whilst we were gone. The lounges were packed with officers who were also waiting for our boat, impatient to get home to their families for Christmas. At the bar I had the excitement of buying my first packet of English cigarettes, some chocolate and tablets of good toilet soap, using a chit I had been given in Hamburg. At last, towards evening the fog lifted and we were taken to the boat. Manny and I were given a comfortable double-berth cabin. Although it was dark I had not the heart to restrain him from carrying out a thorough exploration of the boat – the first he had ever seen. He rushed up and down the gangways and corridors, chattering nineteen to the dozen in German all the time. He was wearing a little shoulder-bag (the one he used to carry his lunch in to the kindergarten) and every now and again he came back to the cabin to unpack this bag which was bulging each time with sweets and chocolate given to him by the soldiers.

After Manny had been at large for long enough, I went to look for him, and found him coming down from the top deck. He had just noticed the water gleaming white as it splashed up in our wake now that we were getting up steam. Standing on the steps, completely enthralled, he was calling everyone's attention to this wonderful sight. I had never seen him so excited about anything before. During the night we rolled about quite a good deal in the North Sea and Manny began to feel a little sick. As soon as I mentioned this to the steward in the morning, he brought him a light breakfast to the cabin after which he felt quite all right again. It was a Swedish ship which was supplied with food from Sweden and we were served with the most lavish meals.

I had often told him stories about England, my home and my people, but to him of course they remained 'stories', not distinguishable from the fairy stories he also loved to hear. Little Red Riding Hood or Hansel and Gretel were just as real to him as were my father or his aunts, uncles and cousins. The brightly coloured pictures in his books were no less alive than the photographs I showed him of my relatives.

We had to wait for high tide and it was dark before we slowly steamed into the harbour. Mu had been waiting for us in Hull all day, at one time seriously disturbed by news which came through that a leave-boat had been involved in a collision in the fog and the name of the boat was at first not reported. The docks where we were to land were at some murky spot, several miles out of the town. There seemed to be no end to the long drawn-out process of landing. Officials came on board to check our papers – such as they were. Considering the difficulties involved in gaining entry into England, it might be imagined that we would be given a sheaf of important documents to present to the authorities on our arrival, instead of which I merely had one narrow slip of paper to prove our identity. The only question I was asked was whether we were being met and had accommodation for the night. If not, everything would be arranged for us. I was handed another slip of paper (or it may even have been the same one) which I was told to take to our local Food Office who would make out our identity cards and ration books. Being English-born, there was no need to register or report to the police. I would be allowed to work now, when and where I liked in England. It seemed that once the initial entry permit had been granted, the portals were flung wide open. Yet it was with a certain fear that I surveyed the future. Had England and the English changed? Our experiences had differed so widely that difficulties might well be expected to arise in finding a basis for common understanding. Perhaps the six years spent in opposite camps would always lie between us, thrusting up spears of rancour at unguarded moments. Would the current hatred of Germans be reflected in the attitude of the average English person towards us? Would Manny be subjected to unpleasant treatment from children because he only spoke German? Would we feel like strangers and be treated as such? Or would individuals be as magnanimous as the State had been in admitting us to the fold without reserve? If we were not accepted on an equal footing we might find it overwhelmingly difficult to make headway and to adapt ourselves to the different mode of life. Supposing my official status as a German citizen prevented me from getting a decent job – an all-important question, considering that the main responsibility of bringing up Manny and educating him would inevitably rest on my shoulders? Until I was reunited with my people it was impossible to gauge their reactions. What would it be like at home without my mother? Now that we approached our destination, the bleak unknown loomed very close ahead. But surely we had nothing more to lose?

I was seized with many conflicting emotions as we leaned over the rail waiting to disembark, watching the rain patter into the gleaming puddles on the quayside – relief and anxiety, pleasure and pain, a longing to be safe and a fear of sacrificing independence.

We had only been able to leave Germany because Kurt and I were divorced and because England was on the winning side. The blows which had been rained upon us and the cataclysm which overcame Germany had relentlessly driven us across Europe towards my country. Nine and a quarter years earlier I had left England with a husband and considerable worldly possessions. Through a strange, inexorable sequence of events I was back where I started, except that I was practically penniless, and instead of a husband I had a son. I grasped him firmly by the hand and led him down the gangway. The wheel had turned full circle.

EPILOGUE

After our momentous journey from Hamburg, Manny, Mu and I spent one night in Hull, and arrived on Christmas Eve at my father's house in Uckfield. It was flowing with the warmth of our family gathering amidst the bright decorations and the logs crackling in the open fireplaces – a sight which was new to Manny. As soon as he had taken off his coat in the hall he walked straight into the dining room, knelt on the hearthrug and gazed into the flames. Then he turned to me with a slightly anxious expression and asked (in German), 'We're home at last, Mummy, aren't we?' When I replied, 'Yes, darling, we're home at last,' he smiled with relief and then wandered, entranced, from room to room. He and my father, jovial and still young at heart, at once became the best of pals. My sisters, Gwen and Mu, and Mu's husband Joe, were kindness itself. Now, after all our past traumas, Manny and I felt safe and secure.

Early in January, through a lucky coincidence, I was offered a job, as private secretary to the Hon. Mrs Ionides, the owner of Buxted Park, whose borders extended to the bottom of our lane. As well as the house, the estate included the park with its herd of fallow deer, a farm and glorious gardens. The house was full of the works of art which Mrs Ionides had collected herself, and she welcomed museum curators, art dealers, authors, artists and actors from all over the world. Queen Mary, herself a connoisseur, was a frequent visitor.

Manny soon learned to speak English again. He settled down well at a nearby school and later gained a place at Christ's Hospital, one of our greatest, most ancient boarding schools. Thus, to my enormous relief, his future was assured. He made good progress, which he has continued to do throughout his chosen career, and he and his lovely wife are my best friends.

I stayed with Mrs Ionides until her death, seventeen years later. For seven years after that I worked for a Tunbridge Wells antique dealer and interior decorator, but retired at sixty to look after my father. He was in his ninety-eighth year and failing in health, though still mentally alert, and as kind and loving as ever. Gwen and I nursed him at home until he died peacefully a few months later, surrounded by all his children and by Manny. After that I took part-time or temporary jobs in the area, helping people with their correspondence and accounts, until Gwen needed my full-time care at home, and she died in 1984. Since 1988 I have been the sole survivor of my generation in the family.

Soon after my return to England, I contacted all my friends and once a month I went up to London for singing lessons with my former teacher Dulcie Nutting at Morley College. Manny came with me and I showed him the sights of London. I was able to return to my old haunts, especially the opera houses. At home we had many joyful family parties with aunts, uncles and cousins, all longing to see Manny and hear our news. We spent delightful summer holidays at Reg's country cottage in Ayrshire with him, Win and their children, Mike and Wendy. It was there that Win (an author and playwright) persuaded me to start writing my memoirs.

Before Manny and I left Germany we in Hamburg only knew of the whereabouts of friends who had fled to our area when the Russians advanced on Bydgoszcz (previously called Bromberg), but gradually news seeped through of some who had arrived safely in other parts of the British zone of occupation. Others died en route or vanished for ever in the break-up of Europe after the war. The Petersens and I became increasingly alarmed about the Krönke family. Then, one week before Manny and I were finally booked to leave for England on 21 December 1945 (having been prevented from doing so on the 13th because Manny developed bronchitis), Gerhard and Ilse turned up on the Petersens' doorstep. The postponement of our departure, although it left no permanent mark on Manny and me, altered the course of the Krönkes' lives, because without my help it is doubtful whether they would have gained permission to stay in Hamburg. We had heard no news of them since the fateful night of our flight from Bromberg on 20–21 January, when Gerhard left in an open pony trap harnessed to the mare Weichsel. There was still no post functioning between the East and West zones and no other means of communication, except through word of mouth by chance encounter. Scarcely a week passed without some acquaintance drifting in from the East, but none of them had seen the Krönke family. All these refugees brought stories of rape and plunder by the Russians, starvation and persecution. Many had had to flee for their lives. They slipped over 'the green frontier' by night, avoiding patrols, and arrived penniless, with no possessions, and of course with no jobs. None were allowed to stay permanently in Hamburg.

Ilse and Gerhard came alone, having left the children in the care of Gerhard's parents for the time being. They begged us to help them get a permit to stay in Hamburg. Whether this would prove possible or not they had definitely decided to go back to fetch the children out of the Eastern zone because life there had become unbearable for them. Towards the end of the war they had been encircled by the fast advancing Russian troops and had finally found themselves marooned in a tiny village where they lived in a tumbled-down, deserted cottage. Gerhard had managed to get temporary work in a neighbouring village, which meant leaving Ilse alone all day. Even disguised as an old woman it was not safe for her to make an appearance in the street if Russians were about. Whenever there was a loud rap at the door she fled upstairs whilst the children tried to misdirect the intruders, saying their mother was not at home. Some were more persistent than others in making a thorough search and several times she had to jump out of a bedroom window and hide in a shed until the immediate danger had passed. Although Christine was only seven or eight years old, some of the men had already cast an eye over her. They were cut off from all civilization. They barely managed to get enough food to keep body and soul together and were on the verge of a breakdown. It was the usual story, but none the less poignant for being heard from so many different sources.

The Germans would not give the Krönkes a permit to stay in Hamburg. The only possible way was to try and wangle one through English channels. I spent the whole of my last week in Hamburg trailing around from one office to another, waiting sometimes for hours to be interviewed by some person who *might* be able to help, until eventually, on the obscure grounds that Gerhard had been born in what was now Poland, we got the coveted promise of a practice as dental surgeon in Hamburg.

Frau Seelig was willing to take the whole Krönke family into her house when Manny and I left. The Krönkes jumped at this offer and of course the German Housing Department made no objections because the Seeligs would now be accommodating a family of five in place of Manny and me. Their house would thus remain protected from confiscation by the presence of the three small children.

These arrangements sound quite simple, but in fact I only just managed to settle up everything before I left. In the meantime, Ilse, grateful to her dying day, stayed at home mending, sewing, cooking, packing and looking after Manny, who fortunately recovered quite quickly.

It was possible to write to my friends in West Germany, whose addresses I already knew, as soon as we arrived in England, and also to send them parcels of clothes. I collected left-over children's garments from kind neighbours and posted them to the Krönkes, who by this time were safely in Hamburg with their three children and living in the Seeligs' house. However, one was not allowed to send food.

It was not until 1950 that British citizens (except those with jobs in the Army of Occupation and the Control Commission, or bigwigs on official visits) were allowed to travel to Germany. In that summer I took Manny to spend three weeks with his father, who eventually rose to a high position. I have kept on good terms with him and his second wife. While Manny was there, I stayed with Linda and Manfred Petersen in Hamburg. Here I also met many other mutual friends with whom there was an immediate warm understanding as of old. Following the Marshall Plan, West Germany's economy had started to thrive because, although at first people received low wages, overnight almost, there were plentiful food supplies in all the shops. Therefore they worked long hours to enable them at last to feed their families.

In England most people were still making do with their old cars. In West Germany I saw only new ones, many of the best makes and of different bright colours. The reason for this was that (as in all the heavy industries throughout the country), the factories had been closed for lack of trade and raw materials, and confiscated under the War Reparations decrees made by the Allies. Thus, in the long term, starting from scratch with new manufacturing plants financed by the Western powers, they had a flying start over the British who could not afford to replace their worn-out machinery.

Needless to say, Manfred was one of the first to swank around in his new Mercedes! He had long since been granted a loan (on very poor terms) and permission to build a new block of flats on his bombed-out site. From then on his business expanded rapidly with his pre-war clients returning to him to design and supervise the erection of private houses, a speciality for which he had always had a good reputation.

On that first visit to Hamburg after the war I couldn't believe my eyes that this was the same city of rat-ridden rubble and ruins that I had left only five years earlier. Everything was functioning perfectly. The ancient monuments and churches, where possible, had been restored, shopping areas which had been completely destroyed were built anew and were full of smart goods. Restaurants serving luscious meals abounded, including the Alster Pavilion where a friend of mine, the German liaison officer who used to work with the town majors, was manager. The lakes, surrounded by beautiful gardens and lawns, were full of small pleasure steamers, sailing boats and canoes. Even the Reeperbahn, the ancient red-light district near the harbour, had been rebuilt, but in a rather shabby, gaudy style. Although still a centre for prostitutes, it had become more of a general amusement area where husbands could take their wives for a jolly evening out at a reasonable cost.

Over the years, I spent many wonderful holidays with the Petersens and the Krönkes in Hamburg and at Manfred's shooting lodge, and they came over to see my family and London, also other parts of England and Scotland. After Manfred died in 1976, Linda and I exchanged visits and kept in close touch until, to my grief, she died in July 1994. Ilse and Gerhard died many years ago.

Every time I was in Hamburg after the war I was entertained by my young friend Hedwig Widegreen, who worked for the Displaced Persons Department of the British Army of Occupation when I joined their staff on 29 May 1945 as secretary-interpreter. By 1950 she was married. We were both, as was Ilse Krönke, deeply involved in our common interests of music and literature. A few years after my book was first published Hedwig started translating it into German in a style I greatly admired, all the time giving me instalments for advice and discussion, either by post or in her home. She is still one of my most regular and sympathetic correspondents.

Anne-Marie, the daughter of Herr and Frau Dr Stockmann in Brühl, who was ten years old when I studied German there, still writes to me about once a month. She is now a proud grandmother. I stayed with Frau Else Daniel, my former singing teacher in Bromberg. The first time was in

1955 when she was already widowed and living in a flat alone in Cologne. Right up until she died of a heart attack she retained a great interest in her profession, and we spent all our time talking, singing, listening to records of opera, and she took me to see Strauss's *Der Rosenkavalier* in the new Opera House. As in Hamburg, Cologne had risen from the ashes and was a busy international venue. Pleasure steamers and barges plied to and fro on the Rhine, and the town centre teemed with shoppers and sightseers anxious to look round the newly built art galleries and museums. I was transported back to the first time I had sat in the open-air restaurant facing the Cathedral in 1933. My other friend who had lived in Bromberg, Frau Dr Edith Schwarz, finished up in Tegernsee, Upper Bavaria, where she was head English teacher at the grammar school for boys and girls in the main part of a baroque *Schloss* (Palace) which used to be a Benedictine Monastery, founded 1235 years ago. She lived alone in a flat near the lake, not far from her two sisters and her favourite nephew, the son of her youngest brother who was killed in the war. She was just as deeply involved and happy in her profession as ever and was greatly respected by the staff and pupils. She asked me to talk to some of her classes, which took my thoughts back to our successful experiment in the Dürerschule in Bromberg and obviously delighted the young people. Her frightful wartime and post-war experiences had, however, taken their toll and, sadly, she died not many years later.

I still hear regularly from one of my 500 pupils in the Braesicke-Hochschule for boys and girls in Bydgoszcz, now retired from teaching and married to a Dutchman. We discovered each other by chance a long time ago in Hamburg.

In 1964, after Manny was launched in his career, he took me for a memorable holiday to Poland. We took a return flight to Warsaw and later made our way by train to Bydgoszcz and Gdańsk. We had been issued with visas at the

Polish Consulate in London after we had complied with the currency regulations by arranging with our travel agent to pay in advance in sterling for board and lodging vouchers for our eighteen-day tour. On arrival in Poland these vouchers had to be changed into Zloty (67 to the pound) before we were given accommodation. We splashed out £3. 10s. od. a night in Warsaw at the well-known Hotel Bristol for a pompous suite of rooms! In cheaper hotels a single room cost 25/- with no bathroom. These were all clean and comfortable with good service. In restaurants the food was of high quality and represented the best of the delectable Polish cuisine. However, we soon found out that there were very few Poles who could afford such luxuries and their living conditions were abysmal. Nearly all the milk was skimmed and none of it tuberculin tested. Coal was dumped in a pile on the pavements and the housewife had to carry it into the cellar (probably thankful to get any at all). There were no citrus fruits or bananas, clothes in the shops were shoddy and dreary and very expensive. There were bookshops in nearly all the streets, but there was such a rush for books that they were difficult to come by. The most interesting goods were in state-owned handicraft shops where prices were exorbitant. We saw no clothing using modern styles or fabrics.

In spite of the amazing amount of rebuilding which had been carried out following war damage, the housing shortage was so acute that nobody was allowed more than one room per person. Agricultural machinery was scarce. Horses were used for farmwork and in every town there were horse-drawn vehicles. Roads were good on the whole, because so few Poles could afford cars and there was no traffic congestion.

All through the years, Poles of all classes and political opinions retained their pride in every branch of Polish culture, music and the arts. What impressed us most of all was their restoration of historical buildings. The whole of the old town in Warsaw had been reconstructed exactly as it used to be, stone for stone, brick for brick, with infinite care and skill.

In Gdańsk, the ancient Hanseatic harbour at the mouth of the Vistula, similar reconstruction was in progress in the old town, and it was fascinating to watch the craftsmen at work. The famous crane gate and gabled houses stood again along the waterfront. The old mill in the centre of the town was completely restored and looked just the same as when it was built by the Teutonic Knights in the Middle Ages. In front of the mill an open space had been left, with grass and flower borders, allowing an unexpected and staggering view of the vast structure of the Cathedral, impossible before the war when houses were tightly clustered round it. The façades in the Dlugi Targ Street (Langer Markt), by then weathering slightly, were such perfect replicas of the original seventeenth-century houses that I would have been taken in by them had I not known that the main part of the city had been totally destroyed by the Russians in 1945.

I was able to show Manny a number of beauty spots where his father and I had spent such happy times when we were first married. We stayed in The Grand Hotel in Sopot (Zoppot), about six miles from Gdańsk, facing the sea with a private beach, not far from Brösen, where Kurt and I used to bathe during the summer. We invited some Polish friends to spend a day with us there and later their schoolboy son acted as guide when Manny hired a car to drive us to the Cassubian Lakes – one of our favourite outings before the war – south-west of Gdańsk, which were still entirely unspoilt and surrounded by vast forests where we used to walk for miles without seeing a soul except for the odd farmer or gamekeeper. In those days they were easily accessible by bus to a village where there was a lakeside restaurant, which specialized in delicious crayfish dishes.

Manny and I travelled to other beauty spots along the coast and to Malborg in trains, trams and buses which, although there were plenty of them, were crammed full with Poles who could not afford cars. It was unfortunately not possible to reach Kaliningrad or the Samland coast, which were in the area occupied by the Soviet Union since 1945. We did not fall short of musical entertainments, which were of a very high standard. All opera, ballet, orchestras, theatres and museums and art galleries throughout Poland were heavily subsidized by the State and were very popular.

One of the main objects of our holiday in Poland had been for me to be able to show Manny where we and his father had lived and worked in Gdańsk and Bydgoszcz, which we achieved, with one exception. In Gdańsk the house where Manny was born, on the hill opposite the General Hospital, no longer existed. The rubble and garden were overgrown with weeds and grass. The only relic we found was one stone pillar from the balustrade surrounding my bedroom balcony, which was much too heavy to lug home as a trophy!

Over the next few years, I travelled with groups of like-minded opera fans for short breaks in Paris and Naples, culminating in two seasons at Bayreuth where, on both occasions, I met young people who to this day are my close friends and have joined me at performances in the London opera houses and once a year at Glyndebourne Festival Opera. One of my greatest pleasures has been my long association with this Festival where I have been an usher/programme-seller since 1958, though now in a sedentary capacity, one evening a week in the Organ Room. Thus I have witnessed the opening of the magnificent new opera house, the achievement of the founder's son, George Christie, which lies nestled among my native South Downs.